# A CONCISE HISTORY OF ART

## Part I

*From the Beginnings to the Fifteenth Century*

# A CONCISE HISTORY OF ART

Part I

*From the Beginnings to the Fifteenth Century*

GERMAIN BAZIN

CONSERVATEUR EN CHEF
AU MUSEÉ DU LOUVRE

*with 348 illustrations*
*8 plates in colour*

THAMES AND HUDSON
LONDON

FIRST ENGLISH EDITION TRANSLATED FROM THE FRENCH BY
FRANCIS SCARFE WITH ADDITIONS AND REVISIONS



THIS REVISED EDITION FIRST PUBLISHED IN TWO VOLUMES 1962
SECOND IMPRESSION 1964

PRINTED BY W. KOHLHAMMER STUTTGART WEST GERMANY
ORIGINALLY PUBLISHED IN FRANCE BY
EDITIONS GARAMOND, PARIS

# PREFACE

Anyone trying to write a short history of art is liable to find his work being compared with Solomon Reinach's famous *Apollo* which served as a manual for several generations of students. At all events the task has become remarkably more complicated since the time when Reinach wrote his 'manual' in 1905. Since that date many civilizations have been more fully explored or even freshly discovered. The great Hellenist confined himself to the art of the West, and as his title *Apollo* suggests, his main purpose was to expound the 'Greek miracle' with all its antecedents and consequences. Reinach's work covered mainly the ancient Mediterranean and the Renaissance. But since then we have discovered another 'miracle' which might well be called the 'barbarian miracle', taking the word 'barbarian' in the same sense as the Greeks and Romans did. The primitive civilizations are now admired as they could not possibly have been fifty years ago, and since then we have also discovered the arts of the East. Moreover, we now recognize certain other values to be as fertile as the classicism to which Reinach devoted his researches, in particular the baroque which in his day was still ignored or condemned as a sign of decadence.

The reader may be surprised to find certain variations in the way the different chapters of this book are planned. All those dealing with ancient civilizations or with pre-Columbian archaeology or the Far East, contain an historical introduction which appeared superfluous in the case of the Western civilizations, whose history is sufficiently well known. In the case of the Far East, it appeared advisable to add some account of the religions of the countries concerned, without which it would be hard to understand the artistic works of races whose outlook is so unlike our own.

This book is an historical work, designed to give the uninitiated reader as many precise ideas and established facts as possible. The remarks which introduce each chapter can be read separately, and in each case they provide a short critical and aesthetic survey. In the Conclusion the reader will find an outline of the various ways in which the work of art has been interpreted, from the time when modern man first turned his eager attention to this particular product of human genius.

The illustrations were chosen to accompany the text, but occasionally they diverge from it, especially those accompanying the prefatory remarks and the conclusion: in such cases the plates are intended to bring out resemblances or historical perspectives, and offer the reader the most direct evidence of whatever unifies or distinguishes the characteristic forms of different civilizations.

The author's aim has been to consider the work of art from a genuinely universal, impartial point of view, as something which transcends the limitations of time and place. Whilst he does not claim to have succeeded, he will feel rewarded if his efforts made in that direction are recognized. But unless he has no roots at all, who can hope to escape from his own time, or ignore the claims of the civilization in which he was reared?

GERMAIN BAZIN

## CONTENTS

## ACKNOWLEDGEMENTS

The publishers wish to thank the following for kindly allowing them to illustrate works in public or private collections, or for placing photographs at their disposal:

Acropolis Museum, Athens (Photo: Max Hirmer) (pl. III); Archaeological Museum, Heraklion, Crete (pl. II); Caisse Nationale des Monuments Historiques, Paris (pl. 338); Herbert Felton, Esq., London (pl. 244); Señor G. M. Ojeda (Photo Club), Burgos (pl. 252); Monsieur L. Ollivier, Paris (pl. 337); Oriental Institute, University of Chicago (pl. I); Messrs. Walter Scott Ltd., Bradford (pl. 243); Edwin Smith, Esq., London (pl. 170).

All other photographs reproduced in this volume are identical with those in the French and German editions.

# I. THE ORIGINS OF ART

The earliest known products of human genius enable us to grasp the creative impulse behind works of art at the very source. The perfection of the statuettes of the Gravettian hunters period, and the masterpieces of Magdalenian cave-art show that primitive man had no inner urge to express some preconceived notion of 'beauty' through the medium of forms. Art is only one of the many expressions – though perhaps it is the most specific – of the unique genius which drives man to repeat the creative act of the demiurge in everything he does, so that he must needs excel himself from century to century. If the Gravettian carvings have such a dynamic sense of form, and if the animal figures painted in the French and Spanish caves are perfect works of naturalism that no later civilization could surpass, it is because primitive man, in making them, was convinced that he was genuinely creating. For him the image was no mere imitation. It had the same living faculties as the being of which it was a model, a double. It was thus a work of magic by which man asserted his mastery over the world. We know that our ancestor of the Old Stone Age (the Palaeolithic) painted or carved natural forms with no intention of making a 'work of art': he intended, rather, to ensure the fertility of his prey, to entice it into his traps, or to acquire its strength for his own purposes. The primitive artist was a magician whose drawing had all the virtue of a magic spell, an incantation. If he gave so much attention to the living truth, it was in order to make shapes as lifelike as possible and endow them with the actual qualities of the creature. Thus the vivid naturalism of those early images can be traced to that desire to identify himself with the world, which distinguishes man from all other forms of life. The animal is bound to the natural order and is doomed to be merely one of its blind forces. Man, on the contrary, has an innate awareness of the surrounding world, thanks to which he can break free of it while ceaselessly striving to rejoin it in thought or action. Primitive man was deeply involved in the natural world, and lost none of its inherent energy. Not a thought nor deed of his failed to contact some power in the universe. Man's entire activity was aimed at skilfully intervening in the play of natural forces, in the hope of preserving a balance, attracting 'good' and repelling 'evil' powers.

If works of art appeared so late in Palaeolithic times, it was by no means because man was incapable of making them. The earliest Palaeolithic 'industries' of the Chellan, Acheulean and Mousterian periods show a craftmanship that could well have been applied to art. But a long period was no doubt necessary before man could acquire a creative grasp of the forces underlying the world. The discovery and evolution of language, in itself, is an artistic operation in which verbal forms have to be invented and perfected. Naming things is the first creative act. To the primitive mind, the name has a magic power which identifies it with the object. Thus man had slowly to bring his mental picture of the world into focus, before he could make his inner vision even more effective by reproducing the shapes he saw in nature. But at last certain 'magicians', who were no doubt of a race with an exceptional plastic sense, thought of extending their verbal spells, and giving them more evocatory power, by first of all painting images of the things or creatures they wanted to control. The profound knowledge of nature that can be seen in these works was not the result of the artists' disinterested contemplation, but was drawn from an intimate acquaintance with animal life, learnt in the daily drama of the hunt. Perhaps this explains why human images were so few and relatively crude: the drawing of the human figure was not an integral part of the primitive system of magic. As these paintings, drawings and engravings were executed without a model, often in the depths of gloomy caves and by the light of the feeblest of lamps, the primitive artist needed a marvellous memory to inform his creative imagination with such a power of synthesis. The artist-magician had to enter into a ritual trance, during which he 'emptied' his own soul by an act of intense mental concentration: he then evoked the supernatural powers which identified him with the bison, mammoth, horse or deer, until he was possessed by the soul of the animal itself and could then portray its image on the wall of his cave.

The study of the origins of art has a surprise in store, for the highest level of art was reached when man was living in this primitive state of the Old Stone Age, at a time when conditions had been made arctic or sub-arctic by the advance of the glaciers. From the Neolithic period onwards, civilization tended to become almost entirely materialistic in its outlook. There was a gap of several thousands of years between the cave art of the Magdalenian era (the final era of the Old Stone Age) and the first great civilizations of South-West Asia and the Nile valley.

## PREHISTORIC AND PROTOHISTORIC CULTURES

Though its chronology is not firmly established, it is safe to say that the long prehistoric era during which man left little or no account of himself, lasted for hundreds of thousands of years – perhaps about 500,000. In the Palaeolithic phase, the largest part of man's prehistorical development, men existed by hunting and fishing, making most of their tools by chipping stone, especially flint. They lived in isolated tribes always in close contact with animal life. In the final, most recent periods (Upper Palaeolithic) men built summer huts and also, in regions where rock-shelters were not available, winter houses half-dug into the ground.

*1 Stags. Rock-Drawings, Lascaux (France). Upper Palaeolithic*

Man's elementary equipment did not change drastically in the Mesolithic phase (Middle Stone Age). In the Neolithic phase (New Stone Age), the age of the greatest refinement of stone tools, there were swift changes in man's development, and towards 5,000 B.C., in the Near East, human effort was increasingly and ever more rapidly directed towards civilization, that is to say the framework of an organized society: industrial specialization involving endless improvements in tools; the emergence of new techniques such as pottery and mining (for flint); the development of trade; the discovery of agriculture; the domestication of animals; and permanent, collective settlements on land or lake.

### *The Upper Palaeolithic Period*

The oldest examples of art date from the first millennia of Upper Palaeolithic times, a long period of the East-West migration of *Homo sapiens* into Europe, where he replaced less advanced stocks. His rupestral art in the naturalistic style, consisting of carvings, drawings, paintings and engravings on rock-faces, is found concentrated in the south-west of France and in northern Spain, and is therefore know as 'Franco-Cantabrian'.

Aurignacian invaders and settlers (named after the French site at Aurignac, Haute-Garonne) first evolved drawing, engraving and painting. In early cave-works (e.g. La Pileta cave, Malaga) animals are silhouetted in pure profile, with only one leg to represent a pair and no indications of detail.

Gravettian mammoth hunters from Russia and Eastern Europe (named after the rock-shelter of La Gravette, Dordogne) carved, especially out

*2 Venus of Willendorf. Upper Palaeolithic. Vienna*

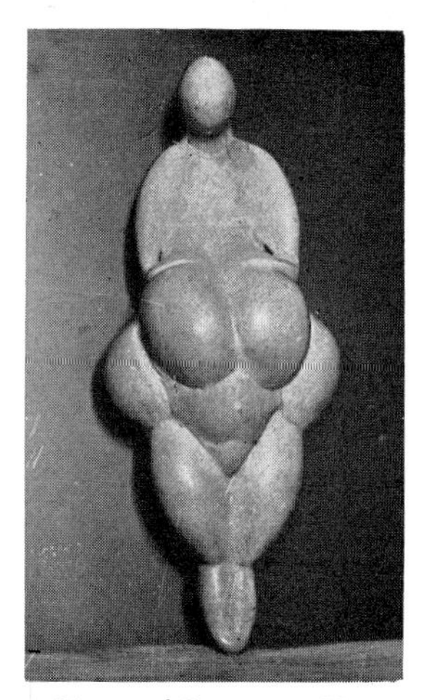

*3 Venus of Lespugne. Upper Palaeolithic. Saint-Germain*

of mammoth ivory, small figures which have been found over a wide area in Eurasia. Some are of women apparently suffering from the fatty degeneration known as 'steatopygia' still found among remnants of the Bushmen in South Africa. While some of these statuettes tend to be representative (Willendorf, Austria, pl. 2), others (Lespugne, France, pl. 3) are almost geometrically stylized. It is not known whether this three-dimensional vision came before or after the portrayal of shapes on a flat surface. In south-western France and northern Spain the Gravettians developed Aurignacian traditions of painting, their pictorial art reaching a climax in the admirable paintings of the Lascaux cave in the Dordogne (pl. 1, 6), discovered in 1940.

The ill-defined Solutrean period (named from the site at Solutré, Saône-et-Loire) is known for leaf-shaped flint tools of astonishing refinement, and for a very few carvings of animals in relief on rock-faces (the frieze of horses along the rock-shelter of La Chaire-à-Calvin, Mouthiers; frieze of horses, ibexes, etc., at Roc de Sers, Charente). Such sculpture was continued in the Magdalenian period (named after the rock-shelter of La Madeleine, at Les Eyzies, Dordogne), for example in the splendid equestrian frieze of Cap Blanc, in the Dordogne, and the frieze of bison, horses, ibexes and female human torsos of Angles-sur-l'Anglin. The 30,000 years or thereabouts of the Magdalenian period (to be compared with a probable span of 50,000 years for the preceding Aurignacian and Gravettian periods) were rich in artistic expression. Sculpture ranged from the large, originally coloured, friezes to small objects in reindeer-horn (pl. 4). The same material was also engraved or incised (pl. 5). However, the pictorial arts became dominant, reaching

*4 Bison. Fragment of a Spear-Thrower from La Madeleine (France). Upper Palaeolithic. Saint-Germain*

their peak in the polychrome animals of the famous caves of Altamira and Castillo (Santander, Spain), Font-de-Gaume (Dordogne), and Marsoulas (Haute Garonne).

The Abbé Breuil's investigations enable us to trace the evolution of this mural art from the simple line-drawing of Aurignacian times to the final polychrome painting, which is late Magdalenian. Whether incised or drawn on rock surfaces naturally covered in soft clay with the finger or 'brush', the line was at first of even thickness, and was only modulated later. Next a tinge of red ochre or black manganese was added, silhouetting the outline of the animal's body. At a later stage the brush or graving-tool would be run over all the finer points in order to bring out the movement, the pelt, or details of anatomy always, though, without the slightest hint of the picturesque. In the advanced

*5 Reindeer on Reindeer-Antler from Loret (France). Upper Palaeolithic. Saint-Germain*

*6 Rock-Paintings of Animals, Lascaux (France). Upper Palaeolithic*

*7 Hunting Scene, Cueva Remigia (Spain). Upper Palaeolithic*

Magdalenian technique the painter finally blended his tones to reproduce the graded colouring of the hide or fur. All these various stages were dictated by a growing urge towards naturalistic truthfulness, yet such a virtuosity was achieved that the painter's hand marked the line down as boldly as a Pisanello, seeking and finding the clear-cut elegance of the arabesque. This thoroughbred art, the product of thousands of years of evolution and intense research, vanished from the Franco-Cantabrian areas while it was still at the height of its perfection, and with hardly a sign of any fall in quality. This may be explained by the amelioration of the cold climate of the Ice Age and the consequent disappearance of the hunter's quarry, which had occasioned Upper Palaeolithic art in all its remarkable forms.

During the Capsian period (named after the site at Gafsa, the *Capsa* of antiquity, in Tunisia) which began during the later Palaeolithic phase and continued into the Mesolithic, the Hamitic peoples of Africa produced a rock-art comparable with that of South-West Europe. Our present inadequate knowledge of the geology and prehistory of Africa makes it hard to settle the time-scale of the engravings and paintings of the Atlas and Sahara regions, or of Egypt, Libya, Nubia and Rhodesia.

*8 War Scene, Khargur Tahl (Libyan Desert)*

However, this art seems to have extended into the historic period. Here we find two distinct styles. In addition to the naturalistic manner, not unlike the Magdalenian, there was also an expressionistic and schematic form of art in which human and animal figures were grouped in dramatic actions (pl. 8). In Magdalenian art the figures were usually separate, and no such complexity of action was attempted. Drawings of the human figure, similarly grouped, are plentiful in the above regions. For the first time the artist had set himself the task of mastering the fundamentals of dramatic composition, and in this he succeeded all the more impressively as his diagrammatic treatment avoided the picturesque; the artist created the impression of whirling *vectors* of movement, pushing his systematization almost to the point of abstract draughtsmanship, the magical figures becoming pure 'signs'.

The peculiar Upper Palaeolithic rupestral art of eastern Spain (pl. 7) is to be related to this aspect of Capsian art, rather than to the developed

Magdalenian art, although it was influenced by art north of the Pyrenees. Thus, from very ancient times, man found a source of artistic inspiration in abstract art as well as in naturalism.

## *The Neolithic Period*

Though it survived in Africa and Scandinavia, the early naturalistic art came to an end in the Franco-Cantabrian region in the Mesolithic period (about 10,000 B.C.) in the Azilian phase. The painted pebbles of the great cavern of Mas d'Azil (Ariège) are evidence of an art verging on the abstract, which was to prevail throughout the Neolithic period. Ceramics, which appeared in early Neolithic times, developed rapidly with the later (Bronze Age) invention of the potter's wheel and was no doubt favoured by the expansion of agriculture. The site of Jericho has revealed an organized society of urban type of the sixth millennium B.C. with a highly-developed terracotta industry.

In the Neolithic (c. 7500 B.C.) and Chalcolithic (c. 3500 B.C.) stages (the latter so named because during it metals were first used), man developed a rudimentary form of architecture which was sometimes impressive in its effects. Such Megalithic (large stone) monuments were usually constructed with colossal, unwieldy pieces of stone, and were intended for burial or for ritualistic purposes. The burial chambers consisted of upright stones weighing several tons each, serving as supports for slabs that were laid across them, the whole being finally covered (though not in all cases) with a mound of earth or small stones. They are of three main types: dolmen, a table-arrangement of stones with no passage leading in; passage grave, a rectangular or more or less circular tomb approached through a narrow

*9 Ritual Circle, Stonehenge. Neolithic*

stone passage, and gallery grave, a covered passage serving as a long burial vault. These underground tombs spread from the Eastern Mediterranean in the third and second millennia B.C. to France, Spain, Portugal, Great Britain and Northern Europe.

Huge arrangements of standing stones, whether set in straight lines as at Carnac in Brittany, or grouped in circles as at Avebury, Arbor Low and Stonehenge (pl. 9), in England, formed impressive sanctuaries which must have required enormous human effort and, at the same time, a fairly advanced social order.

## *Protohistory*

A major event in the history of human techniques was the discovery and use of metals. These seem to have been valued at first for their preciousness. After learning how to obtain gold and silver, and then copper in the raw state (Chalcolithic period), man shaped them with hammers before he discovered the art of casting. The discovery of the blending properties of tin so as to form alloys, enabled him to harden copper, making possible its industrial use in the form of brass and bronze.

The eastern regions of the Mediterranean made the greatest creative contribution. In the third millennium the rise of the Elamite, Sumerian and Aegean historical civilizations coincided with the development of bronze metallurgy, which itself began about 3500 B.C. The peoples of Central, Western and Northern Europe now emerged from their prehistorical stage to enter what is called the 'protohistorical' phase; for although they left no written records of their history, certain echoes of it survive in the traditions handed down by the peoples of the Near East. In any case, so far as metallurgy was concerned they depended on the Mediterranean, for merchants of the Eastern Mediterranean not only exported bronze articles to the West, but imported eastwards the tin they needed for its production. Metallurgical techniques also found their way into Central Europe through the Caucasus route by which the Near Eastern empires went in search of ore. It is not easy to give any strict chronology of the diffusion of metals, for although a relative time-scale may be clearly distinguished, there are no definite, epoch-making dates for the earlier periods. Copper side by side with tools of polished stone was widely in use in the second half of the fourth millennium B.C., while the same phenomenon is to be found in the Aegean area at the beginning of the third millennium, and in the Western Mediterranean by about 1900 B.C. Bronze was in common use in the Near East in the first half of the third millennium, in the Aegean about 2300 B.C., and in the West about 1500 B.C. As for iron, this was still a rare metal in the Near East in the first half of the second millennium. Nevertheless, by 1400 B.C. iron working techniques were evolved in Asia Minor, the centre of dispersion. In the West the Iron Age, which lasted for two thousand years, falls into two periods: the Hallstatt period, taking its name from a site in Austria, which lasted roughly from 1000 to 500 B.C.; and the La Tène period (named after a site in Switzerland), from 500 B.C. to the Christian era.

The protohistoric Bronze and Iron civilizations extended over a considerable area, notably Italy, Spain, Gaul, the British Isles, Central and Northern Europe, Scandinavia, the Urals and the Altaï mountains. The epoch of La Tène corresponded with the westward expansion of the Celts. Although some anthropomorphic sculptures of this period have been found (in France, at Roquepertuse and Entremont; in Czechoslovakia, at Msecké-Zehrovice), the artistic activity of the above peoples showed itself mainly in domestic articles such as terra-cotta vessels (pl. 10), gold vases and jewellery. Whereas the creative imagination of the Mediterranean and Asiatic races found an endless source of inspiration for their plastic art in nature itself, the peoples of Central and Northern Europe seem to have derived more satisfaction from the abstract. The decorative range of their weapons and pots did not go beyond a few non-representational signs, such as the sacred horns of the bull, the double axe symbolizing thunder, the solar disc and its many derivatives – the wheel, the rowel, the star, the S, the spiral and double spiral (pl. 712), the swastika and the symmetrical cross. The head of the horse and swan were also solar symbols.

## II. PRIMITIVE ARTISTIC CIVILIZATIONS

The artistic maturing of the Magdalenians was an isolated phenomenon. For thousands of years the people of Northern, Central and Western Europe, plunged in the obscurity of prehistory until our era, remained static in simple tribal groupings with not a glimmer of political or cultural genius. This entirely materialistic civilization spread as far as the Bosphorus, where the seven superimposed cities of Hissarlik in Troas (unearthed in the 1870s by the German scholar Schliemann – one being the site of Homer's Troy), reveal a striking poverty of the artistic instinct at a time which saw the rise of great neighbouring civilizations.

It was in the Mediterranean area that man made his first great efforts to emerge from his natural state. By inventing systems of politics, culture, religion, industry and commerce, he considerably extended both his practical and intellectual progress. Three great centres of civilization may be distinguished from the fourth millennium onwards. These three centres were in the Nile valley, Mesopotamia (Tigris and Euphrates basins) and the Aegean. All these civilizations were inspired by an heroic resolve to embody their idea of the world in enduring works. The various races who created them seem to have been blessed with a marvellous plastic imagination, and there is nothing – not even the most abstract of concepts – to which they failed to give a concrete form, a figure.

The magical, unorganized setting in which primitive man had lived was now set in order. Man became immune from the elemental powers he so much feared, by personifying them. He worshipped gods; he was no longer in contact with mere things, but with beings he could name, pray to and evoke. Beneficent and maleficent things now tended to crystallize into the abstract qualities of good and evil. The medicine-man gave way to the priest, an intermediary between man and god. Man's relationship to the visible or invisible world became regulated by a code of doctrines and practices; that is to say, religion.

Meanwhile the countless figures with which the Egyptians and Mesopotamians covered their monuments still remained profoundly imbued with the sense of the supernatural which had guided the hands of Magdalenian artists. No civilization carried to a higher point than did the Egyptian the belief in the identity of the image with its original. The host of illustrations, through which we can learn the smallest details of Egyptian life, were meant to add the support of reality itself to the objects and people who had to accompany the dead so as to allow them, in the after-life, to lead the same kind of existence as in their earthly state. These images are replicas – 'doubles' – of the articles and beings they represent, on which magic formulae conferred all the properties of the original model. The invention of images was then, properly

*10 Burial-Urn. Hallstatt Period. Stuttgart*

speaking, a creation; so that in the Nile valley the sculptor was known as 'He-who-keeps-alive'. In Mesopotamia this faith in the power of the image did not result in such a coherent system of imitation, but it was none the less present to the mentality behind the civilizations which succeeded each other in the Tigris and Euphrates valleys. Why did conquering princes so carefully cut the heads off the statues of defeated kings if not to rob them of that power of survival after death which in those days was guaranteed by an effigy? At the beginning of the Sumerian civilization in the first Ur dynasty, apparently it was not enough to paint or sculpt the likeness of a dead man's friends on the walls of his tomb, as was the custom in Egypt: they were actually put to death in the course of bloody funeral rites – wives, princes and servants followed their overlord into death, complete with their weapons, jewels, chattels and chariots of war. Belief in the 'double' later put an end to such holocausts.

This faith in the realness of images brought in its train a whole system of plastic conventions which, more or less empirical in Mesopotamia, assumed in Egypt a rational and sacred character. In order to have the maximum of real power, the image had to reproduce the model in its entirety and not with the incompleteness of our normal vision. The parts on the second and third planes, which remained hidden owing to the foreshortening of perspective, were therefore reproduced with the same fidelity as those which were fully visible. This explains the strange canon of the human figure, observed in religious art in Egypt for thirty

*11 Warriors. Assyrian Relief. About 7th c. B.C. Paris*

centuries, by which a head seen in profile, but with one eye full-face, is planted on a trunk seen from the front, and the trunk set on two legs shown in profile in a walking position (pl. 12). Thus all parts of the human body were represented from the angle at which they appeared most complete. Figures of men who in reality were *seen* in depth, one behind the other, were portrayed each one complete, either in Indian file (pl. 11) or superimposed in ranks (pl. 14 a).

The herdsman milking a cow was represented next to the animal but not against it, so as not to hide its body. In the same way offerings brought to a king by slaves would be portrayed above the basket supposedly containing them. At Khorsabad the famous winged bulls of the palace are shown with five legs, so as to appear equally 'complete' from both front and side (pl. 13). These mighty figures, like those of some of the cows at Hathor in Egypt, are not properly speaking built in the round, but are no more than a profile and a frontal view put together. The artists of those early civilizations had no spatial conception of objects. The sense of depth was as alien to them as the idea of perspective; some objects were portrayed flat while the profile of others was reduced according to the composition, the composition being dictated according to a moral hierarchy in which no account was taken of the relative sizes of the things themselves. Thus a man was always bigger than a tree, and even too big to enter his own house (pl. 14 a, 14 b). Integral realism, dictated by the needs of magic, obliged the artists to defy appearances. They did not see things from a distance as they appear to us, but saw them only as they knew them to be: the object they portrayed was not a spectacle for them, but they identified themselves with it by a process of empathy. Following their hand, their eye rested simultaneously on all the object's planes; they deliberately ignored the fact that certain parts of a thing are farther away than others. Statuary was therefore usually presented head-on, with none of the play of line or forms that would give it spatial life (pl. 63). The name 'law of frontalism' has been given to this slavish convention which makes the statue completely static, giving it the inertia of mere architectural material.

In the images imposed on surfaces – bas-reliefs, paintings – the works were based on the side-view, silhouetted shadow-fashion against the wall; the details of the model were indicated diagrammatically by the chisel, rather than sculpted, and the main outline thus kept all the expressive strength that was characteristic of the cave-art of earlier times.

The architecture of all the primitive civilizations aspired to the colossal. It would appear that from the beginning, thanks to the multiple and combined efforts afforded by slave-labour, man intended his creations to rival those of nature itself. The Egyptian, in the same way as the Mexican or the Hindu, built mountains of stone in the form of pyramids, while the colossi of the Nilotic sculptors are rocks given forms and faces. All of them, Egyptians, Mycenaeans and Peruvians, exploited gigantic materials, while the Mesopotamians, for whom stone was in short supply, built their palaces on artificial hills of dried clay. It seems as though the poorer man was in technical resources, the more he tried to persuade himself of his own supernatural strength. In the art of bonding materials several races – such as the Mycenaeans and some Peru-

*12 Egyptian Wood-Carving. About 2700 B.C. Cairo*

*13 Winged Bull from Khorsabad. Assyrian. 7th c. B.C. Paris*

*14a Schematic View of a fortified Town. Assyrian Bas-Relief*

*14b Schematic View of a Garden. Egyptian Papyrus. London*

vian tribes – used stones of unequal sizes and shapes which they assembled as in a jig-saw puzzle (pl. 44). The Greeks called this the 'Cyclopean' style of building. However, at a very early stage the Egyptians and Sumerians developed a regular style, which the Romans later called *opus quadratum;* this notion of a wall made of identical and interchangeable parts (bricks and stones) implies a great effort of reasoning.

The image-maker of the Nile valley, like the Sumerian, carefully polished the hardest of stones, as once the artist of the New Stone Age had done. Till the decline of the ancient world Egypt prolonged Neolithic art in the manufacture of vases of hard stone, in which Egyptian craftsmen had excelled from the outset.

All Egyptian art may be seen emerging from that technique. Nilotic sculptors first extended their activities from vases to stelae (needles) which they erected over royal tombs. They then took to polishing granite doors for their brick sanctuaries. It was at the beginning of the Memphitic period that they first dared to set up temples and tombs entirely of stone, which they used in enormous slabs. These obelisks were honoured as images of the deity in the temples of the sun during the Memphitic Empire (pl. 15). The menhir had the same function among the Western barbarians, and we know that in Sumeria they worshipped *betyles* of stone, perhaps symbols of the Earth-Mother in her least perishable form. This explains why these artists often showed a religious respect for the original shape of rough stones, which they simply improved with a little abrasion (pl. 16, 17).

It might be asked whether the inclination for mural art, so pronounced in Egypt but also found in the post-Sumerian civilizations of Asia, was a continuation of prehistoric cave-art. Do not the *mastaba* and the pyramid artificially reproduce the prehistoric cave inscribed with images? The second Theban Empire in its turn began to seek subterranean shelter

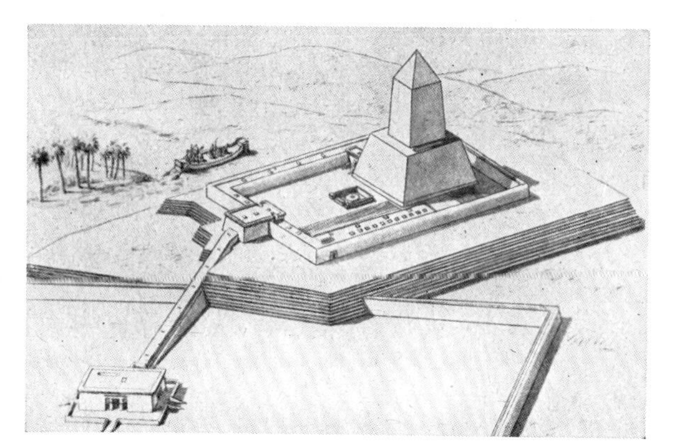

*15 Sanctuary of the Sun of King Niuserrê, Abusir*

for its tombs, and certain Asiatic civilizations (Hittite and Persian) showed a special interest in carving natural rock-faces in the same way as the prehistoric civilizations of the Fezzan and the Sahara had done earlier.

The Egyptian technique of hollow-relief recalls that of engraving in caves, and in both cases, before becoming an independent art, painting was used only as an auxiliary to the carved outline. There is a thread of continuity between the cave-art of Africa which, unlike the European, was pursued well into the historic period, and the mural art of Egyptian civilization, which without doubt had its roots in prehistoric Africa.

The significance given to animals in religion and consequently in art, is another characteristic which links the first civilizations to prehistoric times. At first, brute strength seemed to man to be an attribute of divine power. The lion, the eagle, the bull and the snake played an outstanding part in primitive mythologies. They are to be found in Egypt (at first totemistic) as symbols or, rather, as incarnations of gods. In Mesopotamia they were closely identified with the divinities of the heavens or the underworld. The artists of the Nile, Tigris and Euphrates therefore became adept at the portrayal of animals, like their Magdalenian predecessors. Moreover, the bodies of animals, fused together in daring syntheses, gave rise to what amount to theological and plastic speculations.

This chapter, in which we have tried to discount geographical and temporal factors, so as to give a proper assessment of a primitive stage in the history of forms, must also include some study of the so-called 'pre-Columbian' civilizations. In the strictest sense some of these remained at the Stone Age; others discovered bronze but none of them iron, and the Mexicans erected their enormous stone structures with stone implements. No other evolved civilization shows so pathetically the material and psychological obstacles that had to be overcome by primitive man in order to raise his standard of life. We can only admire how those

*16 Code of Hammurabi. About 1700 B.C. Paris*

*17 Menhir from Les Maurels (France). Neolithic. Rodez*

mysterious races, notwithstanding their backwardness which was no doubt caused by their isolation, managed in spite of their crude technical development to create civilizations superior in some respects to what the Conquistadors were to build on their ruins.

As for the Bronze and Iron Ages, which in Western Europe are shrouded in the mist of prehistory, in the Mediterranean they produced historical civilizations rivalling those of Egypt and Mesopotamia. While we recall that iron was imported from Asia, we are still at a loss to say who invented the alloy of tin and copper – in itself too pliable – which resulted in a far tougher metal, bronze, while facilitating its industrial use owing to the much lower temperature required for casting. No doubt it was via South-West Asia that bronze slowly reached the Mediterranean, where local absence of tin deposits made its use costly and confined it to articles of luxury. For a long time in Egypt and Sumeria it was used only sparingly for statuary, being applied in the form of thin foil on a wooden core, the head alone being cast. The Indo-Europeans, who towards 2000 B.C. invaded the Mediterranean basin and fought and conquered the great powers of the period, no doubt owed their victory to their superior bronze and iron weapons, together with the domestication of the horse. During those ages of metal, the most skilful and highly evolved form of civilization was the Aegean which developed in Crete and later in Argolis from 3200 B.C. to 1100 B.C. It produced no statues, preferring personal articles to durable creations in stone. It excelled in making weapons, jewels, and pottery which were exported all over the East and to some parts of the West. This civilization recalls – though this time it was by the sea – the nomadic habits of those mounted tribes who were rearers of horses. Metal was better adapted than stone to the conditions of a wandering existence that encouraged them to produce only small objects such as jewels, personal finery, and trappings for harness. It was during the second millennium, well before historic times, that these nomad races entered the history of art. In certain sites of Central Asia we are beginning to find the oldest specimens of what is now termed 'steppe' art, which after absorbing the influence of the zoomorphic style from Mesopotamia was to invade the whole of Northern Europe where it held sway until something like A.D. 1000. In style and spirit this art, which gave exclusive attention to the portrayal of animals, must be studied as a rival to the primitive artistic civilizations rather than – as is usually done – as a prelude to the Middle Ages of the West.

The spirit of the Stone Age and the ages of metals is not dead today. It continues to inspire certain communities in Africa, Oceania and America, whose way of life (though degenerating all the time) perpetuates that of prehistoric man. The artistic output of these peoples will therefore take its proper place at the end of this chapter.

## 1. EGYPTIAN CIVILIZATION

### *Historical Background*

Invulnerable on account of its position, with its desert hinterland and its redoubt on the Upper Nile which thrice in the course of history enabled its national unity to be restored, Egypt developed a highly skilled civilization which for thirty centuries maintained a political, cultural and artistic tradition unique in the history of the world. This unshakable tradition, almost devoutly preserved, accounts for its strength and greatness but at the same time for its monotony, though in those long centuries its subtle variations do show a gradual evolution.

The first artistic manifestations of Egyptian civilization – those of the pre-Dynastic era (3197–2778 B.C.) and the Thinite era (1st and 2nd dynasties, after about 3200 B.C.) – show its close relationship to the neighbouring Sumerian civilization, perhaps because Egypt fell under its influence or because they both sprang from some common source. The Memphitic Empire or Old Kingdom (3rd to 6th dynasties, 2778 B.C. –2234 B.C.) carried out in the Delta region the most grandiose constructions to be found in Egypt, the Pyramids, which are the burial-places of the Pharaohs Cheops, Chephren and Mycerinus (4th dynasty, 2650 B.C. – about 2525 B.C.). At that time art was exclusively funerary, while domestic buildings were made of perishable materials, crude bricks of

*18 Sphinx and Pyramid of Cheops*

sun-baked clay, or wood. Statuary, relief and painting appear to have been already properly established. The periods between the Old and the Middle Kingdoms and the Middle and New Kingdoms were troubled times, and are referred to as the First and Second Intermediate Periods respectively. At the end of the First Intermediate Period Egypt was formed anew, and the second period of its history, the Middle Kingdom, was founded at Thebes in Upper Egypt (11th to 17th dynasty, 2065 B.C. –1785 B.C.). Temples remained of modest dimensions and funerary architecture continued to predominate.

The task of recreating Egyptian unity fell to the 18th dynasty, after it had been compromised by the Hyksos invasion. This dynasty founded the New Kingdom (18th to 21st dynasty, 1580 B.C.–1085 B.C.), which was the most brilliant phase of Egyptian art. In this period the wealthy pharaohs, the lines of Emenophis and Ramses, built imposing temples (Luxor and Karnak, near Thebes), while there was a tendency to hollow out tombs in hypogeal form in the cliff-face of the Valley of the Kings. Painting developed and became a completely independent art tending to take the place of low-relief in funerary works. The decorative arts were flourishing, as we can see from the tomb of Tutankhamen. In the first millennium Egypt was several times invaded and lost its independence. Only the dynasties established in the delta at Saïs managed to maintain Egyptian civilization (Saïte period, 26th dynasty, seventh and sixth centuries B.C.). Conquered by the Persians in 525 B.C., then by Alexander, and on the latter's death passed over to Ptolemy (Ptolemaïc period, 285 B.C.–21 B.C.), Egypt, although open to Hellenic influence, never ceased to develop its native art which, though it never regained vitality, was piously respected by the Romans who were the last conquerors of the Nile valley in ancient times.

The Nile valley was the cradle of mankind's earliest social syntheses, and witnessed the first great human endeavour in the art of building. The country's wealth in stone materials, as well as the determination to make the dwellings of the dead last for ever, favoured the birth and progress of architecture. The longing for immortality inspired the first of these works, the Old Kingdom tombs called *mastabas* (shaped like the *frustum* – horizontal section – of a pyramid), and pyramids (pl. 18). The pyramid is, indeed, the most elementary architectural form, the one which most suggests stability and durability. Egypt had inherited from primitive times the taste for the gigantic which stresses the mightiness of man's creations (the Pyramid of Cheops, the largest of all, is 475 feet high, 738 feet wide, its base covers almost 13½ acres and its volume is over 2,500,000 cubic metres). On the outside there is a chapel in which the priest celebrated the funeral rites; it is decorated with mural images, carved or painted, and it has a 'false-door' ostensibly leading into the *serdab* containing the numerous 'doubles' which were intended as material support for the deceased king's soul in the after-life. The corpse, embalmed in the form of a mummy, was deposited in a crypt hollowed-out in the soil or built into the main structure.

After many experiments, the Egyptian temple took its final form in the New Kingdom (pl. 22). It was nothing less than a stone replica of the royal palace, which was made of wood and clay. Like the palace itself, it comprised three sections, the first reserved for introduction, the second for reception, the third for private life *(harem)*. The stone temple was built inside an enclosure of crude brick. There were two monumental 'pylons' or towers (pl. 19), themselves preceded by two obelisks (monolothic needles of stone), leading to a courtyard surrounded by colonnades

*19 Pylons of the Temple of Khons, Karnak. 11th c. B.C.*

*I Painting from the tomb of Mereruka, Saqqara, Egypt*

*20 Courtyard of the Temple of Ammon, Luxor. About 1375 B.C.*

(pl. 20); the great pillared chamber (hypostyle hall) was a sort of throne-room in which the image of the god was shown to the crowds when it emerged in its galley on feast-days; behind it the private quarters were composed of treasure-rooms and sacristies, grouped round the *naos* or sanctuary which enveloped in secrecy and darkness the statue which was the god's 'double'.

Egyptian architecture was hindered in its development by its under-estimation of the arch; though it was not totally unknown or ignored, it was exploited only rarely and incidentally. Nilotic building was based on the system of 'flat-arching', which consists of holding roofs by means of slabs laid on supports. The solidity of the whole rested on the inertia of horizontally superimposed materials; and as stones, unlike wood, cannot take great weights without breaking, the Egyptian had to add the numerous supporting pillars which encumber the interiors, in order to be able to roof spaces of any size (pl. 22). As was later the case with Christian churches, though not with Greek temples, the Egyptian temple was essentially an enclosed space; closed from the outside and partly covered in from above, it hid its mystery behind long blank walls, keeping all its wealth of effects for the inside. The lighting of hypostyle chambers was supplied diagonally by skylights or lantern-lights obtained by giving extra height to the central naves. Its dominant feature of horizontality gave full expression to the notion of immobility to which all Egyptian art was devoted. The stones, well cut, were assembled by means of internal or flush jointing: by a careful coursing which hid the joints the Egyptians strove to give the effect of monolithic blocks. Owing to his urge for strength and his desire to build for all time, the Nilotic architect also made liberal use of massive materials sometimes weighing as much as five hundred tons (as in the high temple of the Pyramid of Chephren).

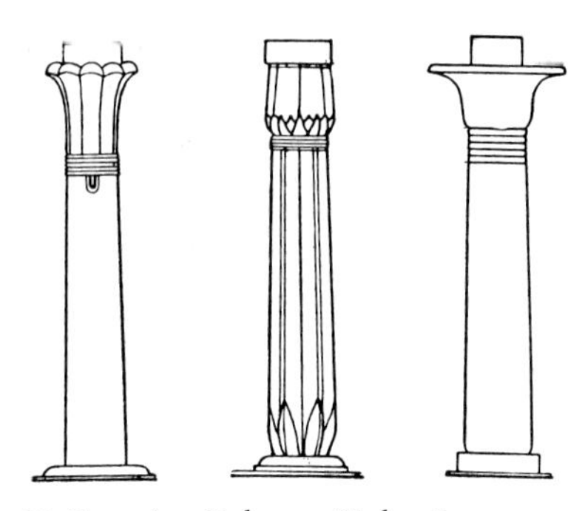

*21 Egyptian Columns (Palm, Lotus, Bell Capitals)*

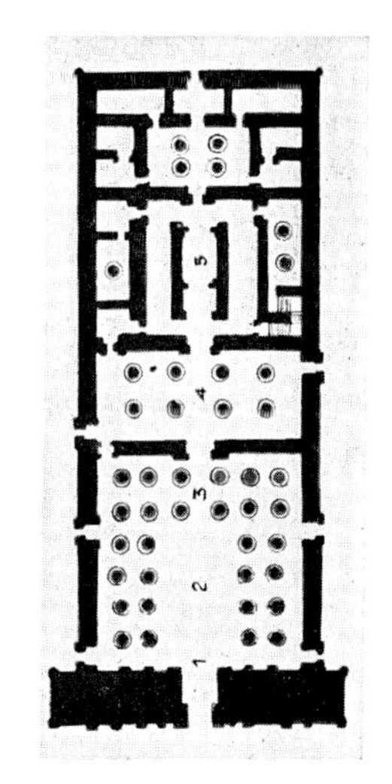


*22 Plan of the Temple of Khons, Karnak. (1 Pylons, 2 Courtyard, 3 Vestibule, 4 Hypostyle Hall, 5 Sanctuary)*

Though he created the art of building in stone, his mind, always after realism, stopped the Egyptian from inventing abstract forms that would have suited the raw material which he was the first to exploit in a rational manner: he contented himself with transposing into harder materials those earlier forms of architecture – in wood, compressed earth or clay – which remained in use for domestic purposes. The walls and towers (pylons) kept the sloped form which was given to mud or brick walls to prevent them from falling; the corners were decorated with a stone beading reminiscent of the sheaves of rushes used for binding dwellings of beaten earth; while the cornices had that splayed form characteristic of the tops of palm-trees. As for the columns themselves, whether palm-shaped, lotus-shaped or bell-shaped (pl. 21), their structure was that of the ancient supports made of sheaves of reeds or rushes, tied together and crowned with floral devices.

### *Sculpture*

The Egyptian sculptor rarely made use of soft stone such as limestone. He preferred the hardest materials such as granite, basalt and porphyry, which are most durable and can be polished. During the thirty centuries of Nilotic civilization statuary never managed to break free from the 'law' of frontality. With the head always on the axis of the bust, and the arms glued to the sides, the statue has all the appearance of being an accessory of architecture. Under the Old Kingdom, sculpture showed a powerfully synthetic modelling and an intensely realistic vision which inspired the greatest masterpieces of that art (pl. 24, 63). But this experi-

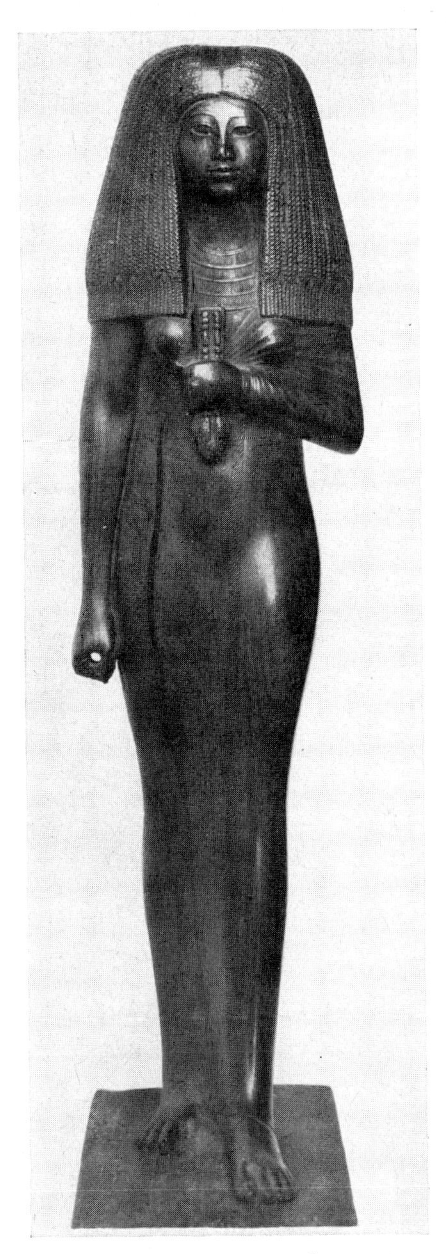

*23 'Lady Tui.' New Kingdom. Paris*

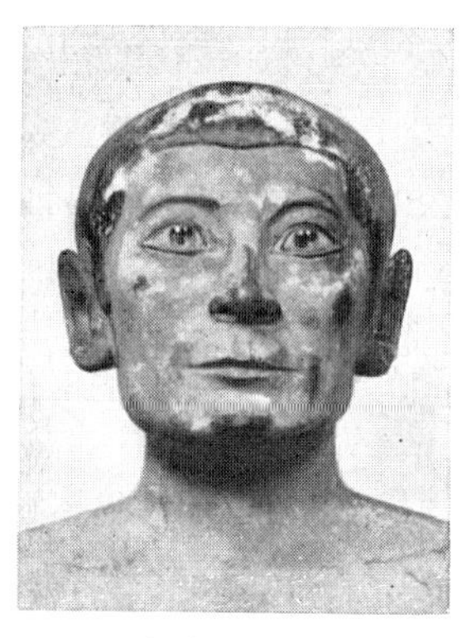

*24 Head of a seated Scribe. About 2400 B.C. Paris*

*25 Head of a Queen. About 1360 B.C. Paris*

mental movement was checked during the first Theban Empire, when it gave way to a classicism rejecting individual characteristics and inclining more towards an ideal of impersonality. This evolution was very much accentuated until the academicism of the second Theban Empire, when an ideal of ease and gracefulness admirably expressed the peaceable nature of the race (pl. 23). The initiative of an heretical pharaoh, Amenophis IV (about 1378 B.C.–1360 B.C.), brought about a revolution in the figurative arts that almost freed Egyptian art from the static style to which dogma had hitherto condemned it.

Challenging all previous sacred conventions, the sculptors and painters of Tell el Amarna (Amenophis IV's new capital) tended to portray forms according to expressionist and mannerist principles (pl. 25, 704). Unfortunately this movement was stifled. The accession of the weak pharaoh, Tutankhamen, who at once re-established the traditional religion and restored power to the priests of Amon, reduced art once again to a theological convention. The ephemeral restoration of the Saïte period breathed new life for a short time into moribund Egyptian sculpture, when it passed through a phase of archaism, renewing the elegant tradition of the New Kingdom and drawing some inspiration from the realism of the Old.

## *Mural Art*

This title covers sculptures in low-relief as well as paintings, which are only an economical imitation of them. The term 'bas- (low-) relief' does not apply very well to mural sculptures, especially in the Middle Kingdom period, when, by making a deeply incised outline, the Egyptian sculptor produced a flat sculpture which did not project beyond the wall's surface and on which he then chiselled minor detail. The con-

*26 Hunting and Fishing. Relief from Sakkara. 6th Dynasty*

ventions governing such compositions with figures have been described in the introductory pages of this chapter. In portraying human beings the face, always impersonal, played no part in the movement, while gesture was always subordinated to a rhythmic cadence that gave it a priestly solemnity. In portraying animals the artist, no longer inhibited by the same theological discipline, could give free rein to his genius for observation (pl. 26).

Curiously enough, the female figures were always more supple and alive than the male; alone of all the pre-Hellenic peoples, the Egyptians succeeded in expressing the voluptuous grace of the feminine body. The execution of bas-reliefs by specialized teams of workers who carved the details once the overseer had worked out the general composition, explains many an imperfection. The colouring of the paintings was extremely sober: red or yellow ochre, a little green or blue. Following a convention established in the infancy of Egyptian art, male bodies were painted red, and female ones yellow.

## *The Minor Arts*

The dry Egyptian soil, preserving whatever sank into it (except iron, owing to the presence of silica), has yielded thousands of specimens of domestic objects, many of them executed in luxurious style by the

*27 Gold Funerary Mask of Tutankhamen 18th Dynasty. Cairo*

artists of the Nile valley and destined for the after-life of important personages. The lucky find of the tomb of the Pharaoh Tutankhamen (pl. 27), still intact, has yielded us royal furnishings of incredible richness. The Egyptians had good taste in finery, the men even more than the women adorning themselves with costly ornaments which often had some magic property or showed their social status. Artists excelled in the working of such jewels, using hard gems set in gold or sometimes in silver, which was both rarer and more valuable. But the purely realistic mode of thought of the Egyptians hampered them in the invention of a decorative system: they reproduced the forms of animals and human beings and even those of architecture, breast ornaments, for instance, taking the shape of a temple tower (pylon) and earrings that of the lotus-type column. The hold of architecture on all the other arts is typical of highly organized societies, in which artists work in teams under the supervision of a foreman or chief who, in his turn, has to carry out the instructions of the priesthood.

## 2. THE CIVILIZATIONS OF WESTERN ASIA

While Egypt was pursuing its unchanging course, Mesopotamia, a frontierless region exposed to envious neighbours on account of its wealth, suffered many historical and ethnical vicissitudes, which now make it hard to follow the histories of successive civilizations in those parts. None the less, the creative impulse of the Sumerians was so strong that we can trace its development through the numerous feudalities and empires of which this 'land of two rivers' became the theatre.

As for the most part these peoples took little care of their burial-places, archaeological evidence remains scarce. The earliest artistic works of this civilization go back to the Eneolithic period and are to be found on the site of Susa at Shush, in Elam, in Iran and in Mesopotamia at El Obeid and Uruk (fourth millennium B.C.). Under the name of 'Chaldean civilization' scholars used to mark out the 'high period' of Mesopotamia, comprising: the 1st Ur dynasty in Sumeria (about 2800 B.C.), which left admirable specimens of the goldsmith's craft in its tombs; the Semitic dynasty set up towards 2470 B.C. at Agade by Sargon the Elder, who united the land of Sumeria with the Semitic land of Akkad (in Syria), and who also founded Babylon (about 2450 B.C.); the period of the Guti invasions (which ended the Accadian empire in about 2285 B.C.), when the shepherd-king *(patesi)* Gudea held court at Lagash (pl. 35) – a city whose site has yielded important works now to be seen in the Louvre; the 3rd Ur dynasty (2124 B.C.), destroyed by Elamite invaders towards 2000 B.C.; the 1st Babylonian dynasty (1894–1595 B.C.), which with Hammurabi (1792–1750 B.C.) represents perhaps the peak of Chaldean civilization. Many people imagine that the Assyrian Empire (beginning of first millennium down to 612 B.C.) with its seat at Nineveh sums up Mesopotamian civilization on account of the important remains which have been found there and its reputation for cruelty; it is on the contrary no more than the expression of its decadence. Achaemenian Persia (sixth to fourth century B.C.) was the political and artistic successor of the Assyrians. In Persia, Mesopotamian art was to lose something of its origins by imbibing the Classical Greek influence. Moreover, the principles of Chaldean art nourished more or less all the peoples of Western Asia, both Semitic and Aryan. Having little gift for original artistic creation, the latter turned to it for inspiration and at the same time helped to sustain it in their periods of success (Hittites, Kassites, Kingdom of Mitanni). The radiation of Mesopotamian civilization spread very far, since towns of the third millennium, showing a distinctively Sumerian character, have been found in the Indus valley (excavations at Mohenjo-Daro and Harappa).

### *The Chaldean Genius*

Whatever may be the attributes common to the two civilizations of the Nile and the Euphrates, of which much has been made by the historians, the genius of the Mesopotamian peoples is strikingly opposed to that of Egypt. An agricultural nation, peaceful in outlook, the Egyptians lived in close contact with the out-door world; the beneficent action of the Nile waters inspired them with an optimistic notion of natural powers, which gave them a belief in the immortality of the soul as well as a deep love of nature, both of which informed their art. Positivistic and with little bent for abstraction, they delighted in the reproduction of natural forms. Egyptian art is one of observation.

Although the flooding of the Tigris and Euphrates, which man learnt to control, gave Mesopotamia at that time a social structure not unlike that of the Nile valley, yet for reasons which perhaps have something to do with ethnical factors of which we know nothing, the races who first occupied these regions did not adopt the same naturalistic optimism.

*28 Hieroglyphs. 5th Dynasty. Cairo*

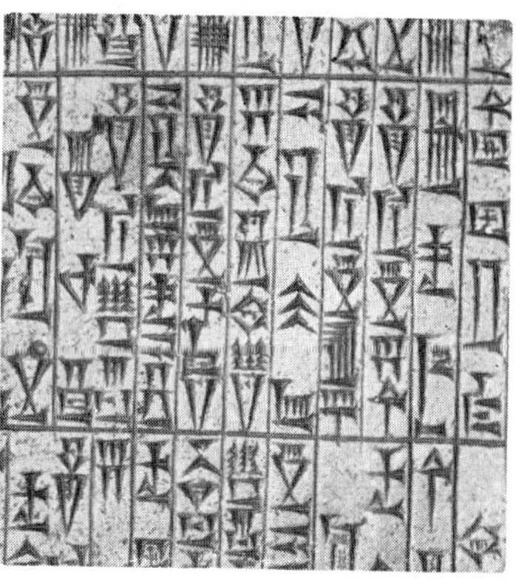

*29 Cuneiform Writing from the Code of Hammurabi. (1792–1750 B.C.) Paris*

If they recognized the benefits of nature – and worshipped it in Ishtar their goddess of fertility – they considered human life to be threatened by demonic powers that had to be exorcised with the aid of magic. Little given to realism, which would have encouraged them to imitate their neighbours, they had an extraordinary gift for abstraction, which made them arithmeticians and astronomers. The genius of each of these two peoples was perfectly expressed in their technique of writing (pl. 28, 29). Egyptian hieroglyphic writing was only an abridged transcription of the forms of natural things; the belief in the identity of the 'double' obliged Egypt right through its history to cling to this cumbersome pictographic method, which in any case was primarily reserved for sacred use. On the other hand, at an early stage, in their cuneiform script the Mesopotamians worked out a syllabic system of abstract symbols, intended for everyday use, and this rapidly made their tongue the language of diplomacy in the East. Art itself became for them a 'script', that is to say not a collection of naturalistic shapes, but a system of signs. The Mesopotamian artist imposed a series of schematizations and metamorphoses on the elements he borrowed from nature, creating purely imaginary forms which, compared with the supernatural powers they evoked, had a sign-value rather than a replica-value as in Egypt.

The oldest expressions of this faculty for abstraction are the admirable prehistoric funerary vases found at Susa and in Elam (pl. 30). The animal shapes on the vases from the oldest stratum, called 'Susa I', are geometrically stylized and thus achieve a most elegant decorative effect, comparable with the Rhodesian cave-paintings or with the first Greek vases (pl. 100). But the real source of this art is to be found in glyptics. For writing-purposes the Mesopotamians used cylinders covered with hollowed-out carvings which, when rolled on a slab of damp clay, gave

*30 Cup in baked Clay from Susa. End of 4th millennium B.C. Paris*

*31 Sumerian cylinder-seal Impression (detail). End of 4th millennium B.C. Paris*

an imprint in relief. These cylinder-seals, which were signets or else magic formularies, were used for all kinds of business or religious purposes. Unlike the monuments of the major arts they have survived in large numbers, and their study can teach us the whole of the evolution of the Mesopotamian aesthetic. From the beginning of Sumerian art these cylinder-seals reveal, already highly organized, the whole formal system of Mesopotamian art.

By skilfully combining animal forms suggested by the ibex, ass, lion, bison, eagle, snake and other beasts, the artists invented 'monsters', that is to say imaginary constructions (pl. 31). While Egyptian monsters remain mere composite entities of an architectural quality, those of Mesopotamia derive an astonishing unity from the nervous energy of their structure, and these imaginary creatures are extraordinarily alive. By ringing the changes on these monstrous shapes by different methods of composition – superimposing, fusing together, antithesis, symmetry and synthesis – the Sumerians created what amounts to a plastic language capable of infinite variation. This vocabulary of forms was to have important repercussions on the history of mankind, whereas Egyptian art reached a dead end and had no successors, which is quite usual with naturalistic art that can only prolong its own perfection by sterile imitation.

This play of metamorphoses on animal themes, invented by the Mesopotamians, was to prove an excellent source of training for others and to be most fertile imaginatively. Iranian, Scythian, Sarmatian, Turanian, German, Viking, Byzantine, and lastly Romanesque artists, were to delve freely into this mine of ideas, enriching it with endless original variations.

In architecture, by their use of vaulting, the Mesopotamians were to give the world a principle infinitely richer in possibilities than the flat roofing of the Egyptians. It required the mathematical mind of the Sumerian to dare project a keyed arch into space, with its radial arrangement of wedge-shaped stones, and its stability assured by nothing more than the force of gravity. From the time when it was applied along with all its implications by the Parthian and Sassanian builders, this principle was to revolutionize architecture and dominate building throughout the West, from Roman times to the Christian Middle Ages.

The Mesopotamians were thus great innovators, great initiators of artistic culture, and no doubt the Egyptians themselves were indebted to them in the initial stages. But whereas Egyptian art was ultimately to become a dead letter, the Mesopotamian plastic code was to remain a living language over many centuries.

## *Architecture*

The scarcity of wood and stone obliged the Mesopotamians to build in baked brick – or often merely sun-dried-brick – for which the silt from rivers gave them plenty of excellent material. Softened by centuries of rain these great heaps of clay now form hillocks (called *tells* by Arabs) which alone serve to break the monotony of the plains.

The most important invention of the Mesopotamians was the true vault. If like many primitive peoples they also made it with superimposed horizontal layers, each jutting out further than the one below (corbelling), which results in a 'false vault', they more frequently built it on the radial principle; tunnel-vaults bonded in this way have survived from the Sumerian period (tomb of a king in Ur). Assyrian bas-reliefs give evidence of the use of the semi-circular and elliptical cupola, but as no such domes have come down to us we cannot say whether the corbel or radial method was used.

*32 Palace of Sargon II, Khorsabad. 713–707 B.C.*

*33, 34 Ishtar Gate, Babylon, and Bas-Relief from the Gate. 7th–6th c. B.C.*

Vaulting increases the possibilities of clearance without recourse to detached struts to ease the overhead weight; but on the other hand it puts a lateral strain on its supports and thereby demands strong shoring which the Mesopotamians usually effected by the enormous thickness of their brick walls. For the stability gained from mere weight and mass in the flat-roof or lintel system, the vault substitutes a system of counter-strains which makes the structure an active organism. If the Mesopotamians did not carry this principle to its obvious conclusions, none the less they deserve credit for its invention.

Unlike the Egyptians, with their spiritual preoccupations, the Mesopotamians gave their architectural skill mainly to temporal undertakings. As well as fortresses they built grandiose palaces that were practically royal cities, as proof of the monarch's power (Sargon's palace at Khorsabad covers 25 acres, pl. 32). Mesopotamian architecture impresses us as monarchic and military, whereas the Egyptian was entirely religious.

The royal palaces were built on hillocks some 30 or 50 feet high which protected them from floods. They formed a rather confused collection of chambers, grouped in blocks round courtyards in the same way as Arab palaces to this day (pl. 32). First there came the reception-halls, then came the private apartments, and lastly public rooms. The palace also contained a building for worship known as the ziggurat. It consisted of seven rectangular storeys of decreasing size, painted in different colours and surmounted by a chapel which also served as an astronomical observatory. The corners of the palaces, like those of the ziggurat, were set according to the cardinal points of the compass. The rooms, though numerous, were of small dimensions – for the Mesopotamian made little use of detached pillars because he had neither wood nor stone to spare. The interiors were lit only by the door. From the outside the palace offered nothing but blank walls, often relieved by buttresses which pro-

*35 Statue of Gudea. About 2250 B.C. Paris*

*36 Relief of Ur-Nina (detail). About 2400 B.C. Paris*

duced some play of light and shade. The principal ornament was a monumental gateway, opening under a long vault between two towers and guarded by two winged bulls with human faces *(kheroubin)* (pl. 13) which served as propitiatory geniuses. These porchways were also used for meetings. In Assyrian and neo-Babylonian days they were decorated with compositions in low-relief or painted clay (pl. 33, 34), arranged in tiered rows round the walls.

The Mesopotamians also discovered the principles of military architecture which, passing from the Arabs to the Byzantines and thence to the Crusaders, survived until the introduction of gunpowder. For the simple passive resistance achieved by the mere thickness of walls, which the Egyptians relied on, the Mesopotamians substituted active resistance. The square towers jutting into the compounds enabled connecting walls to be covered by cross-fire. They were decorated with merlons – embattled parapets between embrasures – which could shelter look-outs who fired from the space between the battlements. A series of courtyards each commanding the other increased the obstacles to be overcome by the attacker, who could never turn an overrun enclosure against the garrison. Finally the complex internal communications, with numerous narrow defiles and tortuous passages, further delayed the besieger's progress. The Hittites improved on this system by building round keeps, better protected from the flanks and more difficult to sap, which had walls sloping at the foot so that projectiles hurled from the battlements would rebound on the enemy (fortress at Zendjirli).

The oldest works of sculpture of the first Ur dynasty *(Relief of Ur-Nina, Stele of the Vultures,* Louvre) are still close to the graphic technique of the cylinder-seals. On the bas-relief showing Ur-Nina and his family the figures, all alike, but with their names carved on their skirts to identify them, are little more than calligraphic symbols (pl. 36). Realism is to be found in the *Stele of Naram-Sin* (Louvre, Agade dynasty) on which the artist skilfully portrayed different actions in a battle. The excavations at Lagash have revealed the only great works of Chaldean sculpture in the round that are so far known to us, those depicting the shepherd-king Gudea (pl. 35). Carved in diorite and carefully polished, works such as this reach a degree of perfection, a synthesis which must have been the result of a long evolution of the stages of which nothing is yet known. The compactness of the statue concentrated within itself and its muscular vigour give an impression of power never achieved by the sculptures of the Old Kingdom in Egypt, in whose works the expression of energy was tempered by serenity and spiritual detachment. Scarcely emerging from the block of stone of which it was made, the Sumerian statue retains all the crude power of rock; it is a menhir in human form. This menhir quality is even more noticeable and was no doubt intended, in the famous *Code of Hammurabi* (Louvre, 1st Babylonian dynasty) in which we can also see writing mixed with sculpture as in certain statues of Gudea (pl. 16, 29).

*37 Relief at Carchemish. Hittite*

The Hittite bas-reliefs (at the sites at Boghaz-Keui and Carchemish, pl. 37) are transitional between Chaldean and Assyrian art. Long series of figures are shown in low-relief on the palace-walls of the Assyrian kings, and displayed at the foot of the wall and not as friezes at the top. This arrangement seems to have first occurred to the Mitannites who in Upper Mesopotamia had unlimited supplies of rock, so scarce in Chaldea. The abundance of this material (a gypsum-like alabaster, unsuitable for building but soft and very easy to shape) allowed the Assyrians full scope for bas-reliefs, as we see from the excavations on the site at Nineveh. Reliefs from the Palaces of Ashurnasirpal (883 B.C. –859 B.C.) and Sennacherib (705 B.C.–681 B.C.) can be seen in the British Museum in London, and from the Palace of Assurbanipal at Khorsabad, in the Louvre. The Assyrian kings' custom of abandoning their predecessor's palace and building one of their own favoured the development of sculpture. It has been calculated that if they were placed end to end, the panels discovered at Assurbanipal's palace at Khorsabad would stretch for 1¼ miles (pl. 38).

The great Assyrian creations are, in historic times, the first examples of artistic undertakings of a purely monarchical character, in other words exclusively devoted to the glorification of a ruler. The art of the Egyptian pharaohs, even at the time of the Rameses, was always conditioned by a religious outlook. The Assyrian kings made images neither for temples nor for tombs, but for their own palaces in the way that Louis XIV was to do in modern times. Those long, monotonous processions in which the king made such a frequent apearance, were intended to stress the wealth, warlike qualities, hunting prowess and cruelty of the sovereigns who for centuries imposed their reign of terror over all Western Asia,

*38 Army of Assurbanipal (669–626 B.C.) on the March. London*

*39 Relief from Agar Quf. 7th c. B.C. Bagdad*

and whose refinements of torture were surpassed only by the civilizations of the Far East. Technically these bas-reliefs, whose very number suggests that they must have been hastily carried out, show a profound decadence especially in the portrayal of the human figure. They reduce this to a play of arbitrary forms with none of the power and noble significance of the Egyptian canon. The limbs are badly articulated, the gestures mechanical and lacking in truth, the faces set like masks. The sculptors always sacrificed life to their cherished notion of superhuman strength, while their instinct for abstraction led them to treat details (beards, curling hair, the folds of clothing, jewels) as decorative themes elaborated for their own sake. All these elements were assembled without being brought into harmony with the main composition, which makes the whole thing a kind of puzzle. Here we see in embryo all the characteristics of the hieratic style so typical of the Asiatic monarchies, which were later adopted in Byzantine art. The principles of the composition of animated scenes followed the conventions described at the beginning of this chapter; it is to be noted, however, that in Assurbanipal's time a certain sense of perspective began to emerge. The different features of the composition were sometimes arranged in depth, each hiding something

*II 'La Parisienne', fresco from the Palace at Knossos, Crete*

of the other; but this progress towards optical truth remained unusual and was not part of general practice.

The real distinction of Assyrian art was in the representation of animals. The Assyrians' innate love of hunting and cruelty (being a people who by comparison with the Sumerians show a relapse into barbarism) helped them to understand the secret workings of animal psychology, much as primitive man had done. The intense truthfulness to life of their animal figures contrasts with the conventional style in which they portrayed human beings (pl. 39). All the expressions of the hunted animal, as it flees or stands at bay or roars with pain under the arrow or spear, were rendered by Assyrian sculptors with a savage vitality unknown to the Egyptians. The peaceful, pastoral Egyptians were too used to the company of domestic animals, which they painted and sculpted so admirably, to have as much understanding of the ways of wild beasts.

## *The Art of Achaemenian Persia*

Political successors to the pharaohs and to the kings of Nineveh and Babylon, the Achaemenian dynasties (539 B.C.–331 B.C.) inherited a mixed tradition. These rulers of the greatest empire of antiquity prior to Rome built castles in keeping with their wealth, such as those at Parsargadae (Cyrus, 539 B.C.–529 B.C.), at Persepolis (Darius, 521 B.C. –486 B.C., and Xerxes, 486 B.C.–465 B.C.), and at Susa, (Artaxerxes II, 404 B.C.–358 B.C.). For the first time in Asia, these palaces were built

*40 Capital from Artaxerxes II's Palace, Susa. Early 4th c. B.C. Paris*

*41 Stirrup Jar. Late Minoan I*

of stone, though brick was used with it. They consist of an extraordinary number of rooms all built on a colossal stone foundation, the finest rooms being called *apadanas* or throne-rooms, in the hypostyle manner borrowed from Egypt. The *apadana* of Artaxerxes II at Susa, which covered nearly 8,375 square feet, rested on 36 columns 63¹/₄ feet in height. These columns were in the form of a fluted shaft topped with a double series of scrolls, bearing a capital made of two bulls back to back, borrowed from Assyrian art (pl. 40). Other forms such as palm-shaped cornices were taken from Egypt. The Achaemenian buildings were all for secular purposes: the highly spiritual character of the Mazdean or Mazdakite religion forbade the use of temples and considered them as pagan. The fire-cult was celebrated on simple open-air altars *(pyrea)*. The 'kings of kings' also had luxurious tombs built in their honour, some of them being hollowed into rock after the manner of the Egyptian *hypogea* (tombs at Persepolis and Naqsh-i-Rustam).

The figurative and decorative art of the Persians evolves directly from Assyrian art, of which it retains all the monarchical character, much modified however by an element of placidity in keeping with the spirit of Persian civilization, which was one of the most humane of ancient times. At Persepolis and Susa we find the same long rows of soldiers and subject peoples as in Nineveh. The Persians made bas-reliefs in stone or enamelled terra-cotta (friezes from the palace at Susa, in the Louvre, pl. 133)which the neo-Babylonian Empire (625 B.C.–539 B.C.) had already used with great effect. Here the realistic portrayal of animals begins to disappear: the winged bulls and Achaemenian gryphons assume more heraldic, emblematic characteristics. The style of these sculptures has lost the barbarous strength of Assyrian works, and, already influenced by the Greek plastic arts, tends towards a decorative elegance.

## 3. THE AEGEAN CIVILIZATIONS

### *Historical Background*

We call those civilizations 'Aegean' which from about 3000 B.C. to the twelfth century B.C. flourished on the shores of the Aegean, in the island of Cyprus, the Cyclades, Crete and the Peloponnese, where the Achaeans, after conquering Crete, continued its tradition for some time. This civilization was based essentially on the industry and commerce of metallurgy, and the Aegean invaders, who came from Asia Minor, brought copper with them from about 3000 B.C. and by about 2300 managed to perfect its use by alloying it with tin, thereby producing bronze. While the Cycladic islanders were beginning to experiment with sculpting in marble, the Cretans, who began to rule the seas from quite an early date, created a highly skilled civilization comparable with those of the same period in Egypt and Mesopotamia, but one which had an extraordinarily modern flavour; for this nation of seafarers, merchants and industrialists seems to have been singularly free from that obsession with deity which governed every thought and act of the Egyptians and Mesopotamians.

### *Minoan Art*

The Minoan civilization, so named by Sir Arthur Evans who discovered it in Crete, flourished on that island from roughly the end of the fourth millennium till 1400 B.C. It was destroyed by the Achaeans, who came from Argolis (Peloponnesus), people of Indo-European stock who in herited the Aegean love of the sea and for a short time only (1400 B.C. –1100 B.C.) imposed themselves on the semi-barbarous 'Mycenaean' civilization, which the German Schliemann discovered in the Peloponnese.

As with most of the peoples of the Bronze Age, the Cretans made few images of the gods – from which sculpture draws its chief inspiration – and busied themselves mainly with industrial products.

Ceramics and metal-work were the principal occupations in Crete. The Cretans excelled in the working of precious metals as well as bronze, and exported silverwork, gems, gold, weapons, bronze ingots, to Asia Minor, Egypt, Peloponnesus (see the gold vessel found at Vaphio, south of Sparta, pl. 42), and also to the West. With them, ceramics had none of the crude industrial character it had with the other Bronze Age peoples (Hissarlik pottery); the prestige of metal was so great that potters began by imitating bronze vessels, giving the pots slim or gracefully curved shapes and covering them with a dark glaze. Artists prized elegance of

*42 Gold Cup from Vaphio. 1580–1450 B.C. Athens*

contour and relied on painting for decorative purposes (2400 B.C.–2200 B.C.). The vases of the Kamares style (about 1800 B.C.–1700 B.C.) bear geometrical patterns. Among the finest are the vases of the Middle Minoan III period (1750 B.C.–1580 B.C.) and those of the Late Minoan I (1580 B.C.–1450 B.C., pl. 41) in which realistic motifs are used, taken from floral or marine forms (cuttle-fish, octopus, coral, nautilus, sea-urchin, anemone, actinia); but the geometrical impulse took over again in the Palace style (Late Minoan II, 1450 B.C.–1400 B.C.).

The art of painting, probably begun on terra-cotta, found free expression in the frescoes adorning Cretan palaces. The imagery is borrowed from everyday life (dancing, bull-fighting), from nature (dolphins, flying-fish, flowers) and from more conventional designs (double-spiral, pl. 43). The bull, which left evidence of its importance in the Greek legend of the Minotaur, figures very frequently. The style is one of great ease, full of lively realism. Inspired by Egyptian and Sumerian art it is none the less more subtle and worldly; its jovial expressionism, its humorous, worldly realism foreshadow the hedonism of the Greeks, who were to deliver mankind from its fear of supernatural powers.

Cretan art has left no large-scale sculpture. The only works in the round, which are well-executed, are earthenware figurines (snake-goddesses) and figures in bronze or carved in hard stones. These were all for domestic decoration.

After the year 2000 B.C. the Minoans built great towns and palaces (Knossos, Phaestos, Hagia Triada, Mallia) where a very carefully planned system of sewers and canals and the size of store-rooms and cellars show an awareness of town-planning problems. The Minoan palace, composed of suites of rooms grouped round inner courts, was no doubt influenced by Mesopotamian palaces. The complexity of the lay-out of the chambers was perhaps responsible for the Greek myth of the labyrinth. These buildings were made of stone and wood, while numerous

*43 Fresco from the Palace of Tiryns. 1400–1100 B. C. Athens*

*44 Lion Gate, Mycenae. 1400–1100 B.C.*

isolated supports were used. The column appeared about 2000 B.C., with its shaft narrower at the base than at the top. The cushion-capital is thought to be a forerunner of the Doric style.

### *Mycenaean Art*

The Achaeans who destroyed Cretan civilization inherited its might, but unlike the Minoans these hardy pirates were of a quarrelsome and warlike temperament, as Homer reminds us in the *Iliad*. Their warlike

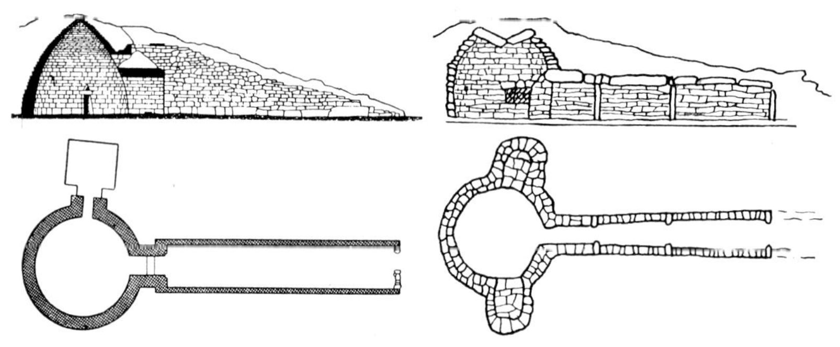

*45 Treasury of Atreus, Mycenae* *46 Neolithic Grave, Portugal*

instinct led to the construction of the strongholds at Mycenae and Tiryns (pl. 44). Owing to their colossal stonework, made of irregular blocks in what the Greeks called the 'Cyclopean' style, these buildings belong even more to megalithic architecture than they do to the Cretan Palace style, although their masonry is more regular. Their tombs (Treasury of Atreus at Mycenae, pl. 45, and the Tomb of Orchomenus), like certain Celtic or Celto-Iberian burial-places (Tomb of Alcalar, Portugal, pl. 46), consist of a covered passage leading to a burial chamber, the latter being hut-like in shape and topped with a sort of cupola made of slabs superimposed corbel-wise.

The decorative art of the Achaeans, so far as we can see from what has survived, appears to have been inspired by the Cretan, of which it is a degenerate form. Like the Cretans they knew the crafts of metalwork and had a great taste for silver and gold trinkets.

## 4. THE ART OF THE NOMADS

Central Asia, an immense reservoir of human energy, has never ceased pouring hordes of nomads into Euro-Asia. They were always ready to swoop like birds of prey on the pastoral settlers who built up the great historical civilizations of China and South-West Asia. These mounted barbarians had a vast territory to overrun in every direction. In the wide strip of the steppes from Budapest to Mongolia every race was represented with all its tribes: in the eastern steppes there were the Turco-Mongols (Ordos, Avars, Huns, Turks), while the western steppes were inhabited by peoples of Indo-European stock (Scythians and Sarmatians in central Russia, Satians [Saces] and Sogdians in Turkestan). But whatever their origins, their similar way of life imposed similar characteristics both in space and time on their chosen forms of artistic expression. As their nomadic habits restricted them to making small

*47 Gilded bronze Plaque. Scythian*

chattels, such as carpets (almost all of which have disappeared), gold ornaments and trinkets (buckles, sword-hilts, brooches, discs and badges for sword-belts) or harnessings for chariots and horses, they perpetuated the customs of the Bronze Age. As with the Magdalenian hunters, the animal represented the primordial power of nature for these tribes of hunters and shepherds: they gave something of the living suppleness of the animal to their ornamentation, which was all composed of curves and counter-curves to which the malleability of metals, whether gold, silver or bronze, readily lent itself. However, if their imagination was capable of creating an original style, their ornamental and zoomorphic art derives from the more civilized arts of Mesopotamia. It was by way of Iran – the great historic point of focus and communication between South-West Asia and the steppes, and melting-pot for so many races – that the tribes of the steppes came to know the ornamental style of the Sumerians and Elamites.

*48 Plaques of cloisonné Gold-Work from the Grave of a Saxon Chieftain, Sutton Hoo. About A.D. 650. London*

*49 Bronze Statuette. Luristan. Paris*

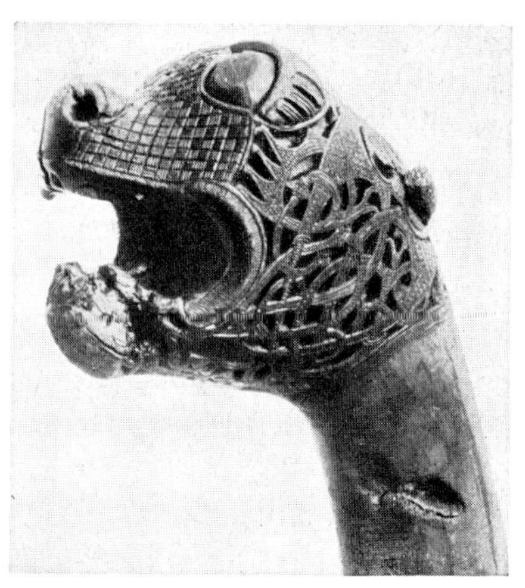

*50 Wooden Staff from the Death-Ship of Oseberg (detail). About A.D. 850. Oslo*

Excavations in the Luristan mountains, which form the frontier between Mesopotamia and Persia, have done much to enable us to understand how this intricate compounding of forms came about, by revealing to us the art of the earliest Iranian settlers who had formed communities by the eleventh century B.C. After their nomadic phase they still retained their skill in the arts of metalwork; in their standards and their trappings for harness they transposed into bronze with wonderful elegance the monstrous, intertwined heraldic forms of the Chaldean cylinders (pl. 49). Among these tribes of the steppes (Ordos, Huns, Scythians), in daily contact with animal life, the zoomorphic style lost its monstrous character and showed a renewal of realism, though this was soon affected by the passion for ornament which filled the barbarians with a longing for fantasy, their nomadic way of life luring their imagination into a perpetual, onward flux.

It is their tombs which have revealed this art of the steppes. Graves were covered by mounds called *kurgans,* in which the tribal chiefs were buried with their wives, servants, horses, chariots and jewels in the same way as in the oldest Ur dynasties, which they were no doubt imitating. These have been examined especially in the steppes of Siberia and southern Russia, which were inhabited by the Scythians some centuries before the Christian era. The Scythians created a dramatic art in which animals are entwined together in furious combat, such violent themes resulting in fine modulations of pattern (pl. 47).

While Scythian art became debased by its contact with the Greek goldsmiths of the Black Sea region, a new zoomorphic art began to appear in Central Asia: that of the Sarmatians, which spread as far as China in the Han period (202 B.C.–A.D. 265) and which appeared in graves in south Russia in the Christian era. Sarmatian art spread to other hordes which were to invade the West, notably the Germans, Huns, Goths and Franks. Among these latter races this form of art tended to become increasingly aniconic (imageless) and abstract, losing sight of the animal realism of its origins. They favoured interlaced patterns, a kind of indecipherable ornamental knot, as well as cloisonné work in gold, the setting of glass beads or gems (garnets, sapphires, emeralds) in gold, and inserting gold filigree into another metal (known as damaskeening). They might well have been influenced by the fine gold craftmanship of the Sassanians or Sassanids, who came to Persia after the Seleucids (A.D. 227–641). However, the jewelry of the Ordos and Scythians seems to suggest that the steppe tribes knew this technique earlier. These Nordic barbarians made much use of an ornamental system derived from the circular motif (wheels, helixes, spirals, roses, six-petalled marguerites, swastikas) which the Sumerians had invented. This abstract art, which consists of handling any living form as a purely ornamental motif, was to flourish once more among the Scandinavian Vikings until the ninth century A.D. (Death-ship of Oseberg, about A.D. 850, pl. 50). It also gave vitality to the first artistic productions of the Christianized West – those of the Franks, Merovingians and Saxons, pl. 48) and more especially the Irish monks of the seventh and eighth centuries (pl. 162). It was one of the sources of Romanesque art, and, as such, of fundamental importance in the advance of the arts in the Western world.

## 5. THE PRE-COLUMBIAN CIVILIZATIONS

### *The Pre-Columbian Mentality*

The cultures which flourished on the American shores of the Pacific ocean before the European conquest were historically contemporary with our own Christian era, and yet even more than the older civilizations of Egypt and Mesopotamia they remained deeply enslaved to the primitive mentality. In no other part of the world did any civilized race remain longer at the mercy of terrifying supernatural powers: nowhere did man have a more tragic awareness of his fragility in a hostile world. He imagined he was on earth only to pay blood-tribute to deities lusting for death and murder, and the sun itself had to be fed its daily ration of human blood in order to continue on its course. The terrors of the millennium left a memorable scar on our own civilization, so that we can only imagine what the psychology of such a race as the Aztecs, who were plunged every fifty-two years into despair lest the world come to an end, must have been. The ritual sacrifice of young women, children or captured enemies – for warfare often had no other purpose than to

*51 Frieze of Plumed Serpents from the Temple of Xochicalco. Aztec*

replenish the altars – has left the Aztec civilization with a gruesome reputation.

Although they were more humane, the civilizations of Peru and Bolivia also practised, though with a little more restraint, similar liturgical sacrifices. But no other evolved civilization made death the very principle of a cosmological, magical or religious system. As though the survival of the species in a terrifying universe could only be ensured by the sacrifice of an enormous number of its members! Those who were privileged to live had themselves to pay the horrible levy, being obliged for instance to make blood gush from their ears, or to draw a string covered with thorns through a hole pierced in their own tongue.

The works of the Peruvians are certainly imbued with some humane spirit, but this was never the case with the images made in Central America. The gods represented by the Maya, the Toltecs and Aztecs are all monsters, while the men are in the image of their gods. No art has ever symbolized so dynamically the inhumanity of a hostile world, no race ever erected such figures as these of the demoniacal powers that primitive man imagined to govern the world.

The strange formal structure of these pre-Columbian works – whose only parallel is to be found in old Chinese bronzes – is made up of a jumble of features all imbricated onto each other without the slightest continuity (pl. 51). The introduction of some unifying principle, of some ordered sequence in the chaos of appearance is the very hall-mark of rational thought, which has the capacity of projecting intellectual, guiding lines into the manifold discords of the world. The Egyptians and Sumerians had this gift, which expressed itself in their art through the still entirely intuitive conception – of which the Greeks became fully aware – of the unifying principles that govern the various elements of which a work is composed, by subjecting it to the laws of rhythm, cadence and proportion. The instinct of cruelty arising from fear of malevolent powers seems not to have existed from earliest times. The

*52 Temple called 'The Castle', Chichen Itza. Maya-Toltec. 8th to 9th c. A.D.*

early civilizations discovered in the Valley of Mexico (at Tlatilco, about 900–300 B.C.) produced smiling terracotta figures full of grace and good humour, showing that this primitive people believed in benevolent powers. The smooth modelling of their statuettes confirms by contrast the demoniac significance of later pre-Columbian modelling.

These races are the only ones to have knowingly given artistic expression to the mentality of primitive man, hurled into a universe whose powers he knew not how to harness, through works which for grandeur and beauty invite comparison with those of Sumeria and Egypt. They show us the highest level of civilization that is attainable by mankind without the aid of national thought, without that marvellous intellectual instrument which in different ways made possible the scientific and philosophical awakening of India, China and the Mediterranean peoples. They were also retarded perhaps by their isolation on a continent cut off from the great centres of the world's civilizations. Yet with no more than the most rudimentary tools, the pre-Columbians sought and contrived to overcome by energy alone a universe that appeared more hostile to man there than in any other part of the globe.

## *Historical Background*

The two empires of the Aztecs and Incas, which dominated the greater part of civilized America at the time when the Spaniards arrived there, succeeded for a long time in concealing the rich complexity of the civilizations they had enslaved. In fact these two empires were both agents of political unification (like the Roman Empire) which were creative mainly at the material level, but which in spiritual matters depended on those they had conquered.

Pre-Columbian America may be divided into two main spheres of influence: Central America, and the Pacific side of South America.

Central America comprises the present territories of Mexico and the Republics of Honduras and Guatemala. The numerous cultures that flourished in this region had several elements in common, notably the use of the terraced pyramid as a base for the sanctuary; the ritual game of *pelota;* the frequency of human sacrifice; the use of hieroglyphic writing; the calendar based on eighteen months of twenty days, making cycles of fifty-two years. The two most creative races of this region were the Toltecs and the Maya. The birthplace of the Maya, who appear to have reached the higher degree of culture, was in Honduras and Guatemala, where in the early centuries of our era they built numerous townships which are now being unearthed in the forest by archaeologists (Uaxactum, Palenque, Quirigua, Copan). After a time of decadence the Maya Empire revived towards the end of the tenth century A.D. in the Mexican peninsula of Yucatan, and its greatest period lasted for two hundred years (987–1191, cities of Uxmal, Mazapan, Chichen Itza, Kabah, etc.). The empire fell owing to civil war; in the eleventh and twelfth centuries the neighbouring Toltecs seized Chichen Itza and created a mixed art, Maya-Toltec, which shows a great profusion of forms.

The high plateau of Mexico was a very active centre of civilization right from early times. Several peoples settled on the shores of Lake Texcoco, now dried up, the site of Mexico City. Several centuries before our era one of these tribes founded the city of Teotihuacan, which fell into decay in the tenth century A.D.; about the time when the invading Toltecs built the city of Tula. The Toltecs paid particular honour to the god Quetzalcoatl, the green-plumed serpent, who was god of the wind, then later god of the arts and of civilization (pl. 51). It is not certain at what date (perhaps the thirteenth century) the Aztecs, coming from the north, settled on the central plateau; the date when Mexico City (Tenochtitlan) was built is variously put at 1325 or 1370. Their principal deity was the cruel god of war, Huitzilopochtli, whose thirst for human blood surpassed all others'.

On the two ocean slopes of Central America lived satellite peoples of the Toltecs, Maya and Aztecs: on the Atlantic shore were the Zapotecs (city of Monte Alban) and Mixtecs (city of Mitla, founded in the fifteenth century), while on the Gulf of Mexico were the Totonacs (sites of Tajin, Cempoala, between sixth and twelfth centuries).

The cultures of South America are less known owing to the absence of written evidence, since the peoples there had no system of writing. They have been revealed mainly by burial-places containing excellent pottery and utensils. Their chronology is still obscure. It is usual to distinguish between the pre-Inca and Inca cultures. The Andean plateau (Peru and Bolivia) was the birthplace of American metallurgy, gold, silver, copper, then bronze. The Aymara built the gigantic monuments of Tiahuanaco to the south of Lake Titicaca. On the Peruvian coast, several peoples succeeded each other in an order which is difficult to establish chronologically: in the north, the Chimu (site of Chanchan); in the centre the builders of the city of Pachacamac near Lima; in the south, those who modelled the fine works in terra-cotta since discovered on the sites of Ica and Nazca. In the twelfth century the Kichua appeared, sunworshippers who established, over different races occupying a region over 2,500 miles long, a vast empire with a very advanced material civilization: the empire of the Incas which was to be destroyed by the Spaniards.

### *Architecture and Sculpture*

The architecture of the pre-Columbian peoples has proportions which strive after great monumental effects, but its range of expression is limited by the absence of the vault and the rarity of the disengaged pillar. The tribes of Central America (Aztecs, Toltecs, Maya, Zapotecs) erected their monuments on artificial terraced mounds, and, for religious purposes, they built high pyramids, step-wise with tiled facings (pl. 52). The summit was reached by way of four steep staircases, giving access to the sanctuary containing the idol and the sacrificial altar. These monuments were often on a colossal scale: the Pyramid of the Sun at Teotihuacan still measures 212 feet in height and covers an area of 53,820 square yards, with a frontage of 700 feet. The largest of these remains yet found, the Pyramid of Quetzalcoatl at Cholula, 1,463 feet

*53 Gateway into the Palace of Labna. Maya*

*54 Stele of Peidras Negras, Guatemala. Maya*

wide, has a far greater volume than the Pyramid of Cheops in Egypt. The architects who built the palaces show a prefence for halls, long rather than wide, so as to limit the span of beams and slabs for roofing. The most highly developed and richest architecture was that of the Maya, who were the only ones who dared build corbelled 'vaults' (pl. 53) and made frequent use of the detached support.

The Andean region has kept intact a much larger number of civil and military buildings. The monuments of the Peruvian coast, built in adobe (dried clay), have left very few remains (Chanchan). On the plateau, on the contrary, are to be found enormous works dating from the pre-Inca and Inca periods: paved roads, huge walls crossing the mountains, strongholds, palaces and temples. The city of Cuzco (in Peru) stands to this day on the foundations of the Inca city. The pre-Incas made free use of colossal monoliths (Gate of the Sun, Tihuanaco). Both polyhedral and regular stonework was so carefully assembled that today it is impossible to insert a pin between the interstices. The stones were often bound with copper cramps.

Sculpture was rare with the Peruvians, but the Central Americans made considerable use of it both in isolated carvings and for facing walls. The figures are ferocious, composite monsters, of which the best known is Quetzalcoatl, the plumed serpent (pl. 51). In the sunken reliefs they are accompanied by a background of geometrical patterns. The finest school of monumental sculpture was that of the Maya (pl. 54). Whereas the Toltecs and Aztecs followed the ideographic conventions common to primitive peoples, only the Maya came anywhere near optical truth in their construction of the human figure; the rhythmical beauty of their works sometimes recalls Greek art.

## *The Minor Arts*

The pre-Columbian peoples excelled in the minor arts such as textiles, the working of hard stones and precious metals, which they lavished on their monuments (Temple of the Sun at Cusco), and especially ceramics (pl. 55, 56). The finest Central American ceramics are the burial urns of the Zapotecs, with their statuesque lines and flamboyant ornamentation,

*55 Chimu Vase from Peru. Paris*

*56 Nazca Vase from Peru. Paris*

and the smiling heads of the Totonacs; these works witness the ascendancy of sculpture over the other arts, which is normal in an artistic society governed by its feeling for the monumental. The Peruvian potters, on the other hand, sought curves better adapted to the needs of the vase, of which numerous specimens have been preserved undamaged in tombs. In polychromatic tones, on red or black slip, the Inca pots are adorned with a geometrical pattern, and those of Nazca with a demoniacal symbolism not unlike that of Central America. The anthropomorphic Chimu pottery perfectly adapts realistic observation to the curve of the vase, and their works are the only human representations to be found in the Americas. The Chimu potters, and above all those who made the earlier Chimu or Mochica pots, with their red foundation, left some admirable portraits. The later Chimu pots, with their black ground, show a withering of realistic inspiration.

## 6. THE ARTS OF THE 'UNCIVILIZED' PEOPLES

In the tropical zones, far removed from the great centres of civilization, peoples of negroid race who go about naked under the hot sun, pursuing a primitive way of life, still give the work of art the sacred and magical meaning that it had in earliest times. These peoples form two great cultural groups, dispersed across Africa and in the chain of islands scattered across the Pacific, from Australia to Madagascar and Easter Island.

Though these races have no known historical relationship, they hold in common an aesthetic notion which exalts the painted or sculpted form into a revelation from the beyond, a sign fraught with supernatural powers. This is true not only in the case of ancestral images, fetishes and totems evoking beneficent spirits and evil demons, or the masks used for ritual dances and ceremonies, but also in the case of objects of everyday use whose stylized patterns have symbolic value (for instance, figureheads on Polynesian canoes); for primitive man lives at all times in contact with the beyond. The attitude of the negroid or Oceanic artist is thus anti-realistic. When he evokes the form of a bird, a crocodile or a human being, he is pursuing an idea, not an image, accentuating some traits, stylizing the lines and volumes; the visual truth of the object is profoundly affected by his sense of magic and mystery. Contrary to the practice of primitive or barbarian peoples of the white race, in negro and Oceanic art the human figure plays a preponderant role because of the ancestor-worship they have in common. The mask is the essential object of these civilizations: the wearing of the mask produces a veritable transfer of personality in the man who assumes it. In funeral or ritual ceremonies, which are masked dances, the primitive man ensures the passing-over of the deceased ancestor, or else possesses himself of his virtues.

This art is also characterized by having no history. Objects collected by explorers before the contact of modern civilization caused rapid decay in native cultures, are objects in recent use whose origins have long been forgotten. Only some parts of Africa are able to provide any historical perspective. The African continent, cut off like an island, seems to have had no communication worth mentioning with the Mediterranean civilizations or with those of Asia, except in the North, which was conquered by Islam, and in Egypt, where a highly skilled civilization developed, and in Abyssinia, which, converted to Christianity, pursues to this day the primitive Christian art from Egypt, known as

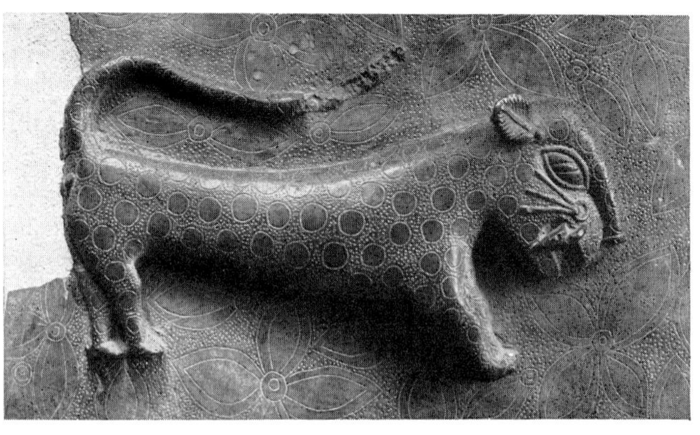

*57 Bronze Plaque from Benin. 16th c. A.D. Paris*

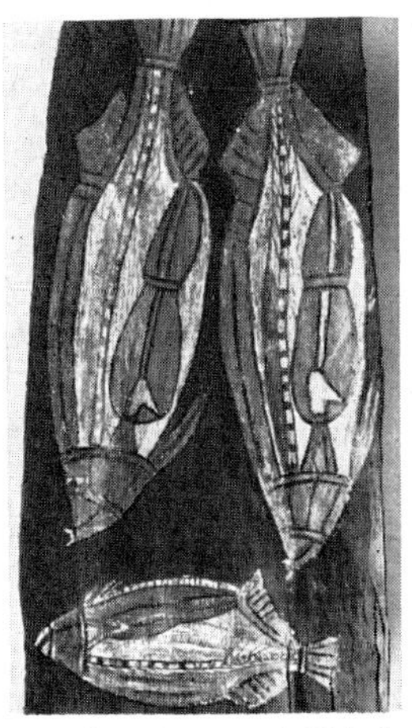

*58 Bark Painting of Fish from Arnhem Land, Northern Territories, Australia*

*59 Wooden Statuette from the Belgian Congo. Tervueren*

Coptic art. Cave-paintings whose traditions go back perhaps to a period contemporary with those of France and Spain have been discovered in the north-west Sahara and in Rhodesia. In the latter region ruins of a town have been discovered, that of Zimbabwe, built apparently by the Bantu, probably in about the fifteenth century. The ancient Kingdom of Benin, on the Ivory Coast, whose zenith seems to have been in the sixteenth and seventeenth centuries, produced admirable anthropomorphic and zoomorphic objects in bronze and ivory (pl. 57) – no doubt under certain Mediterranean influences. However, surveys and excavations carried out in West Africa (at Ife, Jebba, Tada) have brought to light magnificent bronzes that antedate the arrival of the Portuguese and are therefore older than those from Benin. They demonstrate that negro Africa produced highly-developed artistic civilizations before tribal art degenerated. The most productive negro tribes are to be found in Central Africa, in the Sudan, on the Guinea Coast and in the Congo region. African art, which devoted itself chiefly to wood-carving, is full of grandiose and tragic meaning which shows itself in a harsh and dry stylization, giving priority to the straight line over the curve, and the whittling-down of the statue into clear-cut geometrical volumes (pl. 59). It is these characteristics which appealed to the Fauve and Cubist painters of our own period.

Oceania has produced works which are more suggestive, less elementary and have a more mystical and poetical meaning. The Oceanic native has a particular bent for whorls of curves and spirals (pl. 60) and on this basis makes very subtle formal patterns, whereas the forms of African art are always dramatically isolated from each other. These patterns are,

*60 Carving for the Entrance to a House from New Zealand*

incidentally, not unrelated to those of pre-Columbian art. The stylistic interpretation of the Oceanic artists is even farther from nature than that of the African. He is a sculptor, but he also has the painter's temperament, which expresses itself in paintings on bark (pl. 58) and in the colourings of masks and statues. The art of the Pacific offers great variety from island to island. The finest works are to be found in Melanesia, New Caledonia, the Solomon Islands, the New Hebrides, New Zealand and the Marquesas. Easter Islands, the last link in the chain of islands stretching towards America, has some five hundred monolithic statues of unknown origin, in the human image.

The Red Indians of North America show no signs of the same artistic gifts as the peoples of the same race in the centre and South of the continent. In the Rio Grande, in New Mexico, the Pueblos culture is a derivative and provincial centre of the aristocratic civilizations of Central America. These peoples have left towns built in stone on a semi-circular plan, sheltered under rocks or at the foot of cliffs. Farther to the north the Indians have remained in the nomad state, and they are painters rather than sculptors, making coloured patterns in feathers or paint.

In South America, in the upper Amazon as well as on the Atlantic coast, primitive peoples carried on a degenerate form of pre-Columbian art, sometimes mingled with influences that appear to have come directly, across the chain of islands, from Polynesian art.

# III. THE CLASSICAL CIVILIZATIONS OF THE MEDITERRANEAN

The Egyptian, Mesopotamian and Aegean civilizations are the work of the Semitic and Asiatic peoples established in the Mediterranean basin or in Western Asia long before 3000 B.C. The Indo-Europeans who gradually infiltrated into the Mediterranean, mainly after 2000 B.C., spent a long period as parasites of the civilizations they came to overthrow. For over ten centuries neither the Mitannites, the Kassites nor the Hittites made anything really original. The Achaeans battened on the cultural remnants of the Cretans and later the Persians, on whom fell the mantle of the Assyrians, made little more than a pale imitation of the royal art of Nineveh.

However, in the course of that protohistorical phase of the Aryan peoples, a slow assimilation was being accomplished, a blending of elements that was to produce the miracle of Greece. Whether they were pushed back by the Dorian invasion, which was the last wave of Aryan migration to penetrate Greece proper towards the year 1200, or whether in the preceding centuries they had fled from the misery caused in their own cities by social crises of their own making, whether they came from the North, or rather, as some now think, from the Middle East, the Hellenes, who almost immediately proved to have great talent for trading, gradually established colonial centres in both the Eastern and Western Mediterranean and as far north as the Hellespont. They settled more especially in Asia Minor where they founded the numerous cities of Ionia which, succeeding to the Aegean 'thalassogracy' or maritime state, gradually supplanted the Phoenicians' hegemony of the seas and by way of reaction excited the rivalry of the mother cities, Athens and Corinth.

Compared with the ancient great powers, now in ruin, of Egypt and Mesopotamia, or with the Iranian empires of the Medes and after them the Persians who took up all their traditions, the Hellenes who were produced by the ferment of successive migrations represented all the youthful energies of the universe in the seventh and sixth centuries B.C. In them the Aryan genius emerged from its long obscurity, to accomplish one of the most vital revolutions of mankind and lay the foundations of the modern world.

The Greeks broke with the magical bond which had made man, ever since his origins, a power inseparable from the world about him. However mature they were, an Egyptian or Mesopotamian still had the feeling of being no more than a cog in the immense mechanism of the cosmos, so that man's intelligence, the privilege of his species, could do no more than propitiate the play of occult forces by bringing some divine

*61 Assurbanipal hunting Lions. 7th c. B.C. London*

power into action. In order to rise above nature, man has to identify himself with god; the pharaoh assured life and after-life to his subjects by uniting the human and divine in his own person.

We shall never be able to fathom the tremendous effort human genius had to make to upset a scheme of things based on traditions thousands of years old, in order to stand alone, aware of its new-found strength, face to face with the universe. From then on man no longer tended towards self-identification with the spirit of nature, but tried to transcend it by means of reason, so that he could draw knowledge and power from its laws. The creative act, carried out by primitive man only when he believed himself possessed by some demiurge, was now to become pure creativity. Man stopped being the creature of God, and began to create God in his own image. The Greek Pantheon brought under its roof all the personifications of the faculties and attributes of the human soul: intelligence (Athena), sensibility (Aphrodite), the aggressive instinct (Ares), the genius of trade (Hermes), the creative gift (Apollo), lyric power (Dionysus); even the cruder instincts, which subconsciously still link man with the beasts, found an idealized image among the demi-gods. Everywhere man began to project his own dimensions into a world suddenly reduced to a new scale. Order was imposed on chaos, for human intellect thought it could discover some law of harmony in the world, some pre-established system. Foreshadowing the spirit of modern discoveries, Pythagoras saw the essence of things in a mechanics which reduced all phenomena to the norm of numbers.

Man's freedom from those shackles which had enslaved him to the laws of the universe broke out somewhat naïvely in archaic statues, evoking a psychological expression which was hitherto unknown to the art of mankind – the smile, a symbol of euphoria, the 'hieroglyph of

*62 Chariot Race. Ionic Relief. End of 6th c. B.C. Istanbul*

happiness' as it has been called, which expresses the joy of pure creation and of free discovery (pl. 71, 72).

The magic touch now gave way to rational knowledge, but the latter had not yet felt that austere renunciation which is characteristic of modern times. The Greeks did not reject the supernatural but transposed it into images and mythology. There is as much difference between mystery and myth as between night and day. Not that myths entirely stopped being objects of belief (though for enlightened minds this was to be the case, and the gods of Olympus quickly became the divinities of fable); but such belief was no longer placed in blind powers, holding sway over the universe, but rather in concepts. Primitive religions were born of fear. Greek religion, or rather mythology, sprang from the union of reason with poetry which is perhaps the very essence of the Greek miracle. It was as much through the songs of poets as through theological speculation that the confused legends of primitive times gradually syncretized into cycles of anthropomorphic myths. Eager to pour the world's every aspect into the mould of ideas, the Greek imagination personified everything, the most abstract concepts as well as nature's material forms, all the data of the mind, of history and natural philosophy; and, what is more, all these allegorics were given a human face. The Greeks thought of everything either as concepts or figures. Any study of man's historical evolution will show that there is not a human attitude, whether of the senses or intellect, whether personal or social, that did not find its first representation in some Greek myth. The universe crystallized itself for them in shapes, in a vast system of anthropomorphic images which became an endless source of speculation for the plastic arts, poetry and drama.

The artists of that civilization saw before them an immense field of activity unknown to the Mesopotamians and which the Egyptians had scarcely touched: the discovery of man. The human figure was about to

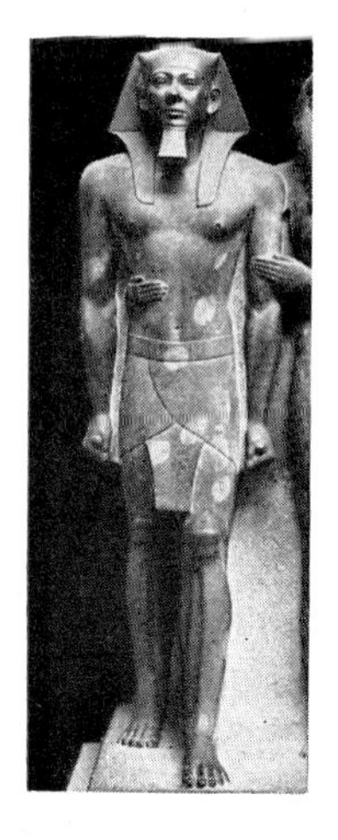

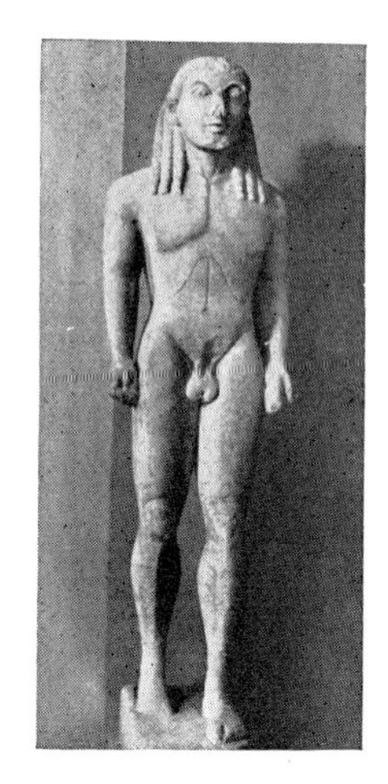

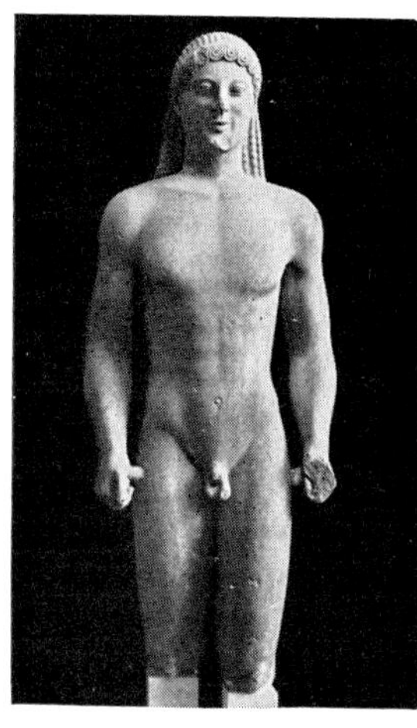

*Evolution of the Athlete in Sculpture*

63 *Mycerinus. Egyptian, 4th Dynasty. Boston*

64 *Athlete (by Polymedes of Argos). 1st half of 6th c. B.C. Delphi*

65 *Apollo from Tenea. 1st half of 6th c. B.C. Munich*

66 *Apollo. End of 6th c. Athens*

dethrone the animal from the sway it had held so long over the imagination and works of the first civilizations. Conscious of his physical weakness, man had at first worshipped the unerring mechanism of instinct to be found in the beasts, and he gave it all his admiration, although he alone enjoyed the privilege of intellect. Formerly man had had to borrow some animal attribute in order to become godlike; but now it was the animal that was translated into man, and the monsters of Greek mythology – centaurs, sirens, satyrs – are all animal forms promoted to the human plane, the plane of intelligence.

This discovery of man was made in two stages: first physically, then morally. It took no less than three centuries to gain experience of the

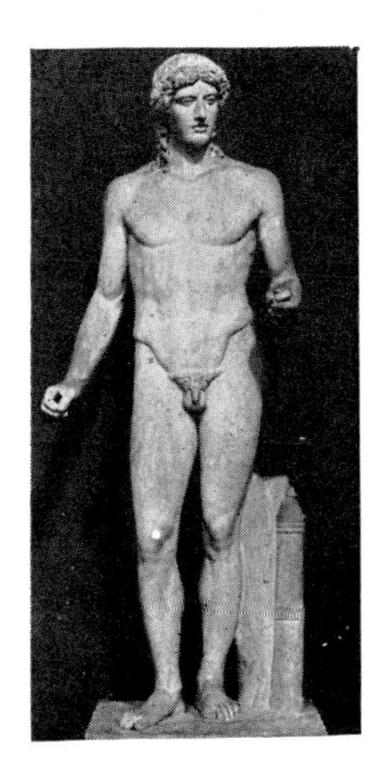
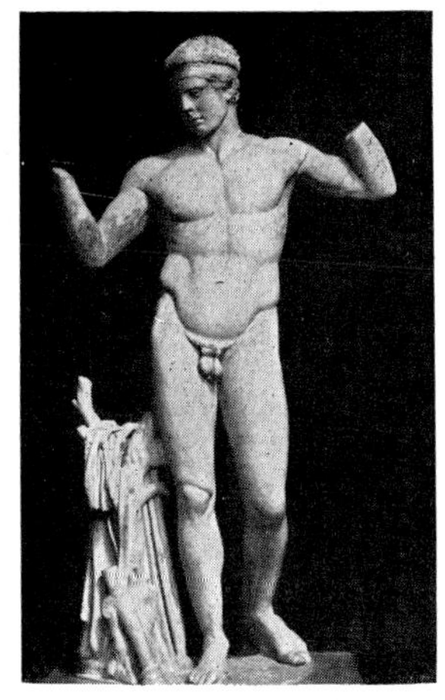

*67 The Cassel Apollo (after Phidias?). 2nd half of 5th c. B.C. Cassel*

*68 The Diadumenos (after Polycleitus). 2nd half of 5th c. B.C. Athens*

*69 Agias (School of Lysippus). 2nd half of 4th c. B.C. Delphi*

*70 The Borghese Gladiator (by Agasias of Ephesus). Early 1st c. B.C.*

human body as such: the sixth and fifth centuries B.C. for male anatomy, the fourth century for the female. After the stadium the artists went on to explore the gynaeceum. Then, having painfully mastered the knowledge of the body, they applied it to expressing the soul. This great investigation into the passions, which they began in the fourth century, ended in the Hellenistic period in an inquiry which, passing beyond Greek man, was directed on to the yet uncivilized world.

The work of art was delivered from that bondage to magic which had made it the slave of narrow conventions by turning it into a means of controlling the supernatural powers. It first became a simple illustration of myths, then very soon an end in itself. The image emerged from

*Evolution of the*

*71 Head of Apollo from Thasos. 6th c. B.C. Copenhagen*
*72 Head of a Figure from the Temple of Aphaia, Aegina. Early 5th c. B.C.*
*73 Head of the Doryphorus (after Polycleitus). 5th c. B.C. Naples*

the sorcery of the temple's darkness to glitter in the sunshine, and as an ornament of cities offered itself as a spectacle to all and sundry, and not only to a few initiates. Costly to produce and carried out by free and paid men, it escaped from that obsession with the gigantic that had been served so well in Egypt and Assyria by hordes of slaves. It was now made to the scale of cities and not of empires. Not that it stopped aspiring to grandeur, but this quality was now sought by the Greeks in matters of proportion and not of dimension.

The conventions which for thousands of years had paralysed the free portrayal of the forms in nature had therefore no excuse for survival. There was no longer any question of endowing the image with the maximum magical power by giving it the largest possible number of attributes of the model. Any resemblance was drawn from mere external appearance. For the first time natural forms were represented as they are seen by the eye, that is to say in their spatial truth, with the foreshortening which deforms them, and in the perspective which hides them or reduces their size. The Greeks' great plastic discovery was that of depth. After defining plane-geometry they laid down the principles of stereometry. Their rationalistic turn of mind was necessary to understand that unlimited space could be reduced to a three-dimensional system.

The intuitive naturalism which prevailed in primitive times became, in Greek art, a rationally planned realism; but it found its own limits in the idealism which led the Hellenes to see an expression of universal order in everything. The Greeks rigorously defined all the ideas of proportion, measurement, composition and rhythm which shape every form – whether abstract like a temple or realistic like a statue – according to the laws of number. In their aesthetic all the parts of a whole

*Face in Sculpture*

*74 Head of Hermes (after Praxiteles). 2nd half of 5th c. B.C.*
*75 Head of Meleager (after Scopas). 4th c. B.C. Rome*
*76 Head of the Borghese Gladiator (by Agasias of Ephesus). 1st c. B.C. Paris*

are in keeping with each other, proportioned according to a common scale: what we call a 'relationship' and what the Greeks called a 'canon', meaning a rule. This canon or standard is the formal principle from which component elements may be deduced according to a series of inter-relationships: for instance, the statue was based on the *dactyl* or width of the finger, while the entire temple depended on the width of the column. This secret order which governs the world and which constitutes beauty had to be reflected externally in art, while the philosopher strove to define its principles. Freed from the magical or theological bondage of its origins, art at last drew its whole mission from itself, much as science did, each of them aiming at the discovery of harmony, that is to say, ultimately and beyond all accidental discords, the pursuit of unity.

The name 'classicism' has been given to this realism which tended towards abstraction and was governed by a philosophy that reduced all things to the measure of man. It had such a universal validity that Greek civilization has remained alive while all its predecessors have long since become extinct.

Hellenism emerged from and returned to the East. The Greek genius was born in Asia Minor. Rich from the start, though still bearing traces of the experiments of the Egyptians, Cretans, and Mesopotamians, it quickly shed them and expressed itself in all its purity in the fifth century B.C., in a few cities of the Greek mainland and particularly Athens, that tiny strip of land which will always glitter like a diamond on the map of the world. Perhaps it was an increased infusion of Hellenic blood, from the ethnical contribution of the Dorian invasions, which produced this crystallization. Once rigorously defined this philosophical and plastic culture was to become the ferment from which future civilizations were to rise. In the Hellenistic period Ionia again took the first place, while Greece, fertilized once again from contact with the East, came into contact with Asiatic mysticism, and brought the speculative and rationalistic instrument it had created to bear on alien metaphysical systems – a synthesis from which Christian dogma was to emerge. The Greek plastic code, conceived in order to express the serenity of deified man, showed its adaptability by conforming to the new spiritual disquiet. Greece gave Rome the spiritual support which enabled it to base its material empire on the foundation of a powerful culture. Rome turned the classical sense of unity into the tool of politics, borrowing from Asiatic Greece that 'imperial' spirit which the latter had inherited from the earlier monarchies. Even Rome's genius for engineering (its main claim to greatness in the domain of the arts) derived from the wealthy cities of Ionia, which the Arabs so thoroughly destroyed that nothing was left but a few bones.

The powerful impulse of Greek genius remained active in time and space. It went to enrich the complexity of Byzantine art. In the West it still remained an unseen presence until it brought about the dawn of the Renaissance. Recent excavations have shown the astonished world that Hellenism spread as far as the Indus, and that Indian art received a definite impetus from the example of Greece.

## 1. GREECE

### *The Evolution of Greek Art*

The evolution of Greek art has been divided into three periods: Archaic, Classical and Hellenistic. Its beginnings and maturity were dominated by two rival principles, the Doric and Ionic, in which the ancients themselves saw the masculine and feminine principles of Greece. The Ionic, springing from the contact of Asian Greece with the East, favours grace, elegance and wealth of ornament; while the Doric, which originated in Greece proper and in western Greece, tends towards severity and rigorous observance of proportions.

*1. The Archaic period*, during which Greece was emerging from the protohistorical period and slowly developing towards maturity, covers a period of several centuries (1200 B.C.–450 B.C.) and has been subdivided as follows:

a) The Geometrical phase lasted from the fall of Mycenae to the eighth century B.C. – five hundred years of darkness which have been called the 'Greek Middle Ages', during which art and civilization languished as a result of the Dorian invasion. It has been called 'geometrical' owing to the decorative pattern found on ceramics discovered in Attica, Boeotia,

*77 Doric Capitals of the Temple of Apollo, Corinth*

Laconia and in the Archipelago, and also the 'cubist' style of carved idols found in the Cyclades. The temples at the time were built in crude clay and wood, with architectonic patterns in modelled and painted terra-cotta.

b) The Archaic phase, which lasted from 700 to 500 B.C., showed the preponderance of the Asian Greeks, which is very marked in their ceramics (workshops at Rhodes, Cyclades, Corinth and Attica) as well as in sculpture, which was already developed by the early sixth century in the form of statuary and monuments (*Naxian Sphinx*, Treasury of Cnidos at Delphi, Temple of Artemis-Gorgo at Corfu, painted limestone relief of the Hecatompedon in Athens). The same century witnessed the first stone temples: the Doric style developed in Greater Greece (Sicily and southern Italy, sites of Selinunte, Syracuse and Paestum), at Corinth (Temple of Apollo) and in the Peloponnese (Heraion at Olympia). Though few traces of the Ionic style remain, we know that it developed contemporaneously in the cities of Samos, Miletus, Ephesus in Asia Minor.

c) The pre-Classical phase (500 B.C.–450 B.C.). The conquest of Ionia by the Persians was to bring about a momentary eclipse there. Architecture flourished in southern Italy, then called 'Greater Greece' (Selinunte, Paestum, Segesta, Agrigentum in Sicily), and in the sanctuaries of Greece itself (Delphi, Olympia). This was the great period of the Archaic Doric, yet the Ionic spirit still inspired such monuments as the Treasury of the

*78 Ionic Capital of the Propylaea, Athens*

Siphnians, at Delphi while the Corinthian style appeared in Sicily. The workshops of Attica took the lead in ceramics. Then, in the course of the sixth century and the first half of the fifth, masculine and feminine types of statuary began to develop, inspired respectively by the Doric and Ionic principles. In the first half of the fifth century monumental sculpture broke free from Archaism with the pediments of the Temple of Aphaia at Aegina, the Auriga at Delphi and the decoration of the Temple of Zeus at Olympia, which is the triumph of the Doric spirit.

2. *The Classical period* (second half of fifth to fourth century) was the period of equilibrium and maturity, dominated entirely by Greece proper. Towards 450 B.C. the Attic Myron and the Argive Polycleitus brought the athletic type to its perfection, the one in the expression of movement, the other by establishing the canon of athletic proportions. The great initiative of Pericles, who with Phidias as his master-of-works undertook to rebuild the Acropolis from its ruins after it had been burnt down by the Persians, was to make Athens the artistic centre of the Greek world. The Doric style found its perfect expression in both architecture and sculpture with the Parthenon which was inaugurated in 438 B.C. and of which Ictinus and Callicrates were the architects and Phidias the sculptor. The Propylaea (437 B.C.–432 B.C.) combines the Doric and Ionic styles, but the Temple of Nikè Apteros (Athene Nikè) by Callicrates (inaugurated 421 B.C.) and the Erechtheum (407 B.C.) are in the Ionic.

The Athenian hegemony emerged shaken from the Peloponnesian wars. In the fourth century the great architectural undertakings were already

*79 Corinthian Capital from the Tholos, Epidauros*

*80 The Parthenon seen from the North. Inaugurated 438 B.C.*

shifted to Asia Minor, which cultivated the Ionic style and showed an Asiatic preference for the colossal (Artemision at Ephesus, Didymeion at Miletus, Mausoleum of Halicarnassus). A new architectural form appeared transposed from wood, that is to say, the theatre (Epidaurus and Athens). Meanwhile Greece kept its pre-eminence in sculpture with Scopas of Paros, Praxiteles of Athens and Lysippus of Sicyon. The arrival of Polygnotus of Thasos in Greece gave great impetus to painting, the imitation of which led to the decadence of the art of ceramics which had been flourishing.

*3. The Hellenistic or Alexandrian period* (third century till the Christian era) dates from the dismembering of Alexander's Empire (323 B.C.) which created great prosperous kingdoms in Asia while transferring the seat of Greek art to the East. New cities such as Pergamum in Anatolia, Alexandria in Egypt, Antioch in Syria, all of which were cosmopolitan in character, furthered the fusion of Hellenism with the East which is peculiar to the Hellenistic period of this civilization. The Doric decayed, and the Corinthian took the lead. From the third century we see the development of official architecture – colonnades, meeting-rooms *(bouleuterion)*, libraries, museums – while large urban agglomerations were built of which the thoroughly explored ruins of Pergamum give us a fair

*81 The Erechtheum on the Acropolis, Athens. Inaugurated 421 B.C.*

idea. Sculpture derived from Lysippian expressionism, which developed towards pathos and realism. The frieze of the Altar of Pergamum (formerly Berlin Museum) of the second century encouraged the 'pathetic' style which was further exploited by the Rhodes school (second and first centuries B.C.). The city of Pompeii, buried in the year A.D. 79 by the eruption of Vesuvius, reveals an Italian reflection of Hellenistic art at the domestic level. The only surviving paintings of ancient times come from this site, and from Delos and Rome.

## *Architecture*

The Greeks inherited flat-roof building. They knew nothing of the possibilities of covering great spaces to be realized by means of the vault; and yet they accomplished a profound revolution in monumental art. A slave to massive walls, the architecture of previous civilizations had to limit itself to such expression of mere strength as could be obtained by colossal dimensions: the monuments of the Nile and the Euphrates were still little more than ordinary buildings coated with decoration. They were derived from the mud-wall which remained the basis of Mesopotamian construction methods until the end, and which the Egyptians continued to imitate in stone even after they had abandoned it. The Greek temple, on the contrary, had its origins in the wooden edifice, wood being a material allowing of large gaps in construction. The column of the hypostyle halls of the Nile was a fragment of wall, whereas that of the Greeks derived from the stake. Building in stone, the Greeks had the idea of masking the nakedness of the full wall with a colonnade which looked far less heavy, and broke the monotonous surface of blank walls by vertical effects which were further accentuated by fluting. They thus invented a gamut of monumental expression by alternating solids and spaces, carried and carrying parts; while by bringing relative dimensions into play (height, width, thickness) in the component elements such as the support (column), the interval (between columns) and the carried surface (coping, etc.), their genius was able to achieve those effects of rhythm and harmony which properly constitute architecture in the real sense, that is, something the Hellenes thought of as a science of numbers.

All Greek monumental art derives from the column. The entire proportions of the temple depended on its strength and slimness, and the relationship between the diameter and height of the column – a relationship known as the 'module' – thus governed the entire edifice. With their scrupulous love of clarity and unity the Greeks reduced the expressions of architecture to three, which were nobility, grace and sumptuousness, to which corresponded the three 'orders', the Doric (pl. 77), Ionic (pl. 78) and Corinthian (pl. 79). These orders differed the one from the other in their proportions as well as in certain elements in their decoration: the Doric capital, with its unadorned moulding, frankly and robustly expresses the architectonic function of the support (pl. 80), while the volutes of

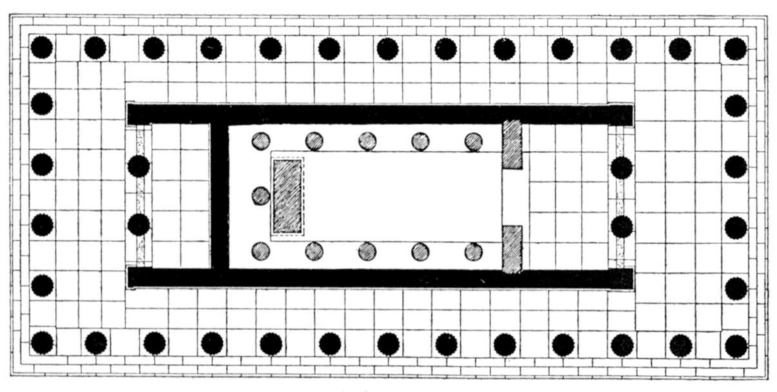

*82 Plan of the Temple of Hephaestos, Athens*

*83 Reconstruction of the Acropolis*

the Ionic capital suggest an elegant impression of elasticity (pl. 81). The acanthus leaves decorating the Corinthian capital contribute an element of ornamental luxury (pl. 79). Originating in Asia, which always favoured serial decorations (Assyrian and Persian friezes), the Corinthian and Ionic orders always have, on their entablature, a sculptured frieze showing a continuous pattern. The Doric order best corresponds with the Western mind, which inclines towards sharpness of definition: the rhythm of the columns and intercolumniation is repeated in the entablature by the alternating of fluted triglyphs and sculptured metopes. The Parthenon is the most perfect of all Greek temples, representing the golden mean between the somewhat heavy strength of the first Doric temples and the fragile gracefulness of the Ionic. With a length of 240 feet and 110 feet wide, it was built according to the Doric order, but has a continuous frieze (on the upper part of the wall inside the colonnade), as in the Ionic order.

The Greeks further enriched the expressive range of architecture by creating a system of ornamental moulding which was extremely simple and logical, dispersed about the monument in such a way as to underline its divisions and define the proper function of each element. Greek monuments were constructed with the greatest care from blocks of marble of moderate size, assembled with scientific skill. The walls were built entirely of ashlar without the use of cement, solidity being guaranteed by sheer weight, though the blocks were often bound with bronze clamps. Greek temples delight us now by the beauty of their marble which glitters in the sunshine, but their architects often embellished them with effects of colouring. This polychromy, applied to all the adornments of the

*84 Theatre, Epidauros. 4th c. B.C.*

Archaic temple constructed in limestone, was more discreetly done when they adopted marble, and was used only to emphasize the main members of the edifice.

The fundamental expression of Greek architecture was the temple (pl. 82). Temples were every city's pride, and were often built either alone or in groups at the highest point in the city, where stood its earliest centre, the Acropolis (pl. 83). The Greek temple, of much smaller dimensions than the Egyptian, usually comprised a blank rectangular wall, with a single or double colonnade *(peristasis)* running all round. Inside, the image of the god was kept in the *naos* or *cella* which was frequently divided into a nave and two aisles: this was preceded by a vestibule *(pronaos)* and followed by a sacristy or treasury *(opisthodomos)*. The rooms were all somewhat feebly lit through the roof. At the front and back (façades) the gently sloping gable-roof made two triangular sections, the pediments, which were decorated with sculptures. All the other monumental undertakings of Greek architecture such as the meeting-room, the market *(agora)*, the portico *(stoa)* incorporated colonnades. The house consisted of a number of rooms grouped round a peristyle containing a garden: unlike the temple, which was a public monument, the house was conceived from the inside, centering on the interior. The Greeks also invented the theatre which they built with an extraordinary simplicity and economy of means. Backing against a hill, the theatre had three main parts: a large segment of a circle with tiers of seats for the spectators, a circular orchestra for the chorus, a proscenium in front of the *skene* or decorated back-wall, for the actors (pl. 84).

The drawback of Greek architecture is its monotony. The monumental perfection attained in the fifth century left little scope for invention in the following centuries. Like all those forms of architecture that lack the arch or vault, Greek architecture could only exploit a limited number of possibilities both at the structural level and by way of harmonic effects. By their use of the arch the Romans were able to give the architect a far wider field of action.

## *Sculpture*

Greek sculpture evolved in such a logical way, and with such a complete exploitation of its plastic and human potentialities, that it is rightly considered as being the most perfect example of the creation of a style.

After the abstract idols sculpted in marble in the Cyclades in the Bronze Age (pl. 85) and without showing any obvious connection with them, sculptors began in the seventh century B.C. to raise the problem of the male type *(kouros)* and the feminine type *(kore)*. The votive and religious statues gave them the pretext for 'still' statuary. Starting from Egyptian frontality, in the course of the sixth century they loosened its stiffness and began to animate their works by exploring anatomical truth as well as volume and movement. Modelling at first showed a geometrical tendency which had little relationship to internal structure; then gradually it began to express what was beneath the surface. Originally the statue was thought of as a front and profile, symmetrically assembled on a strictly vertical axis; then gradually it became a volume turning in space. Workshops all over the Hellenic Mediterranean contributed their share to this slow apprenticeship. The Peloponnese seems to have played a major part in perfecting the naked athlete, a most austere expression of concentrated strength (pl. 63–70). It was Ionia that created the feminine type, with a rather affected charm, whose transparent linen drapery *(chiton* and *himation)* hints at the body's lines. The naked *kouros* served as an experiment for the discovery of anatomical modelling, whereas the *kore* was the basis for discovering draped modelling. At first incised schematically over the volumes, gradually the folds of the dress began to be modelled

*85 Marble Lyre-Player from Amorgos. Bronze Age. Athens*

in hollows and convexities and gave vigorous expression to the reliefs of the figure. The preference given in the fifth century to the monumental *peplos* of Dorian wool, replacing the Ionic linen garment, was to advance this evolution which was completed by Athens. Overcome towards the year 550 B.C. by the 'Levantine' grace of the emigrant Ionians, Athens was to absorb this influence and at the beginning of the fifth century created the grave but unsevere style which was to become its own.

The evolution of 'still' statuary found its perfect fulfilment in the fifth century with the Peloponnesian Polycleitus, who about 445 B.C.–440 B.C. expressed the Dorian ideal of the athletic figure in his bronze *Doryphorus*

*86 Athena, Hercules and Atlas. Metope from the Temple of Zeus, Olympia. 5th c. B.C.*

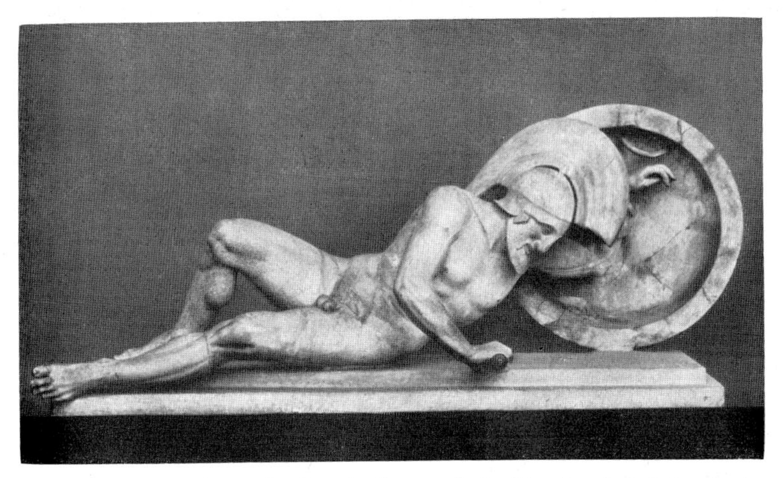

*87 Dying Warrior from the East Pediment of the Temple of Aphaia, Aegina. 5th c. B.C. Munich*

(lance-bearer), which the Greeks called the 'Canon' because the sculptor executed it according to the proportions which he himself had described in an aesthetic treatise of that name. In this work, conceived as the expression of the ideal beauty of the human body, all the problems of volume and anatomy were solved scrupulously but without the slightest stiffness, the harmonious composition of the gestures giving the impression of living suppleness (pl. 73).

It was in monumental sculpture in low-relief that 'mobile' statuary seems to have developed, and it sprang from the need for learning how to group together several figures participating in some common action. Sculpture had been distributed as a uniform adornment but with no particular order, on mural surfaces in Egypt and Assyria; but now it was to become closely involved in the rhythm of the architecture. It was set at vantage-points where architectonic expression needed the balance of relief, such as the metopes between the triglyphs of the Doric temple (pl. 86), the pediments of the façades, the continuous frieze of the Ionic order. The pediments of the Temple of Aphaia at Aegina (about 500 B.C. –480 B.C., Glyptothek, Munich) were the first victory for monumental expression, but still show no more than independent or juxtaposed statues, conceived on the frontal or profile plane (pl. 72, 87). But in the metopes and pediments of the Temple of Zeus at Olympia (472 B.C. –456 B.C.) the figures are associated one with the other by the rhythm of the action and the cadence of the total composition (pl. 86); the three-quarters stance is attempted but not without constraint from recent memories of Egyptian frontality which curbs the natural swing of the torso in rotation. On the west pediment, in Apollo checking the struggle of the

*88 Apollo from the West Pediment, Olympia. 5th c. B.C.*

Centaurs and Lapithae (pl. 88), the 'Olympian' quality appears for the first time; Olympia is the culminating point of the Dorian spirit.

The sculpting of marble in low-relief had favoured a freer expression of gestures, because the forms remained attached to the background or

*89 Zeus or Poseidon of Histiaea. Bronze. About 470 B.C. Athens*

were applied to it as in the case of the pediments. It was the use of bronze which, being both stronger and less heavy, was to help the statue in the round to solve the problem of movement. A gesture like that of the outstretched arms in the *Zeus of Histiaea* (about 470 B.C., National Museum, Athens, pl. 89) could never have been thought of in marble. In his famous *Discus-Thrower (Discobolus,* about 460 B.C.–450 B.C., pl. 90) Myron contrived the canon of movement, just as Polycleitus in his *Doryphorus* had expressed the canon of repose. A synthesis between the contraction and relaxation of muscular effort at speed, this work finds the principles of its harmony in the balance of opposites.

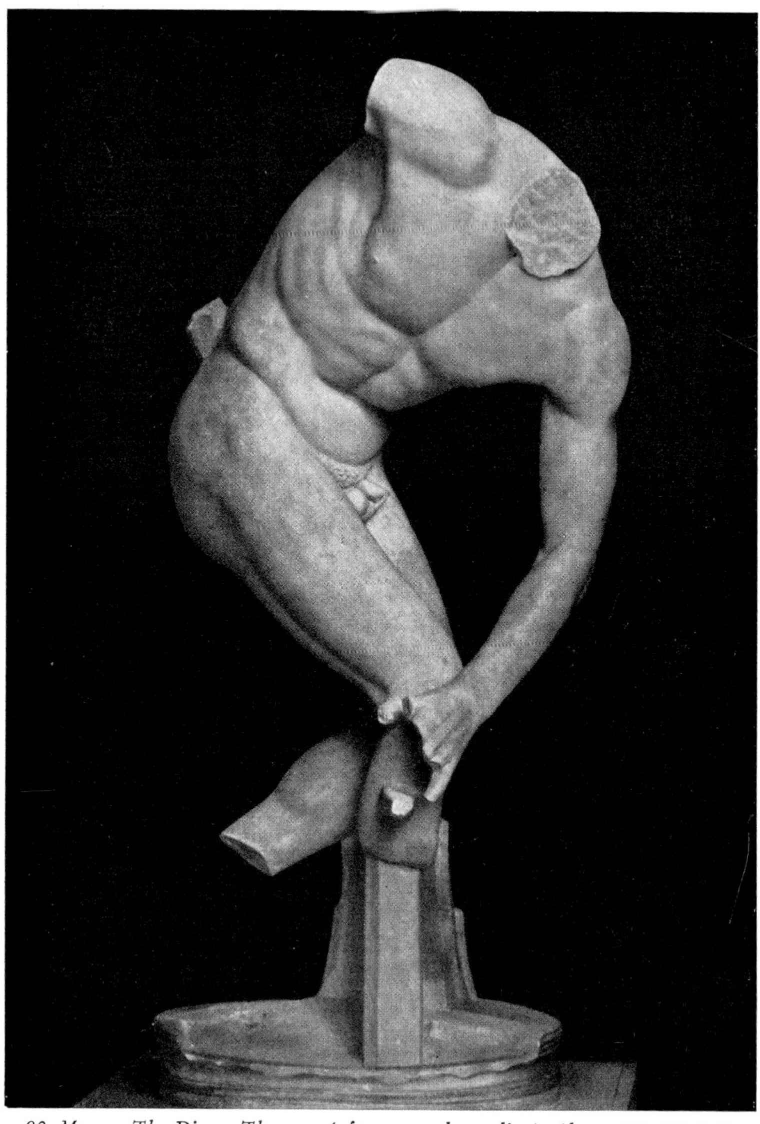

*90 Myron. The Discus-Thrower (after an early replica). About 460–450 B.C.*

All these efforts converged towards Phidias, who from both the moral and plastic point of view represents the supreme expression of the Greek spirit. It was he who gave the most perfect form to that Greek notion of divinity which is known as 'Olympian', a kind of super-humanity whose

*91 Aphrodite and Dione from the East Pediment of the Parthenon. About 447–432 B.C. London*

serenity is untouched by earthly cares. In his famous religious statues in gold and ivory (called for that reason 'chryselephantine') – *Zeus of Olympia* and *Athena Parthenos* – the colossal dimensions (the *Zeus* being 45 1/2 feet in height) as well as the precious sheen of the material, still contained something of the old, magical notion of the deity. But in the monumental sculptures of the Parthenon, the divinity is conceived of in terms of heroic man. In this group (447 B.C.–432 B.C.) in which Atticism brings together Doric gravity and Ionic grace, Phidias achieved a perfec-

*92 Phidias. Fragment from the Frieze of the Panathenaea on the Parthenon. London*

*93 Victory removing her Sandal. Temple of Nikè Apteros. Late 5th c. B.C.*

tion of harmony which no artist has ever surpassed. Each item, taken by itself, is a fluid composition of happily counter-balanced volumes, while the twist of the bodies in space is accomplished with all the ease of real life. At the same time the figures are related to each other according to

*94 Cresilas. Head of Pericles. Berlin*

the principle of an harmonious rhythm (pl. 91). The two pediments *(Birth of Athena* and *Dispute between Athena and Poseidon)* and the ninety-two metopes contain restricted compositions which had to conform with geometrical requirements. The frieze which unfolds at the top of the walls under the colonnade, on the other hand, is a continuous

*95 Venus of Milo*
*2nd c. B.C. Paris*

pattern of related forms, developing like the theme of a melody in music (pl. 92). This is one of the greatest undertakings in all sculpture: 350 human figures, 200 animals (horses and beasts of sacrifice) portray in heroic style the procession of the Panathenaea. Composed of youths on horseback, magistrates, musicians, Athenian maidens, every four years such a procession came to offer the statue of Athena, protectress of cities, a new veil which had been woven specially for her.

The late fifth century lived on the strength of the Phidian aesthetic, which was observed particularly by the sculptors of grave-columns at the Ceramus cemetery (reserved for heroes). The anonymous author of the caryatids of the Erechtheum (between 420 B.C.–413 B.C.) subjected the *korai* (Maidens) to the architectonic requirements of the support. The sculpted parapet of the Temple of Nikè Apteros at Athens (towards 410 B.C., pl. 93) accentuates the Ionian gracefulness of feminine figures. Meantime Paeonius achieved for the Temple of Zeus at Olympia, between 450 B.C. and 420 B.C., an instantaneous glimpse of movement in his *Nikè* (Victory) caught in full flight as she descends from Olympus (original still at Olympia). This effort was renewed in about 450 B.C. by the anonymous author of the Nereids dancing on the sea, discovered at Xanthos (now in the British Museum). With his bust of Pericles, Cresilas created the heroic type of portrait, reduced to the head and bust (pl. 94).

Of the great masters of Greek sculpture, only Phidias is known to us by original works, for, like the masterpieces of Myron and Polycleitus, those of the fourth century were pillaged by the Romans and have disappeared, while scholars have great difficulty in identifying later copies by which they are known.

Between the idealism of the fifth century and the naturalism of the Hellenistic period, the fourth century came as a period of crisis in Greek sculpture. It marks the transition from the mythological to the human. Scopas (very damaged remains of the Temple of Athena at Tegea, in the Peloponnese, about 386 B.C.–370 B.C.) accomplished a revolution by introducing into the Greek plastic code the portrayal of passion violently affecting the body and filling the face with anguish, which hitherto had remained imperturbable even in the moments of action, grief or death (pl. 75). Praxiteles, who first dared to portray the

*96 Zeus fighting the Giants. Altar of Pergamum. Between 197–159 B.C. Berlin*

feminine body entirely naked (the *Cnidian Aphrodite)* was the refined product of the Athenian decadence. He transformed the athlete into the adolescent; moreover the hips of his adolescents, who appear somehow lethargic, destroy the statue's proper balance and drive the sculptor to the use of supports *(Apollo Sauroctonus, Lycian Apollo, Resting Satyr,* etc.*)*. An over-anxiety for gradation, no doubt to be blamed on the influence of painting, weakens the modelling which becomes too smooth and fluid, as can be seen from the *Hermes of Olympia,* no doubt made later (pl. 74). In the time of Alexander, the bronze-worker Lysippus, born at Sicyon in the Peloponnesus, kept a taste for athletic figures, characteristic of his Doric origins; but, obeying the spirit of his age, he debased the Polycleitian squareness by lengthening the proportions (making the body eight times the head, instead of seven). He upset the firm stance of the statue with unstable postures, caught or 'snapped' with a suddeness which twists the bust and gives the whole body an angular uneasiness *(Agias of Delphi,* pl. 69, *Resting Hermes, Athlete with the Strigil).* Forgetting the support which the wall formerly afforded, the statue was now fully modelled from all angles, three-dimensionally, the over-analysis of the anatomy giving the modelling a knotty and episodic appearance detracting from the expression of strength. In the Ionic tradition, which was increasingly active, the Asiatic background seems to have inspired artists to a luxurious fleshiness, well expressed in the statue of the king

*97 Dionysus visiting Icarus. Hellenistic. London*

(Mausoleum of Halicarnassus, British Museum, about 450 B.C.) and the *Venus of Milo* (Louvre, second half of the second century, pl. 95), the latter being one of the most sensual marbles left to us by Greek art.

In the Hellenistic period the Greek plastic code sacrificed every effect of harmony to expressionism and naturalism. The sculptor began to explore the whole gamut of human expression: suffering, death, sleep, laughter, voluptuousness, tenderness, instinct, physical infirmity, old age and infancy. In Alexander's time portrait-sculpture became more individualistic under the influence of painting, while landscape found its way into relief and sometimes became its sole theme (pl. 97).

Hellenistic art glorified brute strength. It created the type of Hercules, a circus-athlete with overgrown muscles, and also showed an interest in types of long-haired barbarians (statues of dying Galatians or Gauls). The beautiful athletes of the Classical period now became professionals of the stadium: *Running Athlete* or *Borghese Gladiator,* (Louvre, first century, pl. 70, 76). Sometimes, on the other hand, they became effeminate to the point of hermaphroditism. But baroque feeling and a heightened realism in the representation of volumes and draperies also have their place, as in the noble *Winged Victory of Samothrace* (Louvre, about 180 B.C., pl. 98).

The largest group of work surviving from that period was the altar built at Pergamum for Eumenes II (197 B.C.–159 B.C.) on which a 'frieze' 390 feet long, arranged as a plinth in the manner of the Persians and Assyrians, portrayed a *Gigantomachia* (Battle of Gods and Giants, pl. 96, 706). This work was in the Berlin Museum before the recent war. The projection of the forms, excessively emphasized, and the chaotic movement

*98 Winged Victory of Samothrace. About 180 B.C. Paris*

of the attitudes, the draped form pronounced to the point of inflation, the melodramatic play of muscle, and the convulsed faces, express all the passions of strife, suffering and death. The taste for pathos led to the composing of groups of statuary bringing together a number of figures in some violent action (group known as the *Farnese Bull*, Naples Museum). The school of Rhodes carried on the traditional theatrical style of Pergamum, which was still very much alive in the famous *Laocoon* group (about 50 B.C., pl. 708) which was the last great work of Greek plastic art. Discovered in Rome in the sixteenth century it had a profound influence on Michelangelo.

## *Painting and the Minor Arts*

Mutilated remains help us to reconstitute the history of Greek sculpture, with many gaps, and painted works of art have likewise disappeared, apart from a few specimens of the later decadent period at Pompeii, Delos and Rome (pl. 99). The latter are extremely beautiful in spite of their clumsiness which was due to mediocre executants. We will thus always remain ignorant of the art of the great painters of antiquity: Polygnotus, Zeuxis, Parrhasios, Apelles. However, we can gain some idea of what the general evolution of Greek painting was like, from the mark it left on an industrial art, that of painted ceramics. The considerable number of specimens (found in tombs) of these products, which were exported all over the Mediterranean, amount to an enormous collection of forms which, better than any other figurative art, enables us to reconstitute the life, customs and general evolution of styles in Greece. Study of the vases shows us that painting was freed from primitive constraints earlier than sculpture, and this increases our regret for the loss of so many great works.

*99 Scenes from the Odyssey. Fresco from a House on the Esquilino. Rome*

*100 Amphora from the Dipylon. Athens*

*101 Corinthian Wine-Jar (detail). Late 7th – Early 6th c. B.C.*

Before the seventh century the enormous Attic vases of the Dipylon (cemetery near one of the gates of Athens) show ceramics to have been under the same influence of the geometrical style as were the temple idols of the Cyclades (pl. 100). The triangular stylization of the human body recalls that of the pottery of Susa in the fourth millennium and certain cave-paintings of prehistoric Africa. This bent for rectilinear stylization, so unlike the fluid formalism of the Cretans, appears therefore to have been the manner of the Doric primitives. We have already seen from sculpture that the Doric spirit always maintained a tendency towards squareness (Polycleitus and Myron). More clearly than sculpture, ceramics prove that the curvilinear style came from Asia by way of Ionia. The pots made in the workshops of Rhodes, Boeotia and Corinth in the eighth and seventh centuries were decorated with dark figures on a light ground, set out in a continuous frieze and composed of animals seen either naturalistically or with a touch of fantasy, and of Phoenician or even Assyrian origin (pl. 101). The seventh century introduced scenes from everyday life which at first were mingled with animal adornments. The growing influence of Athenian ceramics which were to flood markets hitherto in the hands of the Corinthians, freed vases from Oriental influences.

*102 Brygos. Bottom of a Drinking-Vessel. About 490–480 B.C. London*

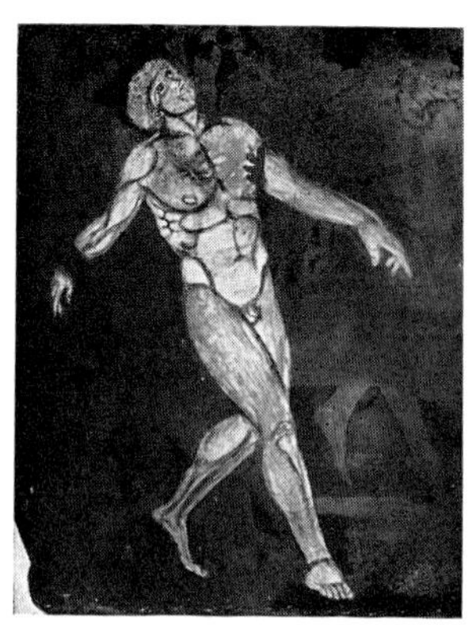

*103 Death of Talos. Bowl from Ruvo. 1st half of 4th c. B.C.*

*104 Exekias. Achilles and Ajax playing Dice (detail of an Amphora). 2nd half of 6th c. B.C.*

Athens used a process of black figures on a red ground (about 650 B.C. –500 B.C.) and, abandoning the lay-out according to zones, adopted the metope style of composition, that is to say rectangular panels blocked out in light red, to take the mythological scenes which were introduced at that time. The lines of the drawing were incised on the black surface of the figure with no attempt at modelling. The beauty of arabesque and elegance of silhouette, the life-like gestures, show that painting was already far in advance of sculpture which was still under the tyranny of the block's mass. A daemonic life animates these figures, which suggest the vitality of the Homeric poems (pl. 104).

The potter Nikosthenes or his colleague Andokides is credited with the invention of the process of depicting red figures on a black ground, towards the end of the sixth century. The light tint of the figures enabled the painter to work them with the brush, to analyse the modelling, perspective, foreshortening, play of light and shadow. The increasing influence of painting pushed the artist towards naturalism at the cost of beauty in decorative style, the figure being no longer conceived as a silhouette but according to the inner modelling. The finest red-figure vases are those of the so-called 'Severe' or 'Archaic' style (late sixth century to about 460 B.C.). The potters Euphronios, Brygos and Douris signed some magnificent pieces in which the balance between realism and style anticipates the harmony of Phidias (pl. 102). Naturalism was stressed

*105 Achilles slaying Penthesilea. 5th c. B.C. Munich*

after the arrival in Athens in 470 B.C. of the painter Polygnotus of Thasos, who introduced perspective effects and psychological expression into his painting (pl. 105). About 450 B.C. saw the beginnings of the 'Fine' style period in ceramics: the aesthetic of Phidias made itself felt in painting and led to a certain degree of academism. During the period of the Ornate style which began in about 420 B.C., its chief exponent being Meidias, ceramics was invaded and led astray by the imitation of painting; compositions included too many figures and became confused, the modelling suggested volumes (pl. 103) and, emulating the painter, the potter began to transgress the decorative laws of his medium – all these defects being further accentuated in the ceramics of southern Italy, whose development coincided with the decadence of Athenian pottery after the Peloponnesian War. The Greek ceramic works nearest to painting that have survived are the funerary *lekythoi* or oil-jars which had a white ground; drawn in firm outline on a limewash background, the figures must have been made in imitation of those found in stucco paintings. The beauty of design of some of the fifth century *lekythoi* only increases our regret for the loss of works by the great masters themselves, since so many of those known to us were from the hands of humble craftsmen.

*106 Greek Cameo. 4th c. B.C. Paris*

The Greeks had a particular bent for the monumental arts and produced little in the way of the minor arts, with the exception of pottery for which they invented some admirable forms, peculiarly suitable for the various functions of the vase, and a decorative style of considerable beauty. The Greek disregard for comfort did not encourage the making of everyday things and furniture, except in the Hellenistic period. Miniature sculpting on bronze was only a reflection of large-scale sculpture, but their bronze mirrors have some beautiful incised drawings. Sober in their tastes, the Hellenes paid little attention to finery, at least in the Classical period. Some fine examples of silverware have survived from the Hellenistic period. Hellenistic artists made some excellent intaglios from hard gems for use as seals, and in Alexander's time they invented cameos (pl. 106), onyx stones cut in relief in which the different coloured layers of the material are skilfully exploited. Their genius for sculpture also came out in the minting of their coinage, the best specimens of this art being produced not at Athens but at Syracuse (pl. 107).

## 2. THE ROMAN WORLD

### *Historical Background*

In the central region of Italy (Tuscany and Latium) Etruscan art, which came before that of Rome, was a kind of provincial extension of Greek art. It sought and found its happiest inspiration in Ionia during the Archaic period (late seventh century B.C. to first half of fifth). The Classical stream (second half of fifth century to fourth) was more banal. The rapid degeneration of this art from the third century produced neo-primitive forms heralding the plastic style of the late Empire, that of the early Middle Ages, or certain aspects of modern art.

The Etruscans imported a great quantity of Attic vases, and imitated the designs on them in the frescoes of their own underground tombs. This

*107 Decadrachm from Syracuse. Late 5th c. Paris.*

they did with a primitive touch, but with a narrative sense remote from the classical spirit, which has something of the Asian sensibility while foreshadowing Roman realism. The Romans were to inherit some of their gift for portraiture. Besides paintings and works in clay (pl. 108), the Etruscans left some fine archaic bronzes (pl. 109). Those structures of theirs that are known to us (city walls, municipal works) are interesting because they show a very precocious use of the arch formed of wedge-shaped stones when it was still unknown to the Greeks.

The Roman art of the Republican period saw a slow infiltration of the Greek aesthetic into Etruscan models. This carried all before it in the last years of the Republic, when the Roman aristocracy were fired with enthusiasm for conquered Greece and vied with each other for originals or copies of the masterpieces of Greek art. Caesar began the great transformation of Rome into the Imperial capital, by enriching it with great monuments: a forum (pl. 110), a theatre, the Basilica Aemilia, the Basilica Julia, the Curia Julia. What is called 'Augustan' art emerged from a great Greco-Roman synthesis of political theory; for Augustus wanted to found a Roman classicism in both literature and art which would be worthy of its Hellenic model and which would become the typical culture of the Empire. The architect Vitruvius Pollio condensed the principles of this classicism in a treatise on architecture written between 25 B.C. and 23 B.C. Augustus had numerous monuments erected in Rome: a forum (pl. 110), triumphal arches, the Theatre of Marcellus, several temples including that of Mars the Avenger, and the Ara Pacis (Altar of Peace, pl. 120). This was the beginning of that great period of building which was to spread all over the Empire and bring so many peoples the benefits of Roman government, peace and comfort. The burning of Rome in the year A.D. 64 enabled Nero – whether he was responsible for the disaster or not – to make the city more healthy and build himself an immense palace (the Golden House). In the first century of our era Vespasian founded the amphitheatre later called the 'Colosseum', which was finished by Titus and had a storey added by Domitian (pl. 111). The Antonine period was one of active building all over the Empire. Hadrian, thoroughly steeped in Greek culture, tried to perpetuate the images of the finest Hellenic works of architecture in his villa at Tivoli (A.D. 127–134) and rebuilt the Pantheon (A.D. 131–124, pl. 113). His enormous mausoleum

*108 Apollo of Veii (Clay Figure from a Pediment). Etruscan. Rome*

*109 Bronze Chimaera from Arezzo. Etruscan. About 500–475 B.C. Florence*

was later incorporated in the Castel Sant' Angelo. Another great fire in Rome in A.D. 191 enabled Septimus Severus and Caracalla to undertake among other things the Baths of Caracalla (A.D. 212–216), one of the masterpieces of Roman architecture. This activity continued until the fall of the Empire (Basilica of Constantine or Maxentius, A.D. 310–312). The whole of the Roman world was covered with monuments. Provence has some very fine ones dating from the first and second centuries (arch and theatre at Orange, amphitheatre at Nîmes, pl. 112, and Arles) and Germany from the fourth (baths, basilica and Porta Nigra at Trier, pl. 115). Africa has ruins of fine buildings at Timgad, Sbeitla and El Djem, while on the confines of the Empire Asiatic Balbec was enriched with colossal monuments. As for Pompeii and Herculaneum, the two cities of the campagna which were buried by Vesuvius in A.D. 79 and rediscovered in the eighteenth century, they are a Western offshoot of Hellenistic rather than of Roman art.

## *Architecture*

It was in the domain of architecture that the genius of the Romans found its most powerful expression. Prolonged peace, the wealth accruing from intense commercial activity, the public works commissioned by an administration anxious for the public welfare combined with the Roman taste for comfort, all created an enormous demand for building all over the Empire.

For religious undertaking the Romans drew inspiration from the Greek temples and from certain Etruscan traditions, showing a preference for the Corinthian order. They also used the Tuscan order which was an Etruscan interpretation of the Greek Doric. They innovated especially in

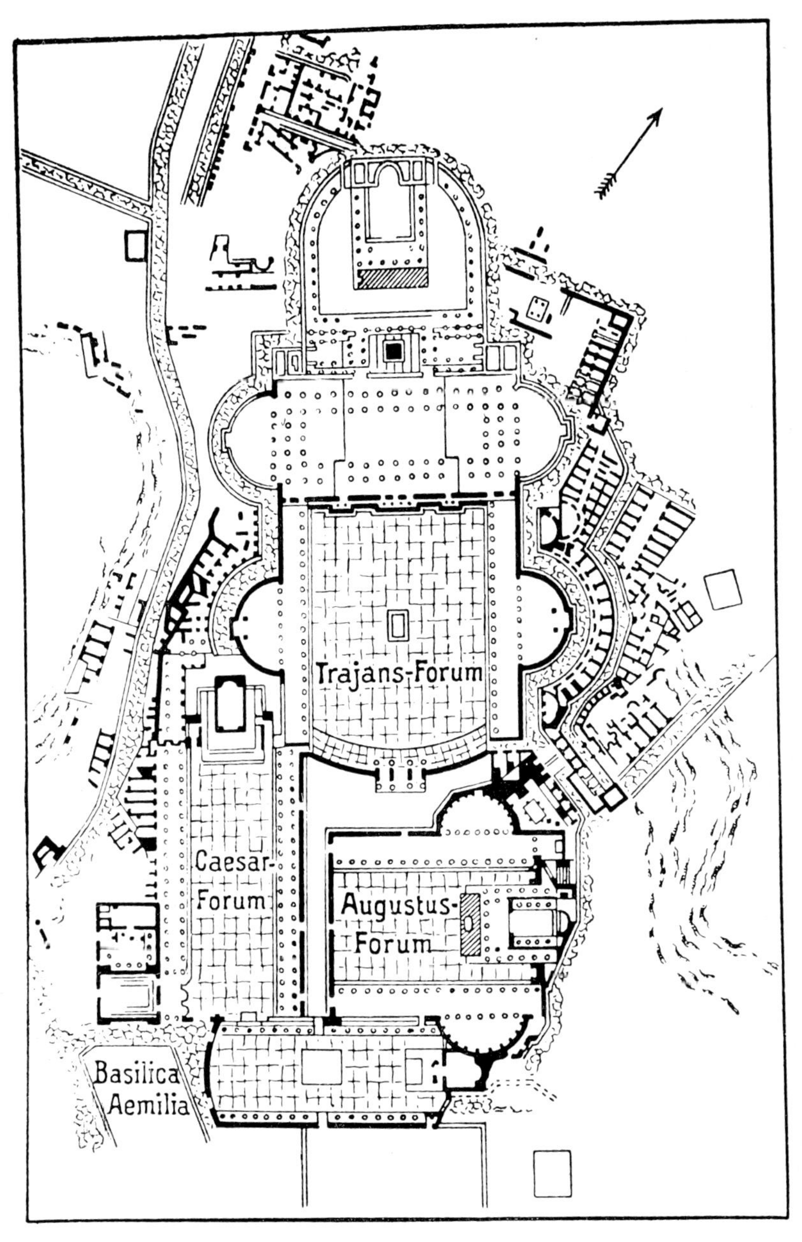


*110 Plan of the Imperial Forums (restored). Scale approx 1 : 5000*

*111 Colosseum, Rome. Flavian*

civil engineering, making buildings which were functionally perfect. The adoption of the arch facilitated the creation of new types of monuments (pl. 113), called into being by the development of public ceremonies and social needs; the possibilities of spanning gaps with arches and vaults, which they made with remarkable skill and science, allowed them to make buildings with the immense roofed spaces required for holding large meetings. Abandoning the Greek manner of building with blocks of dressed but uncemented stone, they adopted a system of building in brick or rubble, having invented a cement of exceptional firmness. This base of brick or rubble they overlaid with marble facings, superimposing the Greek orders one on the other just as they wished (pl. 111), and giving no thought to relating decoration to structure as the Greeks had done. On their strong supports of brick or cement they set huge arches and vaults: domes, tunnel-vaults and 'cross-arches' or groin-vaults. All these principles seem to have come from Asia Minor, and a better knowledge of the Hellenistic cities would perhaps reduce the number of Roman inventions, many 'Roman' architects being of Greek origin, anyway.

*112 Amphitheatre, Nîmes*

*113 Interior of the Pantheon, Rome (after an old print). Hadrianic*

For ceremonial purposes the Romans took from the Hellenistic culture the memorial column and triumphal arch with one or three archways (pl. 118). For public works they also took the basilica from the East; this was a building with a nave, or nave and aisles, often ending in an apse, which they perfected and used as an exchange, a covered market or for the magistracy. The forum was a public place surrounded by arcades used for business purposes, and decorated with memorials and works of art. They took the theatre from the Greeks, but transformed it by building it on open ground, the hemicycle being held and framed by tiers of arched galleries. By putting together two theatres they invented the amphitheatre (pl. 112) which was built in an ellipse and used for circus performances. This is a masterpiece of practical planning. The circuses or hippodromes came from the Greek stadium: they were usually made of wood and have left few remains. The *thermae,* one of the Roman's monumental inventions, contained public baths, games-rooms, all kinds of rooms used for the recreation of the body and the mind (promenades, gymnasia, libraries, lecture-rooms). Provided with a central-heating system of hot air which flowed under the floor and between the walls, the bathing-places comprised a *caldarium* (room for hot baths), a *tepidarium* (a room heated with warm air to induce perspiration) and a *frigidarium* (for the cold

*114 Pont du Gard, Nîmes*

*115 Porta Nigra, Trier*

bath). The ruins of the Baths of Caracalla in Rome, with their enormous arches are the most grandiose of the Empire. Anxious, also, to supply their towns with abundant water, the Romans tapped distant springs, conducting the water by means of enormous aqueducts (pl. 114) made of superimposed rows of arches, to water-towers in the city. Domestic architecture consisted of tenements of several stories as well as private villas. These latter combined the old Etruscan with the Greek form of house. Round a court or *atrium* in the middle of which was an open tank or cistern *(impluvium)* were grouped the service quarters, the public rooms, the master's office or *tablinum;* then behind this part, which was of Etruscan origin, came the private quarters which were exactly the same as the Greek house, set round a garden fringed with columned arcades *(peristyle)* (pl. 116, 117).

The Romans had a splendid sense of monumental grandeur, as can be seen from their amphitheatres and aqueducts. They obtained excellent effects from a combination of straight lines, vertical or horizontal (columns and entablatures), and curved lines (arches and vaults). The great height of some of their structures did not favour the adoption of one particular order throughout; so Roman architects made it a rule to superimpose the three orders, the Doric, Ionian and Corinthian, one on the other. From the combination of the Ionic and Corinthian they made a fourth order, the Composite (often called Roman). Except in religious monuments they usually omitted fluting from their columns, leaving them smooth. The shafts, instead of being set up in segments, were usually cut from a marble monolith. The Romans unfortunately indulged a taste for

*116 Peristyle of the House of the Vettii, Pompeii*

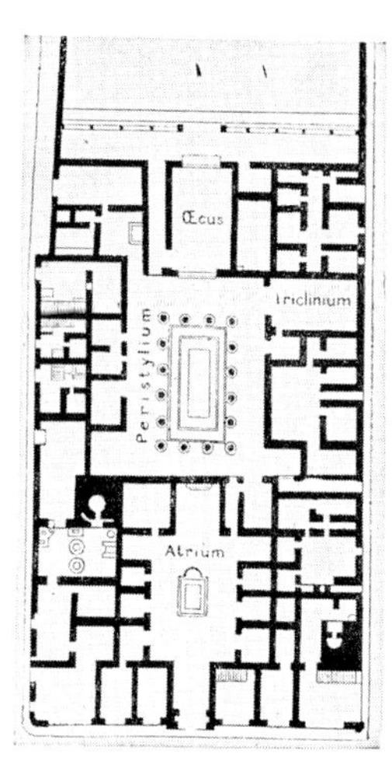


*117 Plan of a Pompeiian House*

the picturesque which diminished the grandeur of their loveliest monuments, and only their later ruin, which stripped them of ornament, was to reveal their honesty and strength of structure.

They made a considerable use of polychromy in their building, combining marbles of different colours which were brought from all over Europe.

Generally speaking they sought effects of luxury and strength, calculated to appeal to the mob's imagination, whereas Greek buildings, intended for a more cultured public, were primarily addressed to the intellect.

*118 Arch of Titus, Rome. Erected A.D. 81 in the Forum Romanum*

*119 Architectural Painting, Pompeii. 4th Style*

The interiors of Roman houses were covered with paintings showing decorative architectural themes (pl. 119) and arabesques, with panels depicting scenes from mythology.

The Roman contribution to sculpture was less outstanding. They admired the Greek plastic achievement, but did little more than painfully copy it. Augustus' initiative resulted in the creation of an official style, nobly dignified, with conventional drapery effects and formal gestures (pl. 120). The practical Roman mind transformed the pathos of the Hellenistic relief into an historical and narrative genre (Arch of Titus, pl. 121, Trajan's Column). Their most original creation was the portrait which, unlike the Greek portrait, reproduced the model without idealizing him, with an exact physical truthfulness (pl. 122): this was the revenge of the old indigenous stock over the Greek aesthetic. In the minor arts the Romans followed Hellenistic models, and made some fine bronze articles of which many were found intact in the ruins of Pompeii and Herculaneum. Pottery, on the other hand, assumed a purely industrial character.

## 3. EASTERN RESISTANCE

Alexander had pushed the frontiers of the Greek world as far as the Indus. The dynasties which succeeded him in Anatolia, Iran and Mesopotamia carried on a superficial Hellenism which stifled native art. The temple-tombs built in the first century B.C. by the kings of Commagene, Mithridates and Antiochus I, which were discovered in 1953–1954 at Nimrud-Dagh and Eski-Kale, reveal a most striking mixture of Greek and Asiatic artistic influences as well as a curious religious syncretism.

After the Seleucid kings, the Parthian dynasty of the Arsacids, who described themselves on their coinage as 'Phil-Hellenes', remained attached to Greek culture. But the revolution of the Sassanians (A.D. 227–641) represents a return to the national tradition of Achaemenian Aryanism, based on the restoration of the Mazdakite religion. The Sassanians, conquering the Romans and Byzantines, drove Hellenic civilization back to the coast, at the moment when they themselves were overcome by the Muslims. Turning their back on the Mediterranean, they developed an art which was to be the basis of the invasions of the West by the East in the form of Islamic and Byzantine art.

In the domain of building the achievement of the Sassanians is more or less parallel with that of the Romans, substituting for Greek architecture with its columns and architraves a system of massive brickwork to take

*120 Group of Figures from the Ara Pacis Augustae, Rome. Augustan*

the thrust of arches. Inheriting Mesopotamian building methods, they perfected the science of constructing arches, barrel-vaults and domes, using the latter with a daring unsurpassed even by the Romans (the great elliptical barrel-vault of Ctesiphon is 84 1/2 feet across, 123 1/2 feet high, and 156 feet deep, pl. 124). They managed the transition from the square plan to the circular plan of the cupola by means of squinches (arches placed

*121 Triumphal Procession with the Spoils of Jerusalem. Arch of Titus, Rome*

*122 Male Portrait. Limestone Head from Praeneste. Berlin*

*123 Hunting Scene from the Inner Wall of Taq-i-Bustan. Sassanian. About A.D. 590–628*

diagonally at the internal angles of the square), or large, curvilinear inverted triangles called 'pendentives', and contrived to set the strains of the vaults one against the other. The plans of their palaces (Ctesiphon, Sarvistan, pl. 125, Firuzabad, Taq-e-Eivan) tend to focus round a higher vault, an idea later adopted by the Byzantines. This vault crowns the throne-room or *divan* which is open at one side, an arrangement which the Muslims followed. Inside, the masses of brick were covered with plates of painted stucco or enamelled terra-cotta in the Achaemenian manner. The Romans likewise covered their walls with inlaid decorations of this kind, but in their case it was used to hide the structural basis and was borrowed from the Greek orders. The monotheistic religion, which had no idols, did not inspire the Sassanians to any great architectural undertakings as was the case in Persia.

Sculpture spread round the walls like a tapestry was a conception foreign to Greek art but was characteristic of the Assyrians and Achaemenians. On the walls of the palaces and rock tombs of Naqsh-i-Rustam or Taq-i-Bustan, warlike or hunting scenes were depicted in tiered rows comparable with the oldest conventions (pl. 123). Although, under Greek influence the relief was more vigorous than among the Assyrians or Persians, the frontal and profile positions inhibited the free expression of volume. Statuary was rare and anti-classical in spirit (pl. 126).

The Sassanians had a considerable influence over Islamic and Byzantine art, and even on Roman art, through their handicrafts (silverwork and textiles) which carried on the Mesopotamian tradition of zoomorphic imagery, whether naturalistic or fantastic, and it was through them

*124 Palace of Shapur I (A.D. 242–272), Ctesiphon (an old view)*

that this fund of imagery created by the Sumerians as long ago as the second millennium B.C., was passed on to the Middle Ages.

Recent researches are revealing in upper Mesopotamia, Syria and Palestine, traces of monuments built by pagan communities, or by Jews or pre-Islamic Arabs. These show, in the early centuries of our era, a widespread revolt against Hellenism. At Dura-Europos, in the upper Euphrates valley, paintings have been found in a temple dedicated in about A.D. 70 to the Palmyran gods. These show already all the attributes of Byzantine hieratic art (pl. 127). The transition towards early Christian art is demonstrated at Dura-Europos itself, by the paintings of a synagogue and in a Christian chapel of the third century. In Egypt, during the

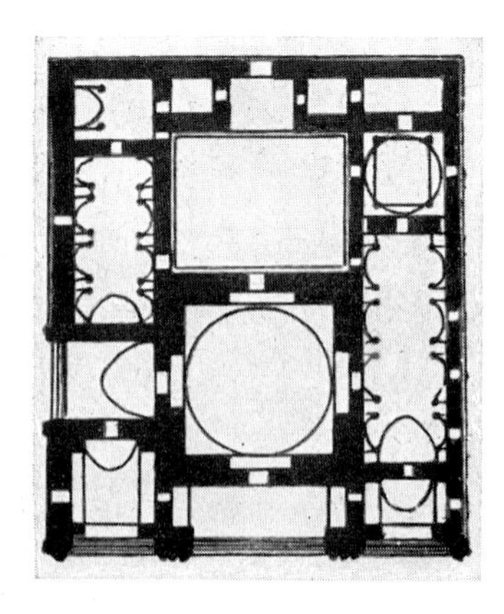

*125 Plan of the Palace at Sarvistan. Sassanian*

*126 Parthian Statue found at Shami (Teheran)*

*127 Sacrifice to the Palmyran Gods. Dura-Europos. About A.D. 70*

Roman period, panels painted in wax or distemper now replaced the masks of mummies in the sepulchres of Fayum and in the region of Thebes. The evolution of these from the first century B.C. to the fourth century A.D. shows the progressive Orientalization of the Hellenic type (pl. 631).

The spirit of the ancient East persisted in the castles, vaulted in the Sassanian manner and no doubt built by the first Omayyad Caliphs, which have been found in the Syrian desert. One of them, at Mchatta, had a great continuous frieze running round the lower part of the external walls, reproducing the Iranian theme of animals and birds sporting among sprigs of vine, of which the early Christians made a Eucharistic symbol (pl. 269).

## IV. EARLIEST FORMS OF CHRISTIAN ART

The decay of the plastic arts of the ancients, which shrank progressively under Oriental influence from the third century A.D. onwards, is one of the most remarkable phenomena in the history of art.

For the first time in the history of world-civilization Greece had given pride of place to all that was *temporal* in human life. The lucid speculation of thinkers, even those of a Plato, projected the light of reason into the dark places of the soul, and the relationship between the soul and the beyond became a matter for pure dialectic and not an article of faith. Once man was delivered from his obsession with the deity, religion gave way to metaphysics.

The religions of the East, which at the end of the ancient world began their onslaught on paganism, reforged the chains of man's submission to God, but by means of initiation they offered the believer a form of participation which united him with the person of a redeeming God. It was by an intuitive and mystical knowledge and no longer a rational form of it, that man was able to cross the gap separating the world of appearances from the beyond. Of all the religions which were struggling between themselves to take over the Empire, Christianity, which triumphed, was the most spiritual: it submitted human destiny to a future life, as was the case with the ancient Egyptians who had some influence on early Christianity.

The pure spirituality which Christianity had inherited from Judaism was to lead its first followers into an aversion from art, which had served the worship of idols only too readily. When the new religion broke new ground and attracted the pagan masses, it had to come to terms with the mind of the illiterate classes who needed images to guide their belief. Having allowed such imagery against its inclination, Christianity had to purge it of that physical emphasis which, ever since the Greeks, had made it a reflection of earthly things. If it was to be no longer an object of worship, but only a means to it, the image was none the less to play a part in the new faith very like the one it had held in the old religions of the East. It was an instrument of theology, the figurative intermediary on which faith leans in order to appreciate the dogma of which the image is only the garment and the representation. While it was an intermediary shorn of that reality which had given it magical power in the ancient religions – though perhaps secretly the layman never stopped believing in that magical property – the image was to enter a new phase by becoming a symbol; and art is a language which translates the truth of dogma into forms, *parlar visible,* as Dante put it.

All that was foreign to the clear transcription of the symbol was eliminated. Landscape was replaced by a few guiding accessories. Some com-

*128 Temptation of Christ. Mosaic in St. Mark's, Venice. 12th c.*

positions were reduced to a few forms linked together like words in a statement, reminding us of hieroglyphs (pl. 128).

Images were now unreally suspended as though in flight, against an abstract golden background; the line of the horizon disappeared, together with the earth itself. Events no longer took place on earth or in the sky, but in the abstraction of an ideal universe. The various features in the composition no longer had the relative sizes that would be theirs in concrete reality, but their size was now determined by the idea behind them: as in the early Egyptian and Mesopotamian arts, the principal person in the composition towered over all the rest, who were grouped like dwarfs at his feet. The composition of landscape was treated with the same severity, a mountain becoming a mere mound of sand, or a building no larger than a footstool (pl. 128). A purely moral hierarchy replaced the material order of things.

This entirely spiritual interpretation of objects, according to which temporal existence is a delusion and the only reality is in the timeless, was to destroy the Greek plastic arts just as it destroyed the Greek aesthetic itself. The Greeks must have seen everything from the corporeal point of view, and this gave all their creations, even in philosophy, the pure edges and the clarity of geometrical forms. Their essential concern was the definition of objects and concepts in their proper dimensions and limits, so that we can understand why their plastic creations were as exactly circumscribed as solids in the three dimensions of space, and why sculpture was for them the major art. The Christian aesthetic was to abolish sculpture, reducing forms to an unreal flatness of surface. The half-profile, or three-quarter view so dear to the Greeks, disappeared and gave place to frontality and to the profile (pl. 129, 131). Modelling was flattened into calligraphy. The artist deliberately avoided any expression of

*129 Head of Achilles (reversed) from a Pompeian Fresco. Naples*
*130 Head of an Angel from a Mosaic in S. Maria Maggiore, Rome. A.D. 352–366*
*131 Head of Theodora from a Mosaic in S. Vitale, Ravenna. 6th c. A.D.*

movement, which would be guilty of imitating life. He fixed his figures in eternal attitudes and gave his compositions the strictest symmetry. The repetition of figures in endless series, so dear to the ancient East (pl. 132, 133) symbolizes that oneness to which the deceptive variety of appearances is reduced in eternity.

While the sense of volume died out, that of perspective which the Greeks had intuitively discovered also vanished, and early Christian art returned to the old mode of representation used in primitive cultures, composition in superimposed layers or rows (pl. 134). To this was added the radiating composition in which all the elements are arranged round a centre (pl. 135). Applied to building methods this radial form gave rise to the central plan which was an outcome of architectural speculation among the Byzantines. On a centred monument the roundness of the cupolas reinforces the idea of gravitation toward a given point, and this became a striking symbol of monotheism (pl. 136).

The whole gamut of primitive conventions now directed against Greek art, plunged the Greco-Roman world back into a type of vision that it had left behind for eight centuries. The eye no longer saw things in an order whose hierarchy was dictated by their true proportions in reality. As in the primitive cultures, everything was now seen for its own sake, in its essence, with the result that the details on a figure were out of proportion, out of scale with the person, who was so to speak 'blasoned' or emblematized by the accessories of his clothing or equipment. The tendency towards series is to be found even in the stylization of draperies and the handling of hair and beards as decorative motifs. Such was the avoidance of the notion of space that very often the perspective was reversed, the figures in the middle-ground being larger than those in the foreground, while the lines of objects converged towards the spectator and not

*132 Holy Martyrs. Mosaic Frieze in S. Apollinare Nuovo, Ravenna. 6th c. A.D.*

towards the background (pl. 137). This aesthetic system reflects a kind of thought which seeks to identify itself with things in their entirety, by an intuitive sense like that of touch; whereas the Greek vision set objects in a perspective comparable with that which the analytic operations of reason impose on ideas.

This conception is so Oriental that the earliest Christian art produced in Rome still knew nothing of it. Without Byzantium it might have seemed that the Classical plastic code was only going to be changed as regards meaing (pl. 130). Quickly developed in Byzantium in the fifth and sixth centuries, the new aesthetic rapidly spread over the entire Mediterranean, then to the still barbarous peoples of the West. The poverty of these latter peoples as regards any artistic tradition made them welcome the Byzan-

*133 Bowmen. Frieze in enamelled Brickwork from Susa. 5th c. B.C. Paris*

tine example only too greedily, without in the least understanding its lofty implications of dogma. For them, it was only a matter of being given a repertory of forms, which they used much as children repeat parrot-wise the sounds of a foreign language. Obstinately hostile to the portrayal of the human figure, even in this conventional form, for several centuries they pursued the purely imaginative speculations they had inherited from their nomadic ancestors, seeing in Byzantine art no more than a vehicle for those Oriental forms which reminded them of their own origins; and all this at a time when Byzantium itself was undergoing a serious disturbance of conscience.

*134 Adam in the Garden of Eden. Ivory Diptych (detail). 4th c. A.D. Florence*

A survey of the Western world and the Mediterranean basin in the seventh and eighth centuries would show, indeed, such a complete regression from the Greek plastic arts that the human person and the figure in general tended to disappear from art entirely, being reduced to a purely ornamental expression. Islam, established on the south and eastern fringes of the Mediterranean, imposed in those regions an outlook hostile to images, strictly observing the spirit of the Koran and opposed to the portrayal of anything human or living. In Byzantium a great movement – the iconoclastic crisis – which sprang partly from Islamic influence, tended to forbid the worship of images as being idolatrous, and to suppress the figurative portrayal of holy personages. In the West, the impulse towards ornamentation thrived and encroached on even the few representations of sacred art that were attempted.

*135 Last Supper. Miniature from a Syriac Codex 12th c. London*

*136 Christ, Angels and Prophets. Mosaic in the Chapel Palatine, Palermo. 12th c.*

However, just when it might be expected that a kind of artistic puritanism was finally about to dominate the world, a simultaneous reaction in East and West restored form and shape to the figure. In the ninth century the Macedonian renaissance in Byzantium and the Carolingian renaissance in the West both aimed at redirecting art towards the spirit of the classical arts. Under this influence the Byzantine hankering after Orientalism was profoundly shaken as it began to long for the harmonious rhythms of ancient Greece. As for Charlemagne, wrapped in his northern mists and far removed from the home of classicism, he only received the classical influence at second-hand, by way of Byzantine art which was fortunate enough to thrive on the very soil on which the ancients had laboured.

The Macedonian and Carolingian revivals, both of them intellectual undertakings brought about by the heads of states, were purely formalistic in character. It is true that they created masterpieces, but a genuine

*137 Abraham and the three Angels. Mosaic in S. Maria Maggiore, Rome. 352–366*

138 *Interior of a Catacomb (Cubiculum with Arcosolium and Loculi), Rome. Early 4th c.*

revival cannot spring from such unspontaneous movements. In eleventh-century France and thirteenth-century Italy, the West, finally emerging from its protracted childhood, was to create a mode of expression as original as Greek art itself.

## 1. EARLY CHRISTIAN ART IN ROME

### *The Art of the Catacombs*

While in the East some figures, though still pagan, already contained elements of the aesthetic which was to triumph with Christianity, in the West the first Christian art was no more than the last phase of ancient art. The earliest images of the new cult are to be found in the catacombs, underground cemeteries made by the Christian during their secret life in the first three centuries of our era, down in the chalky sub-soil of Rome. In the walls of long passages *(ambulacra)* which were practically subterranean towns, the sepulchres *(loculi)* were set in tiers, closed with stone slabs bearing the names of the dead. Occasionally a more imposing tomb cut in the shape of an arch *(arcosolium)* was the resting-place of some notable or martyr, while clearings in the gallery containing *arcosolia* served as funeral chapels *(cubicula)* (pl. 138). The chapels were often decorated with stucco or mural paintings, very fragile because they were executed straight on the unprepared wall, in the manner of the Egyptians or Etruscans. The dominant idea in these decorations was the future life to which the Christian soul was called after shedding its earthly trammels (of which the symbol was the figure of the *orante*), thanks to the Redemption brought by Christ. Subjects taken from the Old and New Testaments were rare and without any historical significance, being used as apologetic

*139 Christ and the Apostles. Wall-Painting in the Catacomb of Domitilla, Rome. 4th c.*

evidence of divine mercy. For the most part the Christians contented themselves with pagan legends and images to which they gave a new meaning. Thus Aristaeus, the god of gardens, with a lamb on his shoulders, became the Good Shepherd, a symbol of Christ. The amorous shepherds and harvesters of the vine found in the villas of Pompeii end their career by symbolizing Paradise and the Eucharist, respectively. Orpheus charming the wild beasts prefigures Christ, while the pagan myth of Eros and Psyche becomes a symbol of the trials undergone by the human soul before entering heaven. Going even farther in their passion for cryptograms the Christians, in order to portray Christ, his Passion and the Redemption, created a whole system of picture-puzzles – and no doubt the persecutions had something to do with this esotericism. Findings in

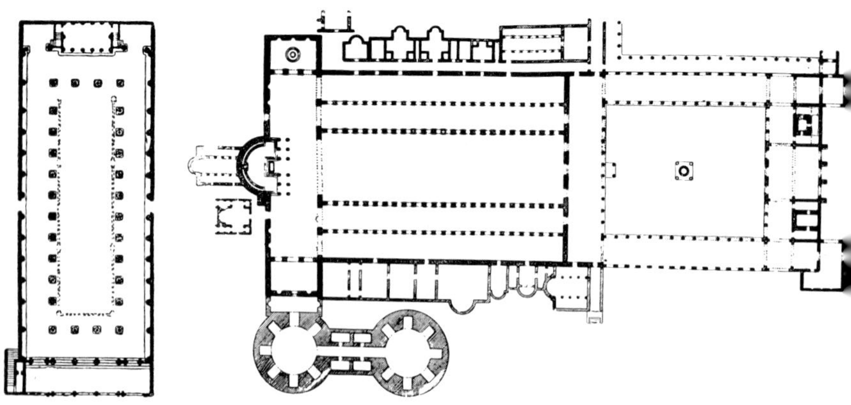

*140 Roman Basilica, Pompeii. 1st c. B.C.*

*141 Plan of Old St Peter's, Rome. Middle of 4th c.*

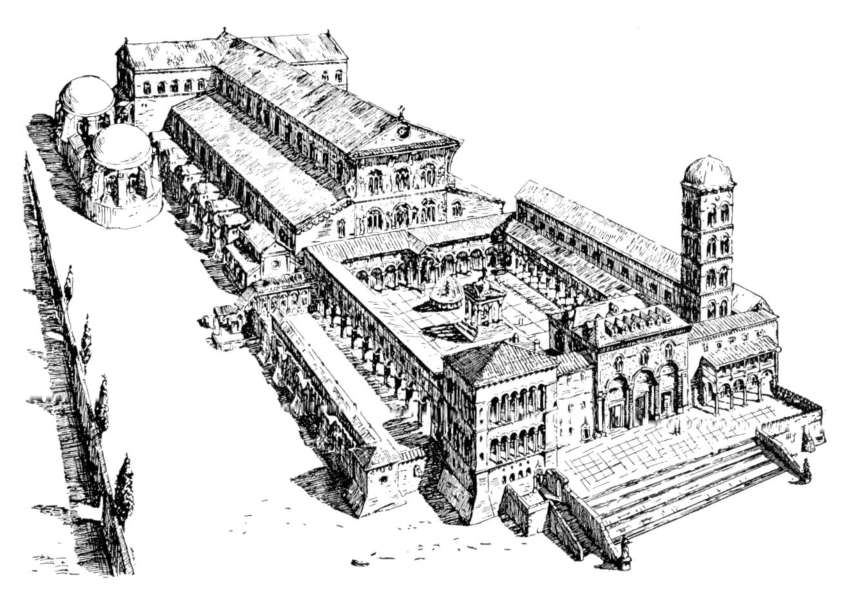

*142 St Peter's, Rome. Reconstruction of the old Basilica. Middle of 4th c.*

the catacombs also include funerary lamps, and gold-bottomed flasks in which the blood of martyrs was kept. A fine bronze medallion of the second century, from the Domitilla catacombs, shows the oldest portraits of St Peter and St Paul, which set standard types for the Middle Ages.

## *Art after the Triumph of Christianity*

### The Basilicas

The early Christians had no interest in forms themselves and were content with the models they borrowed from Hellenistic plastic conventions; all they cared about was the idea behind them. This state of affairs continued until Christianity came out of hiding and became the official religion of the Roman Empire, when it celebrated its victory in an ostentatious way, for which reason the art of the Christian Empire may be called 'triumphal art' (from 313 to the fifth century).

The most noticeable result of this victory was the creation of an architecture to house the new religion. The inconvenience of the Greco-Roman temple as well as its idolatrous associations led the new cult to reject it as a possible form. The temple with its porticos was conceived from the outside, being the house of God to which only priests could have access, whereas the church (*ecclesia,* meaning 'assembly') was a place for the

*143 S. Sabina, Rome. 5th c.*

meeting of the faithful, called without distinction to participate in the worship of the deity. Thus it had to enclose an immense space. The Christians found a ready-made form for this in the ancients' repertory of architectural inventions – the basilica, a long rectangle with nave and aisles, which used to serve as a meeting-place, a tribunal or a closed market (pl. 140). To this they added only a transept or transverse nave, to give it the shape of the cross (pl. 141). The apse, a semicircular or polygonal recess beyond the crossing containing a bench *(presbyterium)*, was reserved for the priests. The altar was at the crossing of the transept and nave, and the ceremonies took place in the main nave, the faithful standing, men to the left and women to the right in the single or sometimes double aisles which at times had a gallery. The church was entered by a narthex in which the catachumens met, and a courtyard surrounded by four colonnades (the atrium), which was the origin of the cloister of the medieval monasteries. In the centre of the atrium stood the *canthare*, a fountain for ablutions which was the origin of our stoup for holy water (pl. 142).

The Roman basilica, like that of the ancients, was timbered over, except for the apse which was given a semi-dome. The pillars separating the nave from the aisles were surmounted by architraves, or more frequently arcades (pl. 143).

*III Girl in sleeved chiton, from the Acropolis, Athens*

*144 Marble Figure of Christ, Rome. 4th c. A.D.*

Symbolic of the Christian soul, which should be completely turned towards the inner life, the brick-built basilican church appeared from the outside as an unadorned structure. Inside, on the contrary, luxurious adornment was spread everywhere to give the faithful the impression of some supernatural place. The columns were of marble, the lower walls were covered with decorative mosaics in precious marble, to which were often added porphyry, mother-of-pearl, onyx and other rare materials. In the upper parts, above the arcades, on the triumphal arch separating the nave from the transept, and in the apse, were frescoes of scintillating mosaics, showing the main figures in scenes from the Testaments. The altar was surmounted by a canopy in worked gold or marble (ciborium), while the choir was surrounded with an incrusted marble screen (chancel) containing the ambos or pulpits for the reading of the Epistle and Gospel.

The principal basilican churches still standing today are, in Rome, S. Paolo fuori le Mura, built in the fourth century and rebuilt after the fire of 1823 (reconsecrated 1854); S. Lorenzo fuori le Mura (fourth to sixth century); S. Giovanni in Laterano (fourth century, much restored); S. Maria Maggiore (fourth and fifth centuries); S. Agnese (fourth to seventh century); S. Sabina (pl. 143). The great basilica of St Peter, with a nave and double aisles, built by Constantine, was destroyed during the Renaissance, and is known to us only from old illustrations (pl. 141, 142).

## New Plastic Conceptions

The plastic language of triumphal art – the art of the Church triumphant – is the same as that of the final period of ancient art. The spirit of Classical sculpture remained until the fourth and fifth centuries in the sarcophagi, great works in marble, in which from the second century onwards the pagans had themselves buried when the influence of Oriental religions, including Christianity, replaced cremation by interment. The Roman sarcophagi were decorated with Christian scenes, vigorously carved in the round but gradually declining under Oriental influence, which was to triumph in the sixth century. The face of Christ was most often taken from the Greek adolescent type (pl. 144).

The real innovation of triumphal art was the figured mosaic. Used in Hellenistic art in the form of pictures for adorning pavements the mosaic, now set upon walls, showed a host of figures spread over a large surface. The oldest mosaics, in the vault of the circular aisle of S. Costanza (after 337), were marble renderings of the symbolic ornamentation of the catacombs. Those in S. Maria Maggiore (pl. 130, 137) date from the fourth and fifth centuries and form the oldest cycle of evangelical and biblical pictures. They still have traces of the ancient aesthetic – figures shown in three-dimensional space, landscape backgrounds, Greek or Roman dress. But the perspective was already changed; the golden background had not appeared here any more than at S. Pudenziana (fourth century) which is dominated by a bearded Christ based on the Jupiter type. The mosaics of the Mausoleum of Galla Placidia at Ravenna (fifth century) are still close to the spirit of antiquity and contrast sharply with those of S. Apollinare Nuovo and S. Vitale, built in the sixth century at the moment when Ravenna was part of the Byzantine Empire and in the grip of the Oriental aesthetic.

## 2. BYZANTINE ART

### *Historical Background*

It was in the East, in the great Hellenistic cities of Egypt, Asia Minor and Syria, that the Christian dogma and ritual were shaped before the Church had actually triumphed, as is proved by the abundance of Greek names in the new religion's vocabulary (Christ, Christian, angel, Apostle, bishop *(episcopus)*, priest, diocese, synod, church *(ecclesia)*, baptism, Eucharist, etc.). It was thus the Eastern Empire that rose from the split in 395, which was to be the most active centre of Christian art. Whereas the Western Empire fell under the onslaughts of the barbarians, the Eastern Empire survived until the fifteenth century. Byzantium (Constantinople), which Constantine founded in 327 was to be its centre; but in the fourth, fifth and sixth centuries, before the Moorish invasions, Christian art flourished all round the Mediterranean fringe, in Antioch, Syria, Palestine – where splendid basilicas were built on the holy sites – and at Alexandria and Ephesus. Generally speaking the coastal cities remained faithful the longest to the Hellenistic aesthetic, while under monkish influence the hinterland developed a more Oriental and primitive art which gradually affected the first type. This was the case in Syria and above all in Upper Egypt (Baouit), where the monks decorated their monasteries with frescoes and

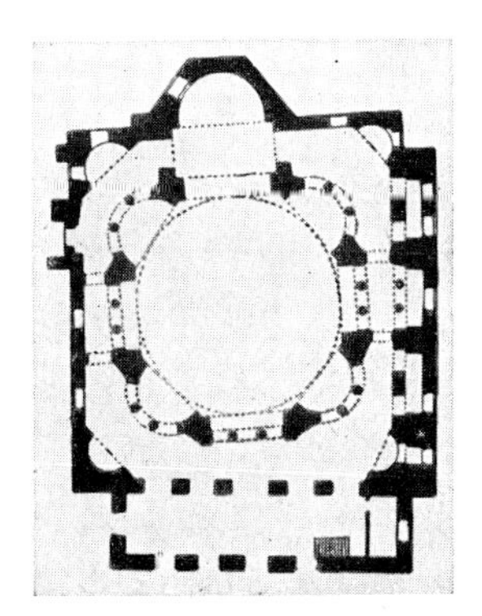

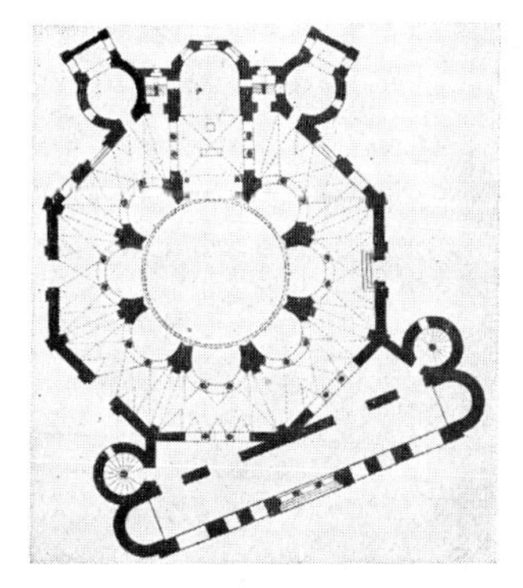

*145 Plan of SS. Sergius and Bacchus, Constantinople. 1st third of 6th c.*
*146 Plan of S. Vitale, Ravenna. 526/534–547*

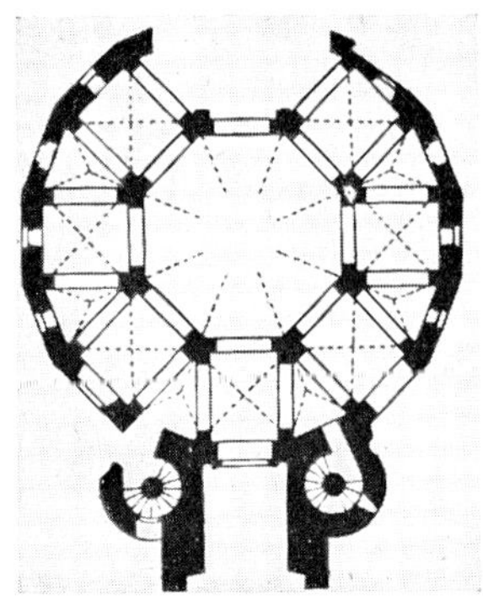

*147 Plan of the Chapel Palatine, Aachen. Late 8th c.*

sculptures full of a primitive vigour already suggestive of Romanesque art (Coptic art, pl. 152).

The period showing the widest extension of the Byzantine Empire and its art was the sixth century, when Justinian retook Africa from the Vandals – setting up many basilicas there – and, from the Goths in Italy, Ravenna (the centrally planned S. Vitale, and the basilica of S. Apollinare Nuovo). In Byzantium itself Justinian built the churches of the Holy Apostles, SS. Sergius and Bacchus and S. Sophia.

After the conquest of part of the Mediterranean by the Arabs, Byzantine art had a phase which is called the iconoclastic crisis. A gust of puritanism, not unlike that of Protestantism later, taxed the excessive image-cult which was widespread in the fifth and sixth centuries, with being idolatrous. In the seventh and eighth centuries, perhaps under the aniconic, anti-image influence of Islam, Byzantine art was reduced to the level of ornamental background. It was reborn in all its splendour from the ninth to the eleventh century with the Macedonian dynasty. The finest monuments were in Greece (Daphni; S. Luke in Phocis); but Byzantium reached into the West, towards Venice (S. Mark's, Venice; churches on Torcello) and, in the twelfth century, to Sicily (mosaics at Palermo, Cefalu, Monreale); and into the East as far as Russia (S. Sophia, Kiev). In Armenia a prosperous Christian community continued building admirable churches in dressed stone; in Asia Minor monks from Cappadocia evolved a popular art, full of pathos, very different from official Byzantine. In the thirteenth and fourteenth centuries Byzantine art spread into Serbia and Bulgaria; its figurative designs were more economically carried out in paint. The finest specimens are in Greece, at Mistra (Peloponnese), on Mount Athos and in the territory governed by the Serbian Tzars, in Macedonia and Serbia (Oratchanitsa, Stoudenitsa, Nagoritchina, Sopot-

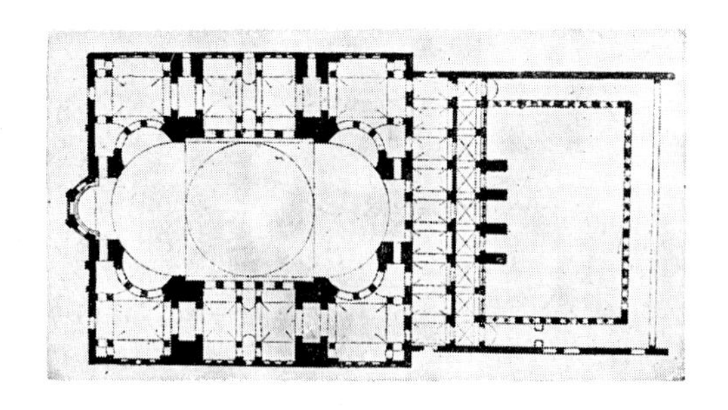

*148 Plan of S. Sophia, Constantinople. 532–537*

chani, pl. 154). Byzantine art endured until our own time in the icons of Russia, Crete and Mount Athos.

The conversion of Prince Vladimir to the Greek Orthodox faith in 989, which at the same time called into existence a new Christian province, directed the artistic activities of the Russian Slavs towards Byzantium. The peoples of Poland and Bohemia on the other hand, who belonged to the Roman Catholic Church, continued to develop under the influence of Western styles.

## *Architecture*

Eastern Christian art in its early stages followed the basilican system, in the Greek churches (S. Demetrios, Salonica), in Palestine (Bethlehem), as well as in Syria, Asia (Anatolia), the region round Ravenna, and Africa (Tunisia). The churches there were all roofed with timber as were the Roman churches, though one or two in Anatolia had tunnel-vaults. But the real creation of Byzantine architecture was the vaulted church, centrally-planned. The central plan often consisted of a simple cupola set on a ring of archways and surrounded by an ambulatory: SS. Sergius and Bacchus, Constantinople (pl. 145); S. Vitale, Ravenna (pl. 146); St George of Ezra, Syria. Then, developing the principle of Sassanian buildings the Byzantines elaborated complex plans in which the domes and tiered tunnel-vaults buttressed each other and took the strain of a lofty central cupola (pl. 149).

The central plan was combined with the basilican plan at S. Sophia at Constantinople, constructed between 532 and 537 by order of Justinian.

*149 Isometric drawing of S. Sophia, Constantinople*

*150 Interior of S. Sophia, Constantinople. 532–537*

The architects were the Anatolians Anthemius of Tralles and Isidorus of Miletus (pl. 148–150). Ten thousand men worked on the building which is the most grandiose structure of Byzantine art; every province of the Empire sent its most precious materials for its decoration. A high cupola (reconstructed after collapsing, 558–562) by Isidorus the Younger (nephew

*151 Byzantine Capital. Gallery of S. Vitale, Ravenna. 6th c.*

*152 Coptic Bas-Relief in Sandstone from Egypt. Probably 4th c. Washington*

of Isidorus of Miletus) is 170 1/2 feet high against a diameter of 100 feet. Its pendentives rest on four great arches set on enormous pillars; at the north and south it is held by two tunnel-vaults and is buttressed at the east and west by two huge half-domes which in their turn rest on retaining recesses or niches. The building is contained in a rectangle, 250 feet by 233 feet. It has two galleries. These vast dimensions reflect a taste for the colossal, at once Roman and Asiatic, in keeping with Justinian's enormous Empire. The Greek spirit predominates in the buildings of the Macedonian period, when, using moderate dimensions, architects sought harmony through pleasing exactness of proportions. They then achieved the perfect central plan in the form of a Greek cross (i.e. with all four limbs of equal length) in which four vaults (either barrel, half-domes or

*153 Detail of an ivory Episcopal Throne. Archbishop's Palace, Ravenna. 6th c.*

cupolas) counterbalance the central Dome (S. Sophia, Kiev; St Luke in Phocis; various churches in Constantinople; St Mark's, Venice; Holy Apostles, Ani in Armenia). Sometimes the cupolas were set on a high drum or circular wall.

Except in Asia Minor and Armenia, where they built with ashlar or freestone, the Byzantine structure was made of enormous solid masses of brick carrying light domes of the same material. The use of freestone led Anatolia and above all Armenia, like later Romanesque art, to the idea of external decoration related to structural meaning, with niches, close-buttresses, plain brick clamping against rough-cast walls; the Macedonian architects also gave thought to external plastic effects. But in the fifth and sixth centuries the Byzantine building showed only a naked structure from the outside. All the decoration was reserved for inside, where it was not built-in but applied to the walls by way of adornment, in the form of marble facings and mosaics. The worshipper found himself plunged into a supernatural atmosphere by the vastness and lightness of the domes which hardly seemed to touch their pendentives; and the luxury of the setting, the wealth of colour-effects, the glinting of the mosaics, were all calculated to transport the worshipper into another world.

At Novgorod and Vladimir Russian architects, building their churches in the form of the Greek cross, made their own original additions: cupolas were surmounted with drums and bulbous domes, which appear from the twelfth century onwards. In Vladimir several stone churches of the twelfth and thirteenth centuries are decorated on the exterior with carved reliefs which appear to have been inspired by Armenian and Georgian churches.

### *The Figurative Arts*

From the sixth century onwards sculpture shows the rapid reabsorption of a technique which had been the chief concern and the main experimental field of Greek art. Sculpture in the round tended to disappear, and only a few capitals, marble balustrades and, at Ravenna, one or two sarcophagi were treated with the hand-drill or bore, but no longer with the chisel. At the same time these features were only decorated with ornamental motifs, not worked in relief but laid on in imitation of the coloured effects of mosaic. Deriving from the ancient composite column, the Byzantine capital evolved quickly until by the sixth century it was no more than a down-turned pyramid covered with open tracery (pl. 151). However, the art of relief survived in small articles made out of precious materials such as ivory and gold. Ivory craftmanship in the fifth and sixth centuries shows a progressive flattening of Greek contours, the immobilizing of attitudes, the schematization of modelling, a tendency which is seen completely evolved in the Throne of Bishop Maximian at Ravenna (sixth century, pl. 153), which came from Alexandria or Con-

*154 Death of the Virgin. Fresco at Sopotchani (Jugoslavia). 13th c.*

stantinople. In the Macedonian period a tentative renaissance of the plastic sense showed itself in ivories.

In the domain of figurative representation, the mosaic was the great art of the Byzantine period. By the unrealness of its gold backgrounds and its glittering colours the mosaic gave the Byzantine artist an ideal medium for his desire to rid the spectator of every naturalistic illusion and suggest the very presence of the supernatural.

The great creations of S. Vitale and S. Apollinare at Ravenna in their totality show the full achievement of the new aesthetic. A hieratic concept of monarchy inspires the mosaics of Justinian and Theodora at S. Vitale. As in the old Eastern monarchies the *basileus* whose person is consubstantial with God has his secular power by divine right, and appears to his subjects surrounded by the superhuman attributes of royal pomp. The heavenly court in S. Apollinare Nuovo shows itself to the faithful in all the ceremonial trappings of the monarch's own court. In the Ravenna mosaics the Oriental aesthetic had overcome the Grecian: the unmodelled forms are flattened into the abstract surface of the gold background; the manifold gestures of life are frozen into a few solemn attitudes; nothing remains of the natural figures but a few stylized outlines; the three-quarter view is replaced exclusively by frontal and profile positions; while the deliberate repetition of gestures and attitudes, the frieze arrangements recalling the enamelled ceramic friezes of the Achaemenians (pl. 132, 133) and the taste for rigorously symmetrical compositions, suggest in the spectator's mind a return of all the forms of creation to some eternal unity (pl. 136). The landscape disappears and a few small accessories serve to suggest the location of whatever scene is represented. When the art of mosaic revived in the ninth century, the apologetic spirit following the iconoclastic crisis imposed a strict iconographic order on

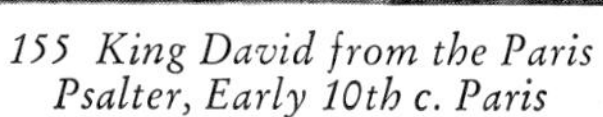

*155 King David from the Paris Psalter, Early 10th c. Paris*

*156 Crucifixion from the Rabula Gospels. Syriac. About 586. Florence*

the distribution of images on church walls. The major works at Kiev (Ukraine, eleventh century), Greece (Daphni, St Luke in Phocis, end of eleventh century), St Mark's, Venice (end of eleventh century) and Sicily (Palermo, Cefalu, Monreale, all twelfth century) show biblical scenes arranged according to the liturgy and surmounted by the colossal, awesome figure of the *Pantocrator* (Almighty) who is set in the central dome at, so to speak, the umbilical point of the church, and has something of the ancient gods in the gravity of his brow (pl. 136). The Oriental conception of superhuman divinity has triumphed here over that of the Greek god, represented on a human scale, which survived in triumphal art (pl. 144). The gospel and biblical scenes are emptied of historical content and have only a symbolic and liturgical meaning. In the Passion, Christ is always portrayed indifferent to pain and insult. The modelling, drawing and arabesque tend to a formal perfection that was to be recaptured by Cimabue in the Trecento (pl. 184, 185).

The more popular art of the fresco – a cheap substitute for the mosaic – shows different characteristics. The monks who decorated the cave-churches of Cappadocia (Asia Minor) from the ninth to the thirteenth century were the first to try and express the human pathos of the gospel. This they did with a naïve violence. Strengthened by Western influences this outlook spread to the Greek painting of Mistra in the fourteenth century as well as to churches in Serbia, Rumania and Bulgaria. The best school of fresco-painters was in Jugoslavia (Sopotchani frescoes, thirteenth century, pl. 154).

In Russia at about the same time mosaic gave way to fresco painting, which was to flourish principally in Novgorod and later in Moscow and Yaroslavl. From the fourteenth century onwards it gradually became the practice to cut off the altar-space from the rest of the church by putting up iconostases, screens to which icons (sacred paintings on wood) were attached in vertical and horizontal rows. By their faithful adherence to earlier models iconographers were to preserve the traditions of Byzantine art for a long time to come.

The various streams to be found in Byzantine art are also reflected in the miniature, the art of book-illustration which began in Egypt in the Hellenistic period. The Alexandrian taste for the picturesque persisted there for a long time thanks to the system of copying prototypes *(Vatican Homer* and *Vatican Virgil,* fourth century, the *Vienna Genesis,* fifth century, *Scroll of Joshua,* sixth century). It took on a new lease of life in the Macedonian period, in the *Theriaca* – a treatise on medicine – of Nicander (eleventh century, Bibliothèque Nationale) and the *Paris Psalter* (tenth century, same library, pl. 155) which astonish us with images that would appear to be contemporary with the frescoes of Pompeii. Side by side with this aristocratic group, a monastic group shows a more religious and more Oriental spirit: this tradition originated in Syriac monasteries in the sixth and seventh centuries, heralding the pathos of the Cappadocian frescoes (*Rabula Gospels,* Florence, pl. 156).

### *The Slavonic Countries*

In the fifteenth century Russian icon-painting became independent, freeing itself from Byzantine influence, a movement which had its parallel in Italy a century earlier. The graceful, delicately refined art of Andrei

*157 a Pantocrator from the Pala d'Oro. St Mark's, Venice. Late 11th–Early 12th c.*

*157 b Rublev. Old Testament Trinity. Moscow. Early 15th c.*

158 *Volcian silver Coin. Paris*

159 *Elusate silver Coin. Paris*

Rublev, active in Moscow at the beginning of the fifteenth century, is reminiscent of the neo-Alexandrian style and spiritualized forms of Duccio (Icon of the Holy Trinity from the Trinity-Sergius Monastery, now in the Tretyakov Gallery, Moscow, pl. 157 b). The Novgorod icon-painters manifest the same delight in pictorial narrative as the Lorenzetti brothers of Siena, and they strive for luminous effects in colour. The portable icons painted in the sixteenth century for the Stroganovs, which reproduce the sensitive delicacy of miniature paintings, call to mind the linear elegance and Persian effects of Pisanello. The movement towards Western realism in the seventeenth century marked the end of icon-painting.

*The Minor Arts*

The Oriental taste for luxury appeared in Byzantium in works of handicraft made all over the Empire for both local use and export; for the

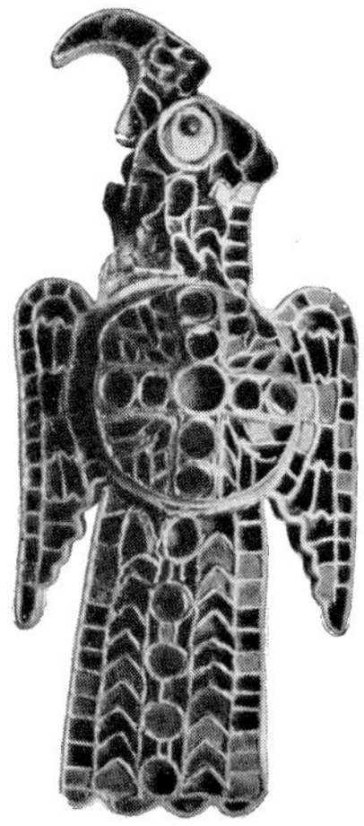

160 *Eagle-formed Buckle in Gold with Garnets from Cesena, Italy. 6th c. Paris*

161 *Decorative Coursing. Church at Selommes, France. 10th c.*

peoples of the West, not yet skilled as craftsmen, readily gave high prices for them. Thus the treasuries of the Western churches have preserved large numbers of ivories, textiles, carved gems and goldsmiths' work. In the sixth century Syria specialized in the production of large, embossed (repoussé) silverware of ancient derivation, while Byzantium exploited the process of cloisonné enamelling. The finest ensemble of Byzantine craftsmanship in gold is the *Pala d'Oro*, the high altar of St Mark's, Venice (early twelfth century, pl. 157 a), which is lavishly worked with gold, gems, pearls and enamels. The fabrics woven in Coptic Egypt and in Syria, then in Constantinople after the Arab conquest, often took their inspiration from old Persian and Sassanian patterns and served as a means of making Oriental designs known in the West.

*162 Initial from the Book of Kells. A.D. 760–820. Dublin*

## 3. WESTERN ART IN THE EARLY MIDDLE AGES

### *Pre-Carolingian*

The artistic tradition of the barbarians who settled in the West in the fourth and fifth centuries, had given them little preparation for the complex works of a permanent civilization. Having been accustomed for thousands of years to the few crafts compatible with their nomadic existence (fabrics, articles of finery and equipment), they were now faced with architectural and iconographical needs for which they had to invent everything themselves.

Tribes of the Goths, the most gifted of the barbarian peoples, founded states in Spain (Visigoths) and in Italy (Ostrogoths). They learnt all they could from Rome and Byzantium. The Franks, who settled in Gaul, and the Lombards in northern Italy, imbibed Oriental traditions through the Greek monks and the Syrian and Jewish merchants who brought them Byzantine and Sassanian merchandise which delighted their luxurious tastes. The influx of these Asiatic peoples revived the ornamental and abstract tendencies which had found expression in Celtic art before being discouraged by the Roman conquest.

*163 Tomb of Theodoric, Ravenna. Early 6th c.*

Any study of early Western art should begin with the minor arts, whose aesthetic dominated even architecture to such a degree that sometimes even the coursing of walls imitated the patterns of the weaver or the silver-smith (pl. 161). The Goths and Franks were to maintain that technique of cloisonné work in gold which was their speciality (pl. 160), both

*164 Symbols of the Four Evangelists. Altar-Frontal of the Patriarch Sicuald. Late 8th c. Cividale*

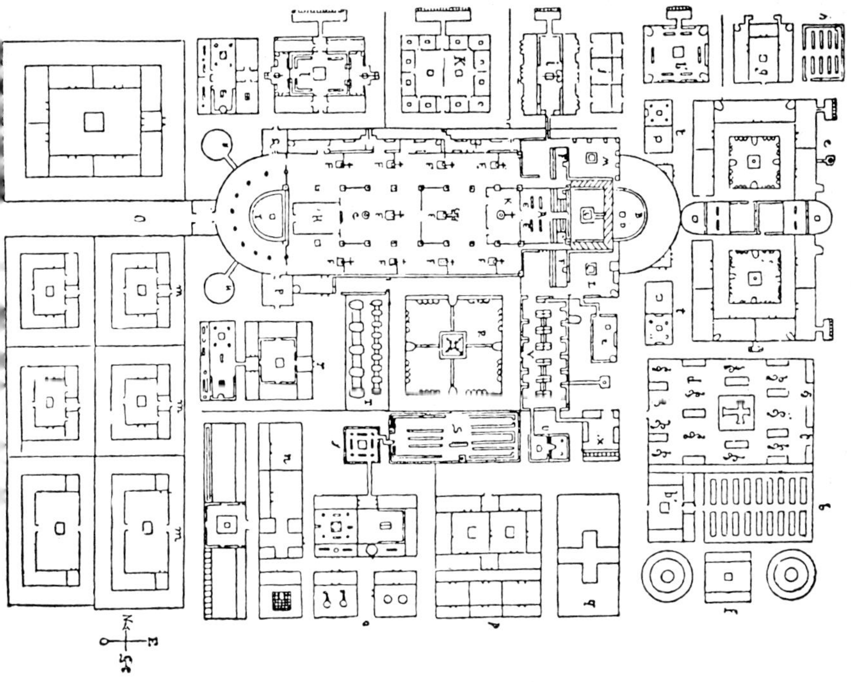

*165 'Ideal' Plan of St-Gall. About 820*

in lay works (crowns of the Visigoth kings, found at Guarrazar near Toledo) and by adapting it to religious needs (shrines and reliquaries). We know from descriptions written at the time that churches were richly decorated with costly works of this kind.

A supremely monastic art, the illumination, was brought to Gaul by monks from Egypt. The monks used it for embellishing holy books (such as missals and gospels) with a pure decorative impulse which disdained mere realism. The chimerical imagination of the barbarians suggested fantastic forms to them, which they intermingled in a sort of indecipherable ornamental pattern which we call tracery. It was in the work of Irish and English monks in the seventh and eighth centuries that this ornamental medium took the most remarkable forms, in which Celtic, Saxon and Mediterranean influences came together. The oldest of these works, the *Book of Durrow* (Trinity College, Dublin, second half of seventh century, pl. 713), has an obvious relationship to the magnificent trinkets found in the graves of Anglo-Saxon chiefs (treasure-trove of Sutton Hoo, about 650, pl. 48). Mediterranean influence is seen in the *Lindisfarne Gospel* (British Museum, between 698–721), while the admirable *Book of Kells* (Trinity College, Dublin, between 760–820, pl. 162) shows – at least in the miniatures showing the human figure – the influence of such Byzantine works as the *Rabula Gospels* (pl. 156) or *Etchmiadzin Codex.* The *Lichfield Gospel* (Lichfield Cathedral, eighth century) is in a similar style to the *Book of Kells.* The *St Gall Gospel* (Bibliothèque de St-Gall, Switzerland, between 750–760) is considered to be a purely Irish example of a style in which the human figure itself became no more than a part of a rhythmic pattern.

Fourth-century Gaul had a period of building activity which resulted in basilicas of the Roman type, decorated with rich mosaics. The mosaics gave way to frescoes after the barbarian invasions of the fifth century. An offshoot of Roman triumphal art, this form still flourished in the fifth century, to judge from the rotunda-style baptisteries which were used for baptism by immersion, and of which a number of specimens survive in Provence (Marseilles, Fréjus, Aix, Riez, Mélas, Valence). At Ravenna in Italy, Amalasuntha built a domed rotunda (after 530) over the tomb of her father Theodoric, king of the Ostrogoths (pl. 163). This cupola is a monolith, 35 3/4 feet in diameter and weighing 300 tons, the last example in the West of the taste for components of colossal dimensions which we noted in the most primitive civilizations. The Visigoth art of Spain, whose capital was then Toledo, has left few remains (S. Miguel de Tarrassa), but some characteristics of this art appear to have persisted in the monuments raised by the Christian kings of the Asturias in the

*166 Chapel Palatine (now Cathedral), Aachen. Late 8th c.*

*IV Christ the Saviour. Apocalypse from Bamberg Cathedral. Munich*

*167 St Matthew. Miniature from the Ebbo Gospel. Between 816–835. Epernay*

*168 Christ. Miniature from the Godescalc Gospel*

ninth century, which also show some Oriental influence (Santullano, S. Miguel de Liño, S. Cristina de Lena, S. Maria de Naranco).

The narrative sarcophagi of Arles, imitated from the Roman in the fourth century, show the last traces of ancient plastic traditions in Gaul, but in a profoundly debased form. Figurative sculpture disappeared in the fifth century. The workshops of the Pyrenees continued to produce columns, capitals, sarcophagi and marble plaques for chancels, all in an exclusively ornamental style. These products of the Pyrenean quarries were exported to northern Gaul (Jouarre crypt), especially in the seventh century when there seems to have been considerable artistic activity; but this industry was killed by the Muslim invasions which ravaged the whole of southern France in the early eighth century. Sculpture in the round tended to disappear all over the barbarian area, being replaced by carved panelling in stone which often imitated the goldsmiths' cloisonné-work (altars at Cividale in Lombardy, pl. 164).

## *Carolingian and Ottonian Art*

The Carolingian reformation showed the same characteristics in art as in politics and literature. It tried to react against the anarchy of the barbarians by a return to the traditions of the Roman Empire. It was in Classical and Byzantine Italy that Charlemagne sought his models for a revival of figurative and monumental art. The famous Chapel Palatine at Aachen (Aix-la-Chapelle) was only a simplified edition of S. Vitale

*169 Tutilo. Assumption and Scenes from the Legend of St-Gall. Ivory Codex Cover. About 900. St-Gall*

*170 All Saints, Earls Barton. Tower about 935*

at Ravenna, but enriched with ancient materials taken from Italy (pl. 147, 166). The Carolingian artists eagerly adopted plans for buildings on the principle of the Greek cross (Church of Germigny-des-Prés near Orléans) and they made great use of the 'double-basilica' plan (with two apses and two transepts). The influence of the monks, who were the guardians of the literatures of antiquity and of the principles of civilization, now dominated everything. Monasteries were built all over the Empire, and the 'ideal' plan, dating from the ninth century and preserved at the abbey of St-Gall in Switzerland, shows us, fully formed, the typical medieval lay-out: monastery buildings set round a cloister flanking a church, together with agricultural, industrial, hospital and teaching accommodation, all giving a good idea of the part that monks were playing in both material and spiritual civilization (pl. 165). The most strikingly ornate example of Carolingian architecture left in England is the west tower of All Saints, Earls Barton (pl. 170).

Carolingian art reacted violently against the formlessness of the barbarians and introduced representation once more. It was often nearer to ancient than to Byzantine art, as can be seen from the frescoes in the crypt of St-Germain-d'Auxerre, or those in S. Maria de Castelseprio which

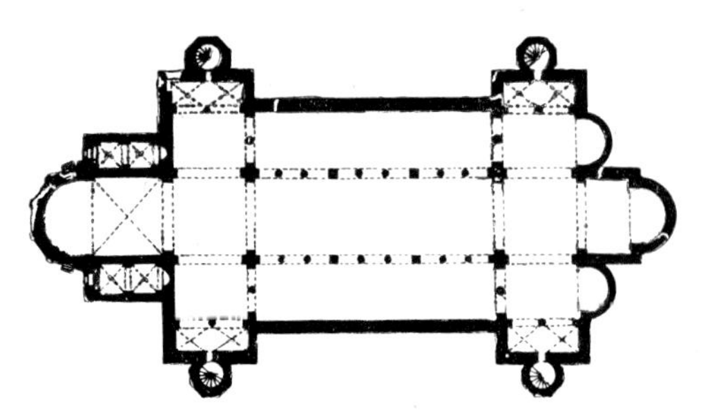

*171 Plan of St Michael's, Hildesheim. Completed 1033*

were rediscovered in Lombardy in 1944. Monastic schools of illumination flourished all over the Empire (at Rheims, Tours, Metz, in France; at Reichenau, St-Gall, Fulda, in Germanic countries). The schools of the East were distinguishable by a romantic, roughish style heralding German Gothic expressionism *(Utrecht Psalter, Ebbo Gospel*, pl. 167, both illuminated at Rheims); while the Tours school *(Bible of Charles the Bald)* or the so-called 'Palace school' which illuminated gospels for the Emperors, sought solemnity of gesture and composition *(Godescalc Gospel* illuminated for Charlemagne, pl. 168, *Gospel of St-Médard*, Soissons).

We know from old descriptions that the churches were embellished with magnificent bronze objects (the so-called *Chair of Dagobert)* but little trace has remained of them. Gold craftmanship is better represented, these objects sometimes attaining a splendour which was not to be improved on in the Middle Ages (Charlemagne's Treasure at Aachen). The Carolingian artists were able to revive the ancient craft of glyptics, the carving of gems. A renewed feeling for relief came out in ivory

*172 Interior of St Michael's, Hildesheim*

*173 Vuolvinio. Golden Altar in S. Ambrogio, Milan. Late 9th c.*

*174 Noli Me Tangere from the Bronze Doors of Hildesheim. Early 11th c.*

carving (ivory bindings for gospels, pl. 169) and through the embossed work that was done in gold (*Golden Altar* in S. Ambrogio, Milan. pl. 173, cover of the *Codex Aureus,* Munich).

The Carolingian impulse was checked in Gaul by the anarchy brought about through the Norman invasions in the eleventh century. Meanwhile in Italy and above all in Germany under the prosperous Ottonian dynasty, Carolingian principles persisted into the eleventh century. At Trier and at Reichenau, as well as at Regensburg, Cologne and Fulda, magnificent illuminated manuscripts were produced in a truly Imperial spirit. The Germanic taste for fantasy appears in the ornamental forms although antique motifs are also to be found. However, in the depicting of the human figure, new and highly individual forms of an extraordinarily moving expressiveness ran counter to the antique art of the South, which had been the inspiration of Carolingian times. No longer did the artist try to portray biblical events in an illusionistic manner, but instead concentrated on expressing their spiritual significance *(Codex Egberti,* Trier; *Gospel of Otto III, Pericopes of Henry II,* both Staatsbibliothek, Munich; *Bamberg Apocalypse,* colour pl. IV; *Hitda Codex,* Darmstadt). While France could now produce nothing better than shapeless reliefs, the plastic sense in Germany expressed itself wonderfully in the eleventh century in the medium of embossed and cast metals (*Golden Altar,* Basle, now in Cluny Museum). Bishop Bernward had a pillar, a chandelier and bronze doors of fine quality made for his cathedral at Hildesheim, which had two transepts, two choirs and two apses (pl. 171, 172, 174), while a little later in about 1060 the craftsman who cast the doors of Augsburg Cathedral, with mythological and biblical scenes, gave them an Alexandrian grace.

*175 Carved pillar in Ste-Marie, Souillac. 12th c.*

# V. THE RISE OF THE WEST

## *Romanesque and Gothic Art*

If any century in Western civilization deserves the name 'Renaissance', then it is the French eleventh century rather than the Italian fifteenth. From the sixth to the tenth century nothing had appeared in the West worth calling a style (we speak of Merovingian or Carolingian 'art', not 'style'). Planting themselves as best they could on the remains of the ancient civilization they had destroyed, and asking Byzantium for lessons which they hardly understood, the barbarians from the sixth to the tenth century never abandoned the tedious ornamental crafts they brought with them from their nomadic past, but failed to fetch from their own darkness that coherent system of constructional methods, architectural, plastic and decorative forms that make a style. But suddenly the veil was torn aside. Architecture in the eleventh century made marvellous strides, a sure sign of a return to building cities. From the basilican church, a building with the unfinished look of a framework covered with temporary

*176/177 Comparison of an Assyrian Cylinder-Seal with a Detail from a Capital in St-Martin-d'Ainay, Lyons*

roofing, emerged the Romanesque church whose vault, dominating the whole economy of the structure, ensured the unification of all its parts. The monument was no longer a mere inorganic set of walls and roofs providing the necessary closed and covered areas. Like the Greek temple the Romanesque church was an articulated organism, all its parts being unified in their functions and proportions. The bay became the standard measurement for length, the storey for height, bringing new basic units to architectural composition to replace the column and entablature of Greek art. With a rhythm punctuated by the tall shafts, the groin-vaults, and the moulding of string-courses marking the galleries – the entire flow obeys a harmonious regulation of spaces, volumes and surfaces. Moving in a leisurely way from support to archway and from storey to storey, the eye impresses on the mind the perfect unity of all the building's constituent parts, which are given as it were a musical measure by the alternating strong beats of the solid parts and the unaccented beats of the open spaces. This constructional arithmetic which the Greeks had understood intellectually, was reinvented empirically, and in another mode, by the Romanesque artists, who are to be thanked for imposing this notion of order and number on the taste for the indefinite and boundless which the barbarians and the East had in common. After a long eclipse the West emerged victorious from an uneasy struggle for logic which had lasted six hundred years.

All the characteristics of Romanesque art stem from this notion of order. The decoration which had been scattered here and there like tapestry on the walls of Byzantine churches was now confined to the major parts of the building, and to emphasize them it was raised into relief, so that a forgotten technique was now revived – that of sculpture in which the ancient world had expressed its faith in the life of the body. Sculpture is the daughter of architecture, arising from its needs and sharing its spirit. By the powerful articulation of its volumes the Romanesque monument was so to speak modelled spatially.

*Subordination of Sculpture to Architecture*

*178 Feast at Simon's. Section of a Tympanum at Neuilly-en-Donjon. 12th c.*

*179 Last Supper. Tympanum at Charlieu. 12th c.*

*180 Last Supper. Capital at Issoire. 12th c.*

Whether it aims at grandeur or harmony – except in the province of Poitou where it lapsed into the picturesque – Romanesque architecture is always sober and restrained in composition. In the few parts yielded to it by the architecture, sculpture, constrained by its narrow frame, wreathes and writhes with a delirious energy. The seductiveness of Ro-

*Humanization of the Holy Face*

*181 Head of Christ. La Madeleine, Vézelay. About 1130*
*182 Head of a Prophet. About 1160. Senlis*
*183 Head of Christ. South Porch of Chartres Cathedral. Before 1212*

manesque sculpture is due to an analytic view of nature before it was frozen into canons, fixed expressions and attitudes; it is a surge of forms elbowing each other, merging one into the other on arch mouldings, pilasters, tympana, spandrels and capitals (pl. 175). Everything from the very beginnings of mankind came together to enrich this marvellous language in stone: pagan myths and Christian scenes, fragments of antiquity, barbarous ornament, Byzantine, Sassanian, Assyrian and even Sumerian forms, for the old animal symbolism of the cylinder-seals of Sumeria and Elam found its final transformation here (pl. 176, 177). Thus Western man, as he started creating once again after six centuries, began by remembering; but he used all the forms that he remembered from the depths of the past as though they were words, creating a new language with them which he spoke with a wonderful oratorical ease. What we have called 'monsters', those composite creatures which the artist invents out of bits and pieces taken from all the civilizations of the world and to which man himself indulgently lent his own body, did not need to be explained away by St Bernard as having little or no intellectual content. Unlike Byzantine art, Romanesque had no very deep religious bearing, and when the glow of inner life shines through the faces on Chartres Cathedral or at St-Loup-de-Naud, that is because the Gothic genius was wakening there already. This fabulous bestiary is a sign of an orgiastic desire to create forms, gripping man's imagination when it was unleashed after six hundred years of abstinence. In behaving thus the Romanesque architect was spendthrift of his inheritance; freed from the pressure of centuries and millennia the Gothic image-maker was able to see nature with fresh eyes and a virginal imagination.

*184 Byzantine Head of Christ. S. Sophia, Constantinople. 11th c.*

*185 School of Cimabue. Head of Christ. Late 13th c. Washington*

Virginal is the term we are tempted to apply to Gothic art. For it is pure creativity. Everything here is new, structure and setting, decoration, inspiration, plasticity. With Greek art, Gothic is the only example in Western civilization of a complete renewal of formal vocabulary through the complete invention of a style. Rome profited from Greece; Byzantium issued from Rome and from the East; Romanesque art was a quadroon product of the East, Byzantium, the barbarian and the antique; Renaissance art and that of modern times borrowed from antiquity its entire architectural and decorative morphology and a great part of its idea of beauty. Gothic art, on the contrary, shook off the burden of well-worn forms which cramped the urge of Romanesque art, and started off from nature. The creative impulse of that admirable twelfth century must have been extraordinarily powerful to inspire such courage in the Gothic artist, filling him with the will to start from scratch at the very moment when all over France Romanesque art was only beginning to flower.

Romanesque art was already a century old and its maturity had hardly lasted thirty years, when the will to create that gave us Gothic art began to stir in the Ile-de-France. The first Gothic cathedrals were erected in competition with the finishing or even the beginnings of the great Romanesque minsters in other provinces, so that critics have jokingly remarked that Gothic art was nothing more than 'Ile-de-France Romanesque'.

The discovery of a new vault, or rather the rational analysis of its properties, allowed Gothic architecture to achieve that Christian dream

*186 Keep at Loches. 12th c.*

which the Byzantine artist had only been able to satisfy by a sort of mirage. Overcoming its weight, the edifice was to soar light and airy, triumphing over matter. The cathedral is a vertical flight just as the Greek temple and the Romanesque church are horizontal in movement. The Romanesque inertia of the surfaces gave way to the vibration of shafts, fenestration, and stained-glass windows, which cause an interplay of lights in a variety of modes comparable with the tones of orchestral instruments. The cathedral is the realization in stone of that symphonic utterance which Germany was to express in pure sound seven hundred years later. In this sense it is the first mature manifestation of the lyrical gift of the North; but in order to take shape it needed the awakening of specifically French genius which was heir to the plastic imagination and the rationalism of the Mediterranean. The cathedral certainly embodies a desire for growth and expansion which causes it to develop organically like a living thing, but it also obeys certain inflecting rhythms, and this development was achieved through a reasoning which, by deduction, exploited a principle to its utmost limits. It was the first appearance of that French logic which later had a sterilizing effect when applied to pure speculation. Here, however, it was marvellously fertile because it was acting on nature itself after having brushed aside everything that went before – just as Cartesian reasoning was to do later in philosophy. Reason governs the Gothic like a queen, not merely creating a system but bringing forth a world; for the cathedral is a manifold world like the universe itself, in which a host of images have their being.

The Western sense of imagery came to life – or to a second life – in Gothic art. If, as M. Emile Mâle has shown, it is true that the image still subserved the idea, it refused to be its slave and lent rather than gave itself. Rejecting the yoke of the Byzantine symbol, the image was no longer a simplified ideogram, but on the contrary it sought to embody some concrete form already in nature. Thirteenth-century France restored Mediterranean anthropomorphism and realism to the West, after it had been temporarily supplanted by Eastern ideomorphism (pl. 181–183). This wonderful evolution, which in its progress takes us from the majestic portals of Chartres to those of Rheims, went through the same phases as Greek sculpture from the sixth to the fifth century B.C. Moreover, from the twelfth century to Claus Sluter, Gothic plastic art followed the same lines as Greek art, from the *korai* of the Acropolis to the *Laocoon;* there could be no better proof of the constants that are to be found in the life of forms as well as in the progress of the Western mind (pl. 698, 710).

The architectural and plastic formulae invented by the Ile-de-France were quickly recognized everywhere, for the logical always imposes itself as obvious. So Europe spoke Gothic as the Mediterranean had spoken Greek. But not all Europe; for Italy refused to absorb the Gothic. After 1250 Italy was working out her own Renaissance without heeding the example of France, and in a different way – not through a revolution but through a renewal of traditions, an 'involution'. Nicola Pisano and Giotto went direct to antiquity for the new inspiration which led them to a sense of nature and of man; at Siena even Byzantine art, with Duccio, was to have its austerity melted into feeling and tenderness. But the overwhelming tyranny of Gothic art came to check this impulse. For a hundred years Italian art was oppressed as though by a foreign occupation. We can understand why the angry men of the Renaissance, in the fourteenth century, denounced that art as *tedesco* (teutonic), a name which was to stick. The Gothic principle acted on the Italian mind like a virus, and when Florence at last shook itself free at the beginning of the fifteenth century, Italian artists had to start from where they had left off in the thirteenth. Donatello's direct precursor was Nicola Pisano, while the innovator Masaccio had, so to speak, to stir the ashes of Giotto.

## 1. ROMANESQUE ART

Romanesque art was born in France in the second quarter of the eleventh century. Its name was given to it in 1823 by M. de Gerville, by analogy with the romance languages. By 1100 it had emerged from the experimental stage, having already created great buildings, and in the twelfth century it went through a striking development which was reflected in many local variations. It gradually died out as it was ousted by the Gothic style towards the end of the twelfth century. It affected all the countries that had not come under Byzantine influence, but France, Spain and England produced its most characteristic forms. In Italy, where apart from some French influence it was little more than a continuation of primitive Christian art, it was known as 'neo-Latin', while in Germany the Rhenish school was the outcome of Carolingian and Ottonian art.

## Architecture

In the eleventh century the demand for works of architecture became heavy, reflecting the changes that were going on in politics and trade. The few civic buildings in stone that have survived are municipal monuments and castles. The latter consist mainly of a large tower or keep, raised on a mound serving as a redoubt or for living in, and surrounded by a wall or enceinte (pl. 186). The finest churches were those of the monasteries, for the Romanesque period was the golden age of monasticism. The monastic communities of Cluny and Cîteaux, both in Burgundy, played a fundamental part in the politics and society of the age – a part which quickly became international.

Although it did not entirely ignore the central plan, Romanesque art gave all its energy to developing the basilican plan. In order to meet the new needs of the faith, the church was considerably extended at the east end: to the simple rounded apse was added a straight part (the choir or chancel, pl. 187) and 'stepped' chapels (Benedictine plan, pl. 188) or chapels lined along the transept (Cistercian plan). In some of the largest and most beautiful constructions, Romanesque art laid down the definitive form for Western churches, by prolonging the aisles of the choir right round the apse (ambulatory) and by making the chapels (apsidal chapels) radiate round this ambulatory (pl. 189). The Western church in the Middle Ages was thus a harmonious combination of the basilican plan with the radiating plan.

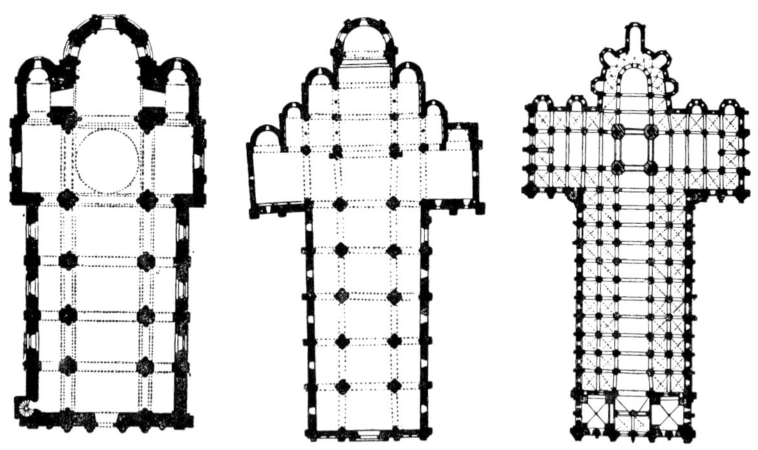

*187 Plan of the Abbey Church, Cellefrouin. 12th c.*
*188 Plan of the Abbey Church, Châteaumeillant. 12th c.*
*189 Plan of St-Sernin, Toulouse. 12th c.*

*190 St-Front-Périgueux. 12th c.*

*191 Aisle of La Madeleine, Vézelay. 12th c.*

Like the Byzantine church, the Romanesque church had all its sections vaulted over. All its characteristics spring from this form of covering. Domes were sometimes used at the crossing, but over the naves, only in a group of south-western churches (Aquitaine school, St-Front at Périgueux, pl. 190); groined cross-vaults (groin-vaults) are usually found only over the aisles (pl. 191). The longitudinal plan led naturally to the use of the barrel- or tunnel-vault (pl. 192); and as this exerts a continuous, non-localized pressure, to take the thrust the architect had to use massive piers, and thick walls pierced with narrow windows. The strain of the nave vault, in the best-planned buildings, was taken by raising the aisle vaults almost to the same height as the nave, thus 'blinding' it as in the Poitou churches (pl. 193). Sometimes, when the nave was very high, it was buttressed by galleries over the aisles (Auvergne school, and large so-called 'Pilgrimage churches'); the purpose of these gallery vaults was perfectly served by basing them on the quadrant, i. e. making them 'half-tunnels' (pl. 195). The arches and vaults were generally round-headed, though the pointed arch was not unknown.

Byzantine architecture sought broad stretches of surface; in the basilican church the arcades made an unbroken series and nothing intervened to disturb the mural surfaces either inside or outside. The Romanesque church, on the contrary, like the Greek temple, tended to knit independent elements which, taken together, result in the total edifice. These elements are the bay on the horizontal plane and the storey on the vertical. The bays are articulated internally by the use of shafts which, applied to the

*192 Nave of St-Lazare, Autun. 12th c.*

*193 St-Pierre, Aulnay. 12th c.*

piers, rise up into the vault and are usually prolonged across its surface, as far as the opposite bay, by lateral supporting arches. The applied-shafts allow the eye to measure the edifice longitudinally, whereas moulded projections mark the storey-divisions in the elevation, constituting main horizontal lines which create a perspective-effect (pl. 203).

On Roman, basilican or Byzantine monuments, the decoration was no more than an adornment stuck on the walls with no relation to the structure. The Romanesque architect, always after logic, achieved a close co-ordination of decoration with structure, to which end he reintroduced

*194 Archivolt of the Porch Andrieu. 12th c.*

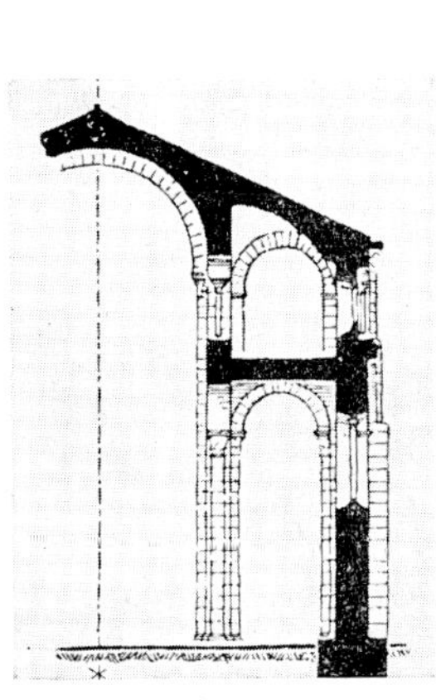

*195 Vertical Section. Issoire. 12th c.*

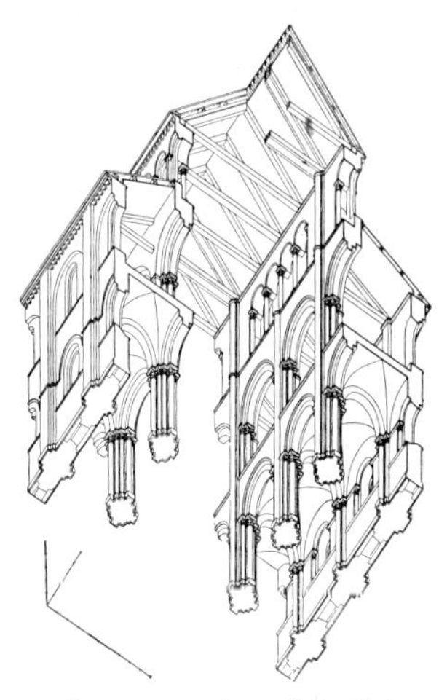

*196 Reconstruction of St-Etienne, Caen. Late 11th c.*

moulding (pl. 194) – a kind of geometrical sculpture that had become stunted in Byzantine art but which Greek art had recognized as useful – in order to stress the main parts of the building. The Romanesque builders liked effects of strength as well as harmony, but occasionally they were tempted by the picturesque, as in Poitou and Saintonge where they overburdened their façades with carvings. They had an admirable feeling for the composition of monumental masses by the forward movement of the

*197 Choir. Paray-le-Monial. 12th c.*

*198 Abbey Church, Fontenay. 12th c.*

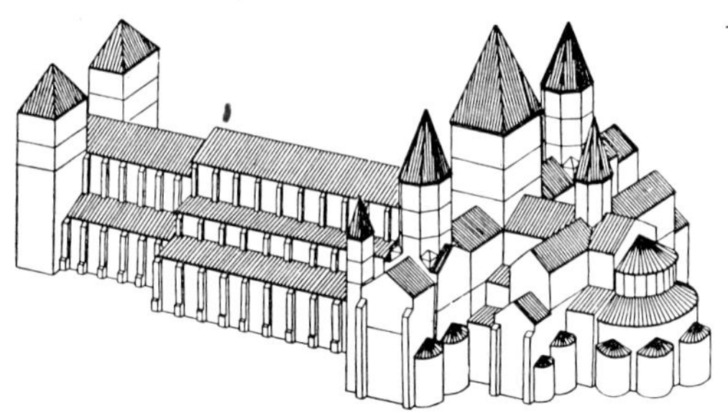

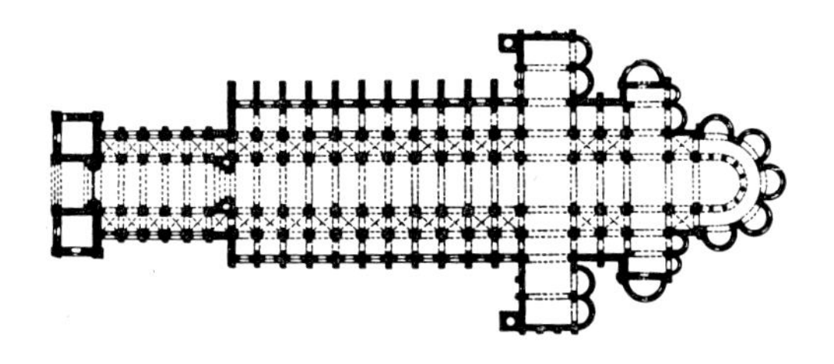

*199 Reconstruction and Plan of Cluny III. Late 11th–12th c.*

nave inside, the radiating rhythm of apse and chapels at the east end (pl. 197) and the tiered arrangement of the façade at the west. A new element, the belfry or bell-tower, often topped with a pyramidal roof, added a vertical emphasis.

The great variety of these schools of architecture is a sign of feudal separatism. When we reflect that in the twelfth century Gothic art was arising concurrently with the triumph of Romanesque, we must agree with the German historians Dehio and Bezold: 'French architecture in the eleventh and twelfth centuries, with its divergent styles flowering simultaneously, is a phenomenon unparalleled in the whole history of architecture.'

The Norman school was the oldest. Between 1025 and 1070 it was already capable of erecting great structures such as Bernay Abbey, the nave of Mont-St-Michel, and, at Caen, St-Etienne (l'Abbaye-aux-Hommes, pl. 196) and La Trinité (l'Abbaye-aux-Dames). It used galleries, but still timbered the naves to which the thirteenth century would have given pointed cross-vaults. The Normans sought very sober, over-all architectural effects and avoided figure decoration.

The Burgundian school benefited from being the home of the two great congregations of Cluny and Cîteaux. The Cluniac order built great churches, lavishly decorated with sculptures. In reaction the Cistercians built very stark edifices (abbey church of Fontenay, pl. 198). The abbey church at Cluny (rebuilt 1088–1120), no longer standing, was then the largest Church in Christendom, with a length of 643 1/2 feet (pl. 199). The Burgundian church had a very daring structure (the nave of Cluny was

$96\frac{1}{2}$ feet tall), while in decoration the Burgundians were influenced by Classical architecture (cathedrals of Autun and Langres).

The Provençal school went in for small buildings but gave them very harmonious proportions (St-Trophime at Arles, Montmajour Abbey); of all the schools this one owed most to antiquity (porch of St-Gilles-du-Gard).

The Auvergne churches were powerfully buttressed by means of quadrant-sectioned galleries which darkened the naves, but they have a harsh grandeur about them (Issoire, pl. 195; Notre-Dame-du-Port at Clermont).

The south-west region (Poitou-Saintonge) built churches with narrow aisles almost as tall as the naves and façades covered with profuse decoration (Notre-Dame-la-Grande at Poitiers).

A group of churches without aisles in Languedoc and in the south-west has several domes over the nave (Cahors, St-Front at Périgueux, pl. 190). The biggest Romanesque buildings belong to an inter-regional type found along the routes used by pilgrims to Compostela (St-Sernin at Toulouse, pl. 189; Figeac, Ste-Foy at Conques, Santiago de Compostela, pl. 203). These churches have double aisles and an ambulatory, suitable for the crowds of pilgrims and already anticipating the Gothic cathedral.

*200 Last Judgement. Tympanum in St-Pierre, Moissac. About 1120*

It was at the end of the eleventh century, after six centuries of inactivity, that monumental sculpture came to life again. Languedoc and Spain show the oldest specimens. The low-relief figures at St-Sernin, Toulouse, (*Christ, Apostles* and *Angels,* pl. 699) and the cloister of St-Pierre at Moissac *(Apostles)* show a still hesitant modelling imitated from Byzantine ivories. Built about 1120, the main portal at Moissac is evidence of a school fully versed in its medium with its tympanum (pl. 200), depicting the apocalyptic vision of St John (Christ shown between four beasts, the evangelist's symbols, which were to appear frequently in Romanesque art).

It was with a generous and lively touch that Romanesque art reintroduced figures into sculpture, which until then had been inhibited by the preference for abstraction of the barbarians. Yet the art of sculpture was not yet practised for its own sake, but waved and twisted in order to fit its frame, lending itself to purely decorative rhythms (pl. 178–180). The Romanesque artists proved to have unlimited imagination in inventing all kinds of ornamental patterns, in which the human figure was reconciled to elements taken from the vegetable and animal worlds as well as from the fabulous code of the East, for the creation of monsters. A frantic vitality enlivens these figures, in their daemonic agitation. One of the most beautiful decorative features of the Romanesque is the capital. Its structure derives from the composite form of the ancients, which certain schools (Provence) carefully imitated; but generally the capitals depict biblical scenes in the form of monstrous shapes which, set onto the capital, cleverly underline its structure (pl. 201). The finest series of

201 *Figured Capital. St-Benoit-sur-Loire. About 1160*

202 *Apocalyptic Christ. Fresco from S. Clemente, Tahull. 12th c. Barcelona*

*203 Nave of Santiago de Compostela. 12th c.*

*204 Nave of Ely Cathedral. 12th c.*

capitals is in the nave of Vézelay in Burgundy, and is the most fertile in picturesque inventiveness.

The great variety of the Romanesque schools of sculpture, reflecting the different architectural schools, may be classified into two main groups. Some of them show a canon of very elongated proportions, a flat and calligraphic modelling of draperies, a hint of convulsion in the movement, and it has been suggested that schools of this type were influenced by the art of illumination. An example is the Languedoc school, the most developed of all, which excelled in tympana with large, grouped compositions (Moissac, pl. 200; Souillac). In the same spirit the Burgundian school (tympana at Autun and Vézelay) made rather more confused compositions, more drily stylized. The Poitou school liked lavish decoration on the façades and especially round the portals. Other schools preferred a system of squat proportions and had a stronger grasp of relief. The influence of gold altar-fronts inspired several segmented tympana in central France (Ste-Foy at Conques, Carennac). The full proportions of the Auvergne

*205 Transept of Peterborough Cathedral. 12th c.*

*206 Puerta della Gloria in Santiago de Compostela. 12th c.*

school probably owe something to the survival of an aesthetic dating from Gallic low-reliefs; Auvergne is the only Romanesque school to attempt carving in the round, in wooden statues of the Virgin which were often overlaid with metal foil. The Provence school (St-Gilles-du-Gard, St-Trophime at Arles) showed a powerful feeling for relief in its imitation of antique sculpture and Christian sarcophagi, which were preserved in large numbers at Arles.

## Painting and the Minor Arts

Romanesque art still had the taste of the preceding centuries for luxurious objects worked in gold. The two main centres of production were in the districts of the Rhine and the Meuse, on the one hand, and Limousin on the other. The Meuse school, influenced by Germanic art, still kept up the Byzantine tradition of cloisonné-enamelling in delicate colours, sometimes derived from Alexandrian colouring (sea-green, lake, azure). The Limousin school practised the craft of chasing metals, which consists of running the enamel paste into grooves cut in a bronze plaque; the colourings, much heavier in this case, (garnet-red, dark blue) originated in the smiths' work of the barbarians.

The same differences in colourings are to be found in the fairly numerous wall-paintings which survive in French churches. The Burgundian school (Berzé-la-Ville) tried to imitate the polychromatic brilliance of the Byzantine mosaic, while the Poitou school (St-Savin) used a palette reduced to red and yellow ochres reminiscent of Oriental hues. In the course of the twelfth century a new contribution was made to the arts of colour in the leaded stained-glass window, an outcome of cloisonné (panelled) metalwork. This developed strikingly in the thirteenth century, though the finest windows date back to the infancy of this art (west front of Chartres, colour pl. V).

### *Romanesque Art outside France*

Romanesque art took a deep hold all over Europe. The closest national school to the French was the English school, which in a sense was the twin of the Norman school, largely on account of the political union between England and Normandy. Thus English Romanesque is known as the 'Norman style'. The great Norman churches (Ely, pl. 204, Peterborough, pl. 205, Durham, Fountains Abbey, Southwell) have the same

*207 Fiesole Cathedral. 11th–13th c.*

*208 Modena Cathedral. 12th c.*

*209 Cathedral and Leaning Tower, Pisa. 11th–13th c.*

characteristics as those of Normandy. They are enormous structures, having galleries, thick walls and massive piers, tall naves, which are generally timbered over, stone vaulting usually being reserved for aisles, and an imposing lantern-tower over the crossing. Certain specifically English features appeared at that time and lasted into the Gothic period, such as the lengthening of the nave, and the decorative arcadings, sometimes of intersecting arches, on the façades. As with the French Norman school, the decoration is almost entirely geometrical, but figures are more frequent than in Normandy. The finest example of this Norman style is the great cathedral of Durham. Durham Cathedral shows a very early use of rib-vaulting, though this does not affect the structure or Romanesque appearance of the building. Rib-vaults were given to the south aisle of the choir in 1096 and to its main bays in 1104, the latter being replaced in 1235. The finest development of the art illumination came in the tenth and eleventh centuries, when the Winchester school's lavish colour and daring draughtsmanship had an almost baroque quality *(Benedictional of St Aethelwold,* British Museum, about 957–980; formerly Devonshire Collection, Chatsworth).

The Spanish school was related to that of Languedoc. It contributed to the revival of sculpture, and from the end of the eleventh century the workshops at Léon and Compostela showed a precocious tendency towards sculpture in the round. The portal of Silo in Castile and cloister at Ripoll in Catalonia, on the other hand, recall Languedoc carving. The cathedral of Santiago de Compostela in Galicia, the goal of the most

*210 Antelami. Deposition. Parma Cathedral. About 1170*

famous pilgrimage in the West, belongs to the lineage of the great Cluniac churches (Pilgrimage churches: St-Sernin at Toulouse, Conques); it has the finest sculptures in Spain on the Goldsmiths' Portal (which have been dated to before 1117) and on the Gloria Portal (pl. 206), finished in 1188 by Maestre Mateo, who brought an already Gothic notion of statuary into Spain. Catalonia had a fine school of Romanesque painting, characterized by a taste for lively glittering colours, particularly red and yellow (manuscripts of the Apocalypse, frescoes in the Pyrenean churches, pl. 202).

Italy persisted in its use of the basilican plan during the entire Romanesque period (pl. 207). In its timbered naves it often used alternating strong and weak piers, practically ignored the ambulatory and for preference placed the bell-towers on either side of the choir. Over bays with this alternate-system, Lombardy shows some precocious examples of rib-vaulting which do not affect the Romanesque appearance (S. Ambrogio, Milan). The finest buildings in Tuscany are the cathedrals of Lucca and Pisa (pl. 209), in Lombardy, S. Abbondio at Como, S. Michele at Pavia, Modena

*211 Bronze Door of S. Zeno, Verona (detail). 12th c.*

*212 Christ healing the Blind Man. S. Angelo in Formis. 11th c.*

Cathedral (pl. 208), and in southern Italy the cathedrals of Trani, Bari, Salerno and Ravello. In Sicily the Lombard influence mingled with Norman, Muslim and Byzantine influences (Cefalu Cathedral, abbey of Monreale). As for sculpture, Italy proved hostile to the Romanesque love of metamorphosis and dynamism and remained stubbornly attached to the sculptural outlook of antiquity. The principal works of Romanesque sculpture in Italy are in the Emilia province (Wiligelmo, duomo of Modena, XIth century, Benedetto Antelami, ambo of the duomo (cathedral) of Parma, 1178, pl. 210). Italy continued using bronzework for its cathedral doors (pl. 211). It created monumental liturgic furnishings (pulpits, ambos, chandeliers, choir-screens) in white marble incrusted with coloured marble mosaics; one family, the Cosmati (a name suggestive of Greek origins), became famous for this art from the early twelfth century onwards. When it reached Rome this art enjoyed great popularity, and the vast stocks of marble to be found in the ancient ruins encouraged its development. In painting Italy remained an apprentice to Byzantium. The fresco now began to develop (pl. 212). In the thirteenth century the Tuscans began painting on panels, taking Byzantine models as a point of departure. The mosaics in Sicily were imbued with the Greek spirit.

Romanesque buildings in Germany are set along the Rhine and the Danube, the most civilized regions of the Germanic countries at that time. The Rhenish school, related to the Lombard, shows the most affinity

213 *Abbey Church, Maria-Laach. 12th c.*

with the earlier Carolingian art. It made free use of the double-basilican plan (cathedrals of Worms, Mainz, Bamberg, Naumburg, abbey church of Maria-Laach, pl. 213), the alternate-systems of 'strong' and 'weak' supports (Speyer Cathedral, pl. 215), and there was a marked centralizing tendency at the east end, with the bell-towers hugging the chancel (church of the Apostles, Cologne, pl. 214). The block (cushion) capitals were mediocrely decorated, if at all (pl. 172), the Germans having little

214 *Church of the Apostles, Cologne. About 1200*

215 *Speyer Cathedral. 11th c.*

216 *Prophet Jonas. Choir-Screen of Bamberg Cathedral (detail). About 1220*

sense of the monumental in sculpture; but to make up for this the relief-work inclines to statuary, and the tradition brilliantly inaugurated in the Ottonian period found its fulfilment in the prophets round the choir of Bamberg Cathedral (about 1220, pl. 216)), one of the strongest assertions of that feeling for pathos which is essentially German.

The Low Countries were attracted by both the Norman and Rhenish influences, most noticeable in Tournai Cathedral.

The Meuse and Rhenish regions show Germanic skill in the metal crafts. Precious objects in brass and bronze, sometimes embellished with enamels, were made at Cologne and round Liége (pl. 217). Between 1107 and 1118 Reiner von Huy made the bronze fonts for St-Barthélémy at Liége, a tradition which was passed on to Gottfried von Huy and Nikolaus von Verdun, whose work was influenced by German expressiveness (reredos at Klosterneuberg, Austria, 1181), while the monk Hugo d'Oignies in the early thirteenth century remained more traditional. On the Rhine and the Meuse there was a faster stylistic evolution than in southern Germany; towards 1200 the *Shrine of the Magi* at Cologne and the stucco reliefs of the choir-screen at Halberstadt (pl. 218) show a far more advanced plastic skill than was seen at Bamberg in 1220.

## 2. GOTHIC ART

The term '*gothique*' is the French equivalent of the expression '*tedesco*', used by the Italians of the Renaissance to decry medieval art. The term has led to regrettable misunderstandings because in reality Gothic was a French creation. It appeared in the Ile-de-France towards 1125 (St-Denis

*217 Chased enamel Plaque. Mosan (Meuse) School. 12th c. Paris*

and Sens) and flourished first in that province, while other regions were still following the Romanesque. Gothic art reached its maturity in the thirteenth century; it quickly spread to England and found its way all over Europe in the thirteenth and fourteenth centuries. Italy was only superficially touched by it and was the first to give it up, when Florence led the way in the early fifteenth century in developing the Renaissance aesthetic. In its belated Flamboyant phase, Gothic art had a strong hold in Northern Europe in the fifteenth century. It persisted in France till about 1530 in religious buildings and in both England and Germany continued in a somewhat debased state until the seventeenth century.

## *The Creation of Gothic Art in France*

The thirteenth century was the great age of Gothic art. The century of St Louis, comparable with the Greek fifth century, saw the first creation in the Middle Ages of a coherent political and social system. Religious dogma and philosophical thought were crystallized in great works of which the most important was St Thomas Aquinas' *Summa Theologica*. The true dogmatic and intellectual centre of Christendom was no longer Rome but the university of Paris, where the Italian St Thomas was teaching. The cathedral was the monumental expression of that demand for order which dominated the fields of fact and thought; it also marks the awakening of the people and a certain secularization of the faith. The intellectual centres now moved from the monasteries to the universities, while the artistic initiative passed from the abbots to the bishops, who were encouraged by a burst of popular enthusiasm. Like the ancient temple, the cathedral was the city's monument, and of all the great monumental forms created by civilizations it best expressed the common effort of a whole society. The gradual expansion of the Gothic style throughout France coincided with that cohesive force which tended to weld the whole territory of ancient Gaul into a strong state centred in the power of the throne.

218 *St Andrew. Choir-Screen of the Liebfrauenkirche, Halberstadt (detail). About 1190*

## Architecture

The decisive elements in the new architectural style were the pointed cross-vault with ribs and the flying-buttress.

Invented by the English and the Lombards, but first exploited in all its potentialities by the Ile-de-France architects, the pointed rib-vault is derived from the groin-vault, and its essential property is the concentration of stresses at four points, whereas the Romanesque barrel-vault thrust down all along the length of the supporting wall (pl. 203, 219). The use of this new vault thus eliminated the carrying function of the walls, which in the thirteenth century were replaced by 'glass screens'. The arches and vaults, being pointed, appeared more slender than the rounded form.

The flying-buttress is a kind of bridge applied to one of the resting-points of the high ogival vaults and passing over the aisle to transmit the thrust of the central structure to a buttress situated beyond the aisle wall (pl. 221). The flying-buttress is in effect a slice cut out of the quadrant-vault which supported the naves of certain Romanesque churches (pl. 195). The equilibrium of the Romanesque church was obtained by

*219 Choir-Vault of Soissons Cathedral. Consecrated 1212*

the resistance of continuous walls; but instead of being surrounded by a rampart of walls, the Gothic cathedral, leaning on its light piers and held laterally by its buttresses, could flood the interior with light through its spacious bays (pl. 229, 244).

This result was only achieved in the thirteenth century. The Gothic cathedrals of the twelfth century (Senlis, Laon, Notre-Dame in Paris, pl. 224) had no flying-buttresses, those visible today on Notre-Dame having been added in the thirteenth; the supporting of the central vaults was still ensured by the use of galleries over the aisles. The internal eleva-

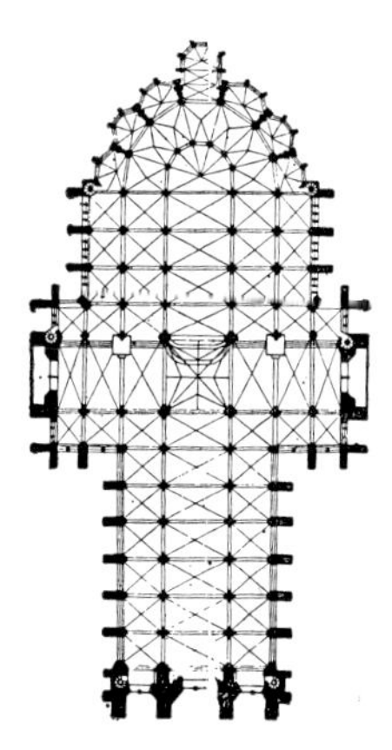

*220 Plan of Amiens Cathedral. 1220*

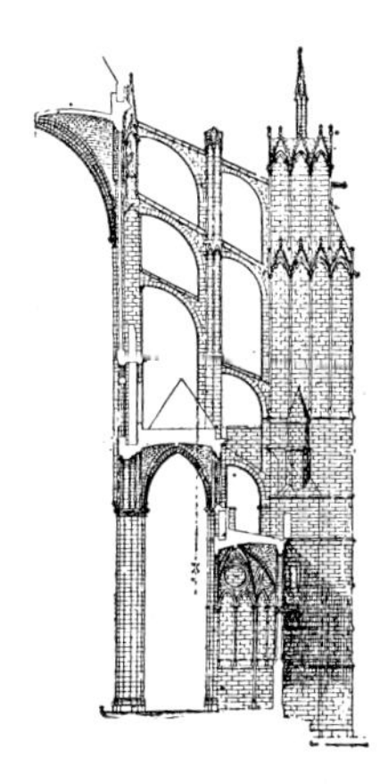

*221 Vertical Section of the Choir of Beauvais Cathedral. 1247*

*222 Nave of Laon Cathedral. About 1150*

tion was in four stories: archways or arcades, tribune (gallery), triforium (small circulating gallery), and clerestory with its windows (pl. 222).

The first great cathedral to be built with flying-buttresses and without a tribune was undoubtedly Chartres which was begun in 1194 (pl. 223). It inaugurated the thirteenth-century type of elevation with three stories (including triforium) which was to be followed at once by Rheims (1211; façade, pl. 225) and Amiens (1220).

Gothic art developed extremely rapidly as though with some vital urge to growth. Its evolution took the form of increasing sparsity of walling, increased elevation, the stressing of the verticality of the naves, the proliferation of images.

In 1240 Pierre de Montereau, who was the architect of the nave of St-Denis, further eliminated stone-work by placing windows in the outer wall of the triforium, which was henceforth to be closely associated with the fenestration; the windows were multiplied in the free space left between supports, and were filled with stained or painted glass. The lay-out of these networks of windows and rose-windows has earned Gothic art of the period 1250 to 1400 the name '*gothique rayonnant*' (pl. 229).

A few figures give ample evidence of the increasing height of vaults: Laon (1150), 78 feet; Paris (1163), 114 feet; Chartres (1194), 119 feet; Rheims (1210), 123 1/2 feet; Amiens (1220), 136 1/2 feet; Beauvais (1247), 156 3/4 feet. Beauvais Cathedral marks the end of this craving for height: with a framework that was insufficiently supported, the choir vault which was finished in 1272 collapsed in 1284, and the structure had to be reinforced by doubling the piers.

The soaring trend followed the growth of vaults, which resulted in taller and taller arcades (32 1/2 feet at Paris, 68 1/4 feet at Beauvais). The effect of this was further marked by the emphasizing of the vertical lines, for increasingly slender subsidiary shafts, attached to the piers, rose from the floor to the vault, while the clerestory window mullions prolonged those of the triforium. From 1250 onwards sharp pediments over porches and windows (gables) contributed further to this impression of upward movement (pl. 229).

*223 Nave of Chartres Cathedral. 1194*

While the nave was raised and cut away, the forms clothing its skeleton were multiplied, every one tending to gain its independence and to produce secondary forms. This instinct for growth can be noticed particularly in the increased complexity of mouldings, sills and window tracery. Still kept in a strict hierarchy by the disciplined mentality of the thirteenth century, these forms ended by covering the whole edifice with an unruly vegetation in the Flamboyant style of the fifteenth century.

The Gothic builders perfected mouldings, which were empirically invented by Romanesque art. They created a coherent system of moulding, obeying strict laws. On capitals and decorative string-courses, the fanciful ornamentation of the Romanesque artists (pl. 201) now gave way to supple and living forms based on plant-life (pl. 226). The same instinct for growth animates these floral decorations. On foliage capitals (the final metamorphosis of the Classical composite style) the buds of the twelfth century burst into leaf in about 1220, and after 1250 became branches.

In the thirteenth century the simple Romanesque castle, influenced by the Crusades, became a scientific and formidable structure (Château de Coucy, pl. 227). The plan usually adopted consisted of a rectangular enclosure with a tower at each corner and with the keep in the centre (Philippe-Auguste's plan, Louvre).

The best-preserved of these castles are in the Holy Land, where the Krak des Chevaliers still stands almost intact with its double stone shell. In the fourteenth century a more advanced civilization thought the fortresses of the preceding age much too bleak, and the castle was transformed into a palace (Château de Pierrefonds). The fifteenth century developed the

*224 Notre-Dame, Paris. About 1200–1235*

hôtel or villa, an urban residence suiting the needs of a new social class, the bourgeoisie (Hôtel Jacques-Cœur at Bourges). The Gothic period introduced many new forms of building corresponding with all the activities of a developed society, in the shape of bridges, hospitals, con-

*225 Rheims Cathedral. About 1240–1260*

vents and monasteries, town-halls and municipal buildings, law-courts, markets and the like.

Gothic art was poorer in provincial variants than was the Romanesque. However, in the thirteenth century the different provinces adopted

226 *Foliage Capital from the North Porch of Chartres Cathedral. About 1230*

the forms created in the Ile-de-France, giving them some local flavour. The Champagne school (Rheims Cathedral) was nearest to Ile-de-France classicism. Thanks to a remarkably durable material (Tonnerre stone) the Burgundian school built structures in which the elimination of walls was pushed to its farthest limits (Auxerre Cathedral, Notre-Dame at Dijon, St-Urbain at Troyes). The Norman school made wonderful cathedrals surrounded by fine spires (Bayeux, Coutances, pl. 228, Rouen, Lisieux) and the abbey of Mont-St-Michel which, perched on a rocky island off the north coast, is one of the most lyrical expressions of the Middle Ages. The Normans showed an exceptional lack of aptitude for figure-sculpture. Anjou gave its attention to the decorative possibilities of multi-ribbed vaults (St-Serge at Angers). Gothic art came to the south of France as a Nordic import, a whole group of cathedrals whose design is due to Jean Deschamps marking this infiltration (Clermont, Limoges, Narbonne, Toulouse, Rodez). However, the native spirit reacted in Languedoc, as it did later in Catalonia, by creating a type of church with a nave

227 *Château de Coucy. 13th c. (destroyed 1918)*

*228 East End of Coutances Cathedral. 13th c.*

of very large dimensions and no aisles (Albi Cathedral). Gothic regionalism disappeared in the fourteenth century when architecture was checked by pedantic formulas (St-Ouen at Rouen), but it revived again in the fifteenth century. The Rouen school was the most outstanding exponent of the Flamboyant style, which sprang up under English influence.

*229 Glazed Triforium of Sées Cathedral. Late 13th c.*

*230 Tympanum in the Porch of the Virgin at Notre-Dame, Paris. About 1210–1220*

*231 Figures from the Royal Porch of Chartres Cathedral. About 1150*

*232 Visitation Group on Rheims Cathedral. About 1230*

## Sculpture

The birth of Gothic sculpture in the Ile-de-France was not much later than that of Romanesque sculpture, since the Royal Porch (Portail Royal) at Chartres was started in about 1140 (pl. 231, 573). Following what was still a Romanesque convention, the figures were raised or flattened to

*233 Labours of the Months in Amiens Cathedral. March: Work in the Vineyard. About 1225*

follow the shape of the column to which they were attached; relief as such was almost non-existent and the modelling of folds mainly calligraphic, but the robes were taken from contemporary clothing and from those stone sheaths sprang heads that were full of personality and life, genuine portraits. The feverishness that twisted the figures at Moissac and Autun was soothed, giving way to calm postures and serene expressions. Sometimes a fleeting smile lit up their faces, and while all over France the Romanesque workshops were making wonderful ornamental fancies, the Ile-de-France sculptors sought a methodical observation of nature and the achievement of harmony. The porches at Senlis (pl. 182), Sens, Laon, and the Porch of St Anne at Notre-Dame (about 1170) are major stages in this growing grasp of relief and truthfulness which recalls astonishingly the transition from the sixth to the fifth century B.C. in Greek sculpture. This rapid advance resulted in the thirteenth century in the almost classical poise of the Porch of the Virgin at Notre-Dame (1210–1220, pl. 230), or the portals and carved porches at Chartres (1200–1240, pl. 231, 701), or the west porch at Amiens (1225–1236, pl. 233). The search for expression is tempered in them by a monumental balance and an idealism which seems to halo the faces with a sympathetic but austere saintliness. If some of these works recall the serene pediments of Olympia, the cathedral of Rheims (west porch, about 1225–1270) is the Parthenon of Gothic sculpture. Its statues are the most perfect works of Gothic plastic art, yet are so close to the supple ease of ancient Greece that critics have even suggested that there was some imitation (*Visitation group,* pl. 232). Facial expressions became more human, optimism was smilingly revealed, but the face lost the lofty spirituality of the previous epoch; worldliness was being introduced into art through the influence of courtly poetry, *la poésie courtoise* (pl. 234). There is no better demonstration of the progress of humanism than the rapid evolution of the types of Christ and the Virgin. Purely a theological concept in the twelfth century, by the end of the

*234 St Modesta on Chartres Cathedral. About 1230*

*235 Philip the Bold. Memorial Figure in St-Denis. Late 13th c.*

thirteenth the Virgin was a tender maternal figure playing with her child. The formidable Christ of the Romanesque tympana was brought down to the piers to welcome the faithful with an evangelical smile at the church door. Under the influence of St Bernard, God was no longer worshipped as the supreme Judge, but the devotion of the faithful was transferred to the New Testament Christ, God become man.

All these works were harmonized with each other, according to the principles of an iconographical programme that required a scholar's knowledge. Byzantine symbolism was a religious symbolism, but that of the thirteenth century had an encyclopaedic character, for it reflected the scholastic philosophy, intent on imposing the logic of thought upon the universe. The cathedral is an immense book which tells the history of the world; Chartres contains no less than 8,000 painted or carved images.

At the end of the thirteenth century the portrait began to appear in recumbents, or funerary statues, whose features are lit up by a smile, a typically French expression (pl. 235).

In sculpture as in architecture the fourteenth century was an academic period. Sculpture became detached from the column or field and approached carving in the round; but the human expression became empty, the modelling conventional and dry, the artist's impotence betraying itself in nervous hesitant poses with the hips unnaturally set (pl. 703). At the end of the century some health was restored to an anaemic art by the vigorous contribution of the Flemish temperament, thanks to Claus Sluter.

## The Arts of Colour and the Minor Arts

If the French school of painting was very inferior to the Italian, this is because painting was not the only form of colour-expression in France, as it was across the Alps. Stained-glass windows, illuminated manuscripts

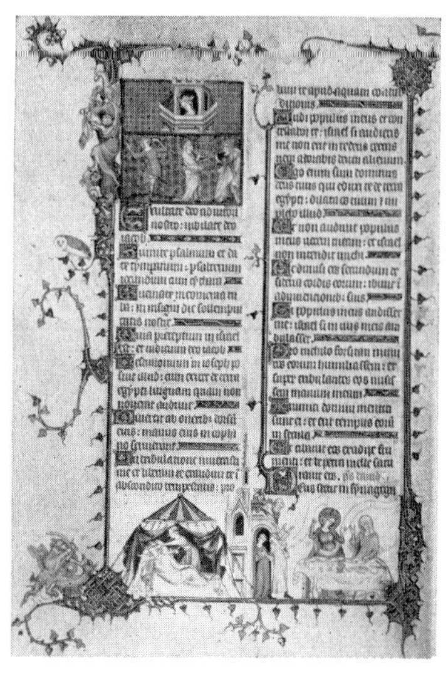

*236 Jean Pucelle. Page from the Belville Breviary. Before 1343. Paris*

*237 Richard II presented to the Virgin by his Patron Saints. Wilton Diptych. About 1377. London*

and tapestries, which were hardly known in Italy, filled cathedrals and princely houses with a fairyland of coloured images. The stained-glass window spread considerably in the thirteenth century in response to the enormous demand from cathedral building-yards. Chartres and Bourges still have their complete sets of windows. This art decayed in the fourteenth century through imitating sculpture, then in the fifteenth under the influence of painting, to achieve only a short lease of life again in the early sixteenth century.

Illumination continued to develop in Paris, which its famous university made the centre of book production. The liturgical works of the preceding period were succeeded by psalters, breviaries and books of hours, all richly adorned for the benefit of the higher social orders, and always executed on vellum. In the thirteenth century illumination was inspired by stained glass *(St Louis Psalter* and *Blanche de Castille Psalter)* while architectural forms also intruded *(St Louis Psalter).* The most elegant works in this art were made in the early fourteenth century in the studio of Jean Pucelle (*Belleville Breviary*, pl. 236). Under Charles V it declined but was to gain fresh vitality from the Flemish contribution at the end of the fourteenth century.

The workshops in which they made both high-warp and low-warp tapestries appeared or are mentioned as being in Paris towards the end of the fourteenth century; the oldest preserved tapestry is the *Angers Apocalypse* (end of the fourteenth century). The Hundred Years War broke up the Parisian workshops, some being moved to Arras where they specialized in tapestries with historical or mythological themes, dense compositions with large numbers of characters. The Touraine workshops, until the early sixteenth century, expressed the poetry of nature in tapestries with a green background.

Painting was less vigorous than in Italy. It remained for a long time overshadowed by tapestries, illumination or stained-glass, and broke free only in the second half of the fourteenth century. The Parisian style then produced some exquisite works, of which only a few have been preserved. On the other hand, before Italy, France appears to have developed a lay art which provided the abodes of princes with hunting and fishing scenes, painted in fresco; an example survives in the Ward-Robe Tower at the Papal palace in Avignon (about 1345). The art of portraiture was in the same vein, and seems to have appeared first in France (*Portrait of Jean le Bon*, Louvre).

The minor arts in the Gothic period were under the tyranny of architecture which imposed its forms on furniture as on gold- and silverwork (pl. 238). Sculpture in ivory was very much in favour, and was also inspired by monumental modelling.

## *The Expansion of Gothic Art*

The finest Gothic monuments, after the French, are to be found in England. The English were quick to understand this new style – to whose development they contributed by their very early use of rib-vaulting in

*238 Shrine of St Taurin in St-Taurin, Evreux. 13th c.*

*239 Lincoln Cathedral. 12th–14th c.*

Durham Cathedral (1096) – and were the only builders to evolve a native form of it in the thirteenth century. The Gothic style was encouraged in England, as in Italy and Germany, by the spread of the Cistercian order. Nothing is more characteristically Gothic than the choir of Canterbury Cathedral, which was built between 1175 and 1184 by the Frenchman William of Sens, who took as his model the cathedral of Sens where Thomas à Beckett had sought refuge. With the exception of Westminster Abbey, which was influenced by the Ile-de-France and Champagne styles and which has an apse with an ambulatory and radiating chapels (chevet), the first phase of English Gothic, known as 'Early English' (Salisbury Cathedral; parts of the cathedrals of Lincoln, pl. 239, Lichfield, York and Wells) is parallel with that of thirteenth century Norman Gothic; but whereas the Norman school increasingly shed its native characteristics as

*240 Vault of the Chapter House of Wells Cathedral. 1293–1319*

*241 Angel Choir of Lincoln Cathedral. Between 1256–1320*

it evolved, the English school stressed its own local features. English builders had a liking for square east ends with an elevation resembling that of the façade, as at Durham, long naves, double transepts, slender forms (such as sharp grouped lancet windows and extremely slender attached shafts). Salisbury Cathedral (pl. 242, 243) which was begun in 1220 and consecrated in 1258, is perhaps the purest and most elegant example of the first phase.

Towards 1260 there came a sharp division between the development of the Norman and English schools. The Norman school lost its personality and was absorbed into French High Gothic. While French Gothic architecture suddenly came to a standstill in the fourteenth century, England, boldly following its own internal evolution, towards 1280 began creating the Curvilinear or Decorated style, which both anticipated and begot French Flamboyant. This style, so fully achieved in the choir of Lincoln Cathedral (1256–1320, pl. 241), Exeter Cathedral (about 1280) and the nave of York Minster (after 1290) is distinguished by a lavish ornamentation spreading even into the vault (renewed in 1890 at York), with

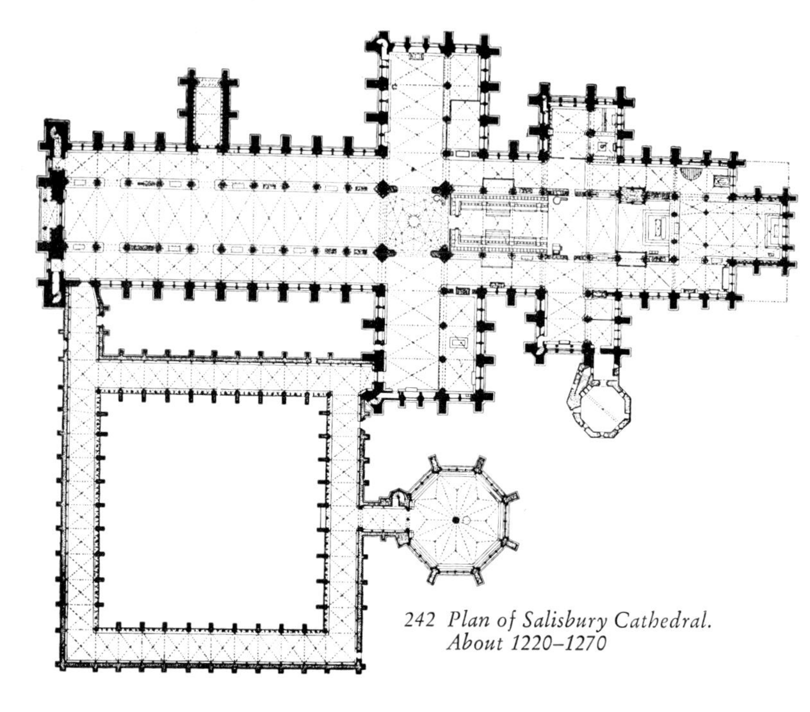

242 *Plan of Salisbury Cathedral.*
*About 1220–1270*

243 *Interior of Salisbury Cathedral.*
*About 1220–1270*

*244 William Torel. Tomb of Eleanor of Castile in Westminster Abbey (detail). 1291*

*245 Freiburg Minster. Tower 13th, Spire 14th c.*

*246 East End of Bamberg Cathedral. Middle of 13th c.*

its intermediate ribs and carved bosses and its structure developing away from the simple Gothic cross-vault. The taste for curves and flourishes was further developed in the fourteenth century (Lady Chapel, Ely Cathedral, 1321–1349), while the chapter houses, built on a polygonal plan with a central pillar, are remarkably elegant (pl. 240). At a time

*247 Choir of Cologne Cathedral. 1248–1322*

*V Madonna and Child. Stained Glass. Chartres Cathedral*

*248 'Stone Harp' of the West Front of Strassburg Minster. 14th c.*

*249 Christ before Pilate. Choir-Screen of Naumburg Cathedral (detail). About 1240–1250*

*250 Head of the Bamberg Horseman in Bamberg Cathedral. Before 1237*

when all fifteenth-century Europe was indulging in elaborate curves, England rejected them to create its Perpendicular style with all the stress on verticality.

During those three hundred years, parish churches for the most part remained faithful to the simple design inherited from the Saxon period, in which the central tower serves as a massive nucleus for four unequal arms: these churches were often roofed with timber.

In the representational arts, English Gothic is notable, in the same way as in architecture, for its leaning towards elegance. In sculpture this meant the lengthening of forms and a slightly mannered gracefulness (Wells, Winchester, Salisbury, Lincoln, Westminster, pl. 244). Craftsmen of Derbyshire, Yorkshire and Nottinghamshire carved portable sculptures in alabaster during the fourteenth and fifteenth centuries, which they exported all over Northern Europe and France. During the thirteenth and fourteenth centuries the miniature achieved great subtlety of line, and the painting of the period derived from it. The *Wilton Diptych* (National Gallery, London, pl. 237), painted towards 1377, portraying Richard II being presented to the Virgin, is one of the most refined works of the Middle Ages. Historians have attributed it successively to the French, English and Czech schools, but all that is certain is that it was executed at the English court. Towards 1400 the miniature began to return to the International Gothic style (*Beaufort Book of Hours,* 1401–1410).

Gothic art in Germany was, on the contrary, an imported art. The earliest Gothic monuments (Limburg an der Lahn, Maulbronn, Bamberg, pl. 246, Naumburg, choir of Magdeburg) appeared during the first half of the thirteenth century in a region that was still Romanesque. Cologne Cathedral (choir begun 1248, pl. 247) was the first real Gothic building in Germany, but it was inspired by Amiens and Beauvais while the nave of Strassburg (1250–1270) was a replica of that of St Denis. The German churches of the fourteenth century were more original. In their profuse decoration they heralded the Flamboyant without having yet conceived its forms. The buildings were entirely clothed in a sort of vibrating tracery (façade of Strassburg Minster, pl. 248, and of Cologne Cathedral – carried out only in the nineteenth century – openwork spire of Freiburg im Breisgau, pl. 245). In the thirteenth century Westphalia pro-

*251 Eckhart and Uta in Naumburg Cathedral. About 1250–1260*

*252 Christ in Majesty. Puerta del Sarmental of Burgos Cathedral (detail). About 1230*

duced a type of church with aisles as high as the nave (Hall churches: Minden, Münster, Osnabrück, Paderborn) which was to spread in the fourteenth century to the Baltic, where brick construction was the rule.

The workshops of Rheims were the source of German Gothic sculpture. About 1235 at Bamberg (Franconia) Gothic sculpture replaced the Romanesque without any transitional stage, after the Romanesque had just expressed itself in the outstanding *Apostles* and *Prophets* of the choir screens (pl. 216). Artists who were no doubt trained at the Rheims workshops took inspiration from its elegant forms and gave them a specifically German intensity (*Visitation, Church and Synagogue, Horseman,* pl. 250). Between 1260 and 1273, the cathedral workshops at Naumburg developed an expressionism which foreshadowed the mood of Europe a hundred years ahead and the pathos of Claus Sluter's sculpture (*Christ before Pilate,* pl. 249, *Eckhart and Uta,* pl. 251). The statues of *Church and Synagogue* in Strassburg Cathedral add a touch of Germanic unreality to the elegance of Rheims. At the end of the thirteenth century and the early fourteenth, the *Wise and Foolish Virgins* from the west front of the same cathedral have a rich local touch which saves them from the academicism that is noticeable in the Prophets of the neighbouring portal.

In Spain, the slight artistic traditions of Castille gave a ready welcome to Gothic architecture from the thirteenth century onwards. The cathedrals of Burgos and Toledo were inspired by the Bourges and Coutances types, while León Cathedral reflects the forms of Rheims and Amiens. Catalonia, where there had been a prosperous Romanesque school, proved more cautious and hesitated between the northern French type with aisles and ambulatory and the southern type with side-chapels but no aisles (Gerona Cathedral). The sculptors' shops at Burgos and León give further evidence of the wide influence of Rheims (pl. 252).

## *The Resistance to Gothic Art: Italy*

### Architecture

Italy was the country most hostile to Gothic art. It never made more than a superficial impression, in its southern French form (lower church of St Francis, Assisi, 1229–1236); the mendicant orders who introduced it also followed the austere Cistercian manner. In the late thirteenth and fourteenth centuries a more personal style was developed but proved to be absolutely opposed to the Gothic spirit, in which the decoration is expressive of the structure; embellishments of polychrome marbles, in the Byzantine manner, covered both the outside and inside of brick-built cathedrals (cathedrals of Siena, Florence, Orvieto, pl. 254). The severe town halls (Palazzo Vecchio, Florence, pl. 253, Palazzo Pubblico, Siena) have a certain Romanesque roughness. The Flamboyant style penetrated

*253 Palazzo Vecchio, Florence. Ascribed to Arnolfo di Cambio. Begun 1298*

*254 Façade of Orvieto Cathedral. 14th c.*

*255 Doge's Palace, Venice. 14th–15th c.*

the north of Italy as well as the Kingdom of Naples. In Lombardy it produced Milan Cathedral, a cosmopolitan work by Italian, French and German architects, which shows an awkward adaptation of Flamboyant sinuousity to the stiffness of its marbles. In Venice the Flamboyant style was mixed with Moorish influence to create a composite art something like the Spanish Mudéjar, resulting in some pleasant constructions (Doge's Palace, pl. 255, Cà d'Oro).

## Sculpture

On the other hand, Italy underwent a plastic revolution in the thirteenth century in both painting and sculpture, thanks entirely to her own creative efforts. She first broke free from Byzantine influence in sculpture, a technique in which Byzantine art produced but little. It was in antique sculptures as well as Christian sarcophagi that Nicola Pisano (about 1225 – before 1284) found his new conception of sculptural density and his heroic sense of man (principal works: Pisa Baptistery pulpit, 1260, pl. 256; pulpit in Siena Cathedral, 1266). This classical tradition came from southern Italy. Nicola Pisano came from Apulia, a region in which in the early thirteenth century there had been an episodic but genuine revival of the classical spirit under the direction of the Emperor Frederick II, a philosopher-prince imbued with scepticism. He admired Arab culture and held a cosmopolitan court at Palermo (Triumphal Arch, Capua, about 1240).

One of Nicola's pupils, the Florentine Arnolfo di Cambio (1232?–1302), both architect and sculptor, made plans for the cathedral of Florence (S. Maria del Fiore) and perhaps also for the Palazzo Vecchio (pl. 253). In his sculptural works (Tomb of Cardinal de Braye in S. Domenico, Orvieto, about 1282), he tried to recapture Roman grandeur, though with a somewhat stiff dignity.

The plastic tradition established by Nicola Pisano was continued in Pisa and Florence during the fourteenth century, somewhat modified and diluted by increasing Gothic influence which was harmful to native expression. Already Nicola's son Giovanni Pisano (about 1245–after 1320) was more inspired by the flexible style of Gothic ivories than by the imposing Roman sarcophagi (pl. 257). Even more obvious in Andrea da Pintedera, also called 'Pisano' (died 1349), French influence made less impression on Andrea Orcagna (died 1368) a painter and sculptor in the Giottesque tradition; but it revived with Nino Pisano (died 1368) whose *Annunciations* derive from the rather sickly elegance of the French, but with an entirely Tuscan preciousness.

In short, the genuine Italian Renaissance, based on a revival of the Classical tradition, was strongly marked in the second half of the thirteenth century, but was held up by the Gothic invasion of the fourteenth

*256 Nicola Pisano. Birth of Christ from the Pisa Baptistery Pulpit. Finished 1260*

century, which amounted to a foreign occupation. In the early fifteenth century the Renaissance had to begin all over again, by first of all driving out the Gothic infection.

## Painting

Meanwhile Italy gave the world a new mode of expression in its painting. A national school broke away from Byzantinism towards 1250, under the influence of the new naturalistic and humanistic outlook introduced by St Francis of Assisi. The first tokens of this were at Pisa and Lucca (school of the Berlinghieri, pl. 258). At the end of the century, Florence and Siena took the lead. The sources of Florentine realism are to be found in certain mosaics, rather than in Cimabue (active between 1272–1302) who paid tribute to the theological spirit of Byzantium in some dignified icons (pl. 185). Through Duccio (active 1285–1308/11) of Siena the antique Alexandrian grace preserved by Byzantium began to show some signs of tenderness (his Madonnas and saints), but his Passion scenes express a growing sense of pathos, as in the *Maestà* (Virgin in Majesty) for the Siena Duomo (pl. 259).

*257 Giovanni Pisano. Birth of Christ from the Pulpit in S. Andrea, Pistoia. 1298–1301*

*258 Berlinghieri. St Francis (detail). 1235. Pescia*

*259 Duccio. Road to Calvary from the Maestà. 1310. Siena*

The future of painting lay in another direction. The true Renaissance was clearly affirmed in Rome by Pietro Cavallini (active 1273–1316) who rediscovered Classical dignity (mosaics in S. Maria in Trastevere; frescoes at S. Cecilia in Trastevere). The Florentine Giotto (about 1266 –1337) carried on the efforts of Cavallini and Nicola Pisano, giving Italian painting its main impetus. His principal works are the frescoes of the *Life of St Francis* in the upper church at Assisi (about 1300); those of the *Life of Christ* in the Arena Chapel at Padua (1305, pl. 261, 262); those of the *Legend of St John and St Francis* in S. Croce, Florence (1311

*260 Simone Martini. Annunciation. 1333. Florence*

*261 Giotto. Betrayal (detail). Arena Chapel, Padua. 1305*

*262 Giotto. Joachim and the Shepherds. Arena Chapel, Padua. 1305*

–1317). First and foremost a monumental artist and fresco painter, Giotto sought the truth of natural forms while never losing the Byzantine longing for clarity which subjects the composition of the work to some central idea. But this idea, which in Byzantium was spiritual, became both dramatic and plastic in Giotto. His concise art is a work of the intellect; he sacrificed the accidental to the greatest expressive concentration. He also brought with him that heroic sense of human life and that taste for virile strength which were to inspire Florentine art until the sixteenth century.

The creative effort of Giotto excited such lively admiration in his contemporaries that it resulted in the academic style of the Giotteschi. However, his successors were to temper his greatness with the influence of Sienese tenderness. Such was the case with Bernardo Daddi (active 1317 –1349).

The history of Italian painting in the second half of the fourteenth century shows an eclecticism striving to blend Giottesque precision with the narrative spirit of the Sienese school and the angular style of the Gothic. Taddeo Gaddi (died 1368) who was a direct pupil of Giotto's remained nearest to his sobriety. Andrea Orcagna was also a sculptor, and this can be felt in his work. In the third quarter of the century, Sienese influences took such a hold in Florence that it sometimes becomes difficult to distinguish Sienese from Florentine works.

At Florence, Giotto imposed on nature a dramatic and aesthetic order dictated by his intelligence. Sienese art on the contrary is all sensibility, seeking in reality only what makes the quickest appeal. Under Gothic influence Simone Martini (1283–1344) opposed the supple grace of his Madonnas to the robustness of Giotto; he achieved intense pathos not by a concentration of means but by accumulating tragic effects *(Story of Saint Martin,* frescoes in the lower church of St Francis – S. Francesco – at Assisi; *Annunciation,* Uffizi, 1333, pl. 260).

In the second quarter of the century Siena itself came under Florentine influence. The brothers Pietro and Ambrogio Lorenzetti (died 1348) assimilated the robust Giottesque plastic language while also developing the feeling for the picturesque which was typically Sienese, (*Allegory of Good and Bad Government,* Palazzo Pubblico, Siena, 1337).

Wearied by this sterile struggle between conflicting elements, the fourteenth century ended in Italy, both in painting and sculpture, in a decadence which gave no inkling of the wonderful example of creative energy that Florence was soon to give the world.

# VI. ISLAM

Islam, which is too often only mentioned casually in histories, or else used as an introduction to the arts of the Far East, is a civilization of the Western Mediterranean. Springing from the same monotheistic source as Christian civilization, Islam developed in rivalry with the first forms of Christian art in Byzantium and in the West. Profiting from the rich cultural traditions of the Syrian, Egyptian and Iranian countries on which it was grafted, Muslim civilization flourished far sooner than that of the West, which stagnated in a state of barbarism until the twelfth century and was outstripped three hundred years earlier by the Arabs. (In the twelfth century the caliph of Córdoba is said to have owned some several thousand books, while four hundred years later Charles V of France, who was very proud of his library, only had nine hundred.) In every domain of civilization Islam was the first to define the values which were to become those of the Middle Ages: chivalry, courtesy and that noble conduct which Joinville called *prudhommie* (integrity) were moral rules already practised in the East in the ninth century. It was by trusting to the speculations of Arab theologians and philosophers that Christian thought achieved what it did in the twelfth and thirteenth centuries. St Thomas Aquinas only knew Aristotle through the commentaries of Averroes of Córdoba. We also owe our commercial techniques to Muslim civilization (such words as cheque, *douane* and tariff being Arab), as well as arithmetic, algebra, the first rudiments of medicine, mechanics, chemistry, geography and astronomy. The awakening West was to take all it could from this magnificent source of art and science, by way of Spain, Sicily and the great Italian ports.

The earliest Islamic works of art were not so unlike those of the West as they might appear. The decorative spirit of the Muslims is nearer that of the early West than was the sacred imagery of Byzantium. Our understanding of Muslim art has been distorted by the accusation that, in obedience to some prohibition in the Koran, it excluded any image of living things. Nothing of the sort is to be found in the Koran, and only in later texts was the artist warned against the realistic reproduction of living things. But if the Muslims created an ornamental system of geometrical devices which perhaps shows their taste for the abstract speculations of mathematics, in everyday decoration they made lavish use of animal, vegetable, floral and even human forms. However, these forms were never 'represented' for their own sake as in the aesthetic which prevailed in the West from the Gothic onwards; they were freely interpreted so as to make a plastic language of infinite wealth, whose terms all strengthen and enhance each other in a system of exchanges at which the Oriental imagination excels. This style of metaphor gives Muslim literature that dream-like quality which is its peculiar charm (the poets compare animals with flowers, flowers with stones and stars; the wound of a gazelle becomes a 'pied flower' and so on). Indeed, this art is closest to Romanesque formalism (pl. 263). The Romanesque and primitive Muslim imageries both sought their forms in the same Oriental sources – Chaldeo-Assyrian, Sassanian and Persian – which had been enriched by the peoples of the steppes and the ornamental instincts of the barbarians. This stock of imagery, further enlarged by observing nature, resulted in a system of infinitely adaptable metamorphoses which allowed the Islamic aesthetic to last almost to our own time, whereas in the West our equivalent tradition was interrupted by the rise of realism in the thirteenth century.

The profound difference between Romanesque art and that of Islam lies in one particular means of plastic expression; for Romanesque art, originating in sculpture, tended towards carving in the round, whereas Islam reduced every form to a surface and expressed itself in polychromy. For the realistic West sculpture was the fundamental art, while for Islam this was perhaps weaving. Whether it be in stucco, plaster, stone, or openwork marble as in India, Muslim monuments are covered in 'tapestries' of forms which drape them like flowing robes (pl. 265).

Starting from myth, Romanesque art seeks the real. During its long life Islamic art never lost the anti-realist instinct of the early civilizations. This instinct rested on a philosophy which denies the very existence of a world in which the whole chain of causality is in the hands of God. Arab thinkers were the first – in the Mediterranean world at least – to formulate the idea of 'nothingness'. This non-reality of things permits every imaginative fancy to both poet and artist; being embroideries of thought upon appearances they imply no consequences, they are no more than fables and tales. The art of Islam is thus a mirage, a fantasmagoria

*263 Tympanum from a House in Kubatchi (Caucasus), 12th–13th c. Washington*

*264 Interior of the Córdoba Mosque. 755*

of images woven on the web of nothingness. The forms so abundantly borrowed from nature are never evoked as anything more than the graceful phantoms of a dream. The scarceness of sculpture in the round perfectly illustrates this aloofness from the real; we are told that a thirteenth-century theologian forbade in his home any 'images that cast a shadow'. Three-dimensional sculpture asserts the reality of the space in which it is set; it was to be the chief art in the West and, when painting came to life, its object was to deceive the eye by creating an illusion of three-dimensional space on a plane surface.

When the Crusaders reached the East they found a decaying society. The decline of Muslim sciences coincided with a revival of puritan

*265 Court of the Lions of the Alhambra, Granada. 1353–1391*

orthodoxy leading to intolerance. Free-throught arose in reaction to this, and the sceptical philosophers, twelfth-century Voltaires, saw religion as a mere drug, an opium used for secular ends to ensure public order. Western Islam – the Maghreb – was aware of its decadence; the refined monuments of Seville and Granada are the decadent forms of an art which in its maturity had produced the great Córdoba Mosque (pl. 264). However, the eastern Muslim region was yet to have its true renaissance, thanks to the new ethnic contribution brought by the Turkish and Mongol invasions. The eagerness of these barbarians for culture led to a brilliant renaissance in the arts and letters; they gave fresh youth to the ageing Muslim art, by bringing from the refined China of the Sung dynasty those elements which, acting like a fermentation on the ancient layers of culture in Iran, produced the exquisite flowering of the Persian miniature. The miniature is a perfect reflection of Muslim literature during those Turkish and Mongol periods when, as is to be expected in an advanced civilization, thought was expressed not so much in the sciences or metaphysics as in literature, history, lyric and epic poems. The human figure now predominated, but in the midst of gardens perfumed with flowers and peopled with graceful creatures it was intangible as a form seen in a dream (colour pl. VI). In the same period, in the first half of the fifteenth century, the miniaturists and certain painters of the West such as Pisanello, were evoking the fleeting images of the declining Middle Ages in their fairy-like, nostalgic creations.

The Turkish and Mongol conquerors had a monumental sense of architecture which raised some imposing works. But perhaps for Muslim

*VI Prince Humay and Princess Humayun in a Garden. Persian Miniature. Paris*

art, whose typical form was essentially 'minor', this was a symptom of decadence. In the West, there is a decline as soon as architecture becomes ornament; but the opposite is the case with Islam. Delicate decorative effects, traceries in marble, china vestments, are no longer in scale with the vast spaces and mighty masses of the Safavid or Hindo-Mongol buildings. On the contrary, in the Córdoba Mosque the arabesques hewn in the stonework are symphonically related to the space, which is so cunningly divided by innumerable columns and festooned by the multifoil arches with their interlinking curves.

The art of Islam ended in an extraordinary capitulation to the Byzantine civilization it had overthrown. In Asia Minor, then European Turkey, and very soon through their empire the Ottomans seemed intent on multiplying large and small replicas of S. Sophia. Islam had been as a spiritual ferment capable of restoring life to the old civilization it overran, to the peoples of every race that it annexed and whose beliefs it respected in its liberal golden age. Marvellous creations arose from those contacts. But from the sixteenth to the eighteenth century Islam was weary and stopped inventing; it kept copying itself and imitated what only yesterday it had conquered.

## THE EVOLUTION OF MUSLIM ART

### *Early Period*

The first artistic manifestations of Islam appeared in Syria under the Caliphate of the Omayyads (665–750) whose seat was at Damascus. Transformed Christian churches (El-Aksa-Mosque at Jerusalem, the Great Mosque at Damascus) owe most of their features to Hellenistic and Byzantine art, but the Damascus Mosque already shows the typical layout of the Muslim sanctuary (pl. 274 a). The few castles of that period remaining in Transjordan (Qasr Amra, Mchatta)* show the same Hellenistic traits. In A.D. 750 the ousting of the Omayyads by the Abbasids (750–1000) resulted in the transfer of the Caliphate to Baghdad and enabled Islam to profit from the Iranian tradition (ruins of Samarra). Islam became more original; under the Caliphate of the Abbasids which soon became only nominal, an Iranian and Turkish feudality developed. Architects turned to brick construction, with great tunnel-vaults, or cupolas, and with applied decorations in stucco or plaster. The encouragement given to all the arts of furnishing by the Abbasids earned Baghdad a reputation for splendour which was to spread into the West.

* These castles in the Syrian desert used to be attributed to Arab princes before Islam, vassals of the Sassanians. The present tendency is to consider them as having been built by the Omayyads; but some doubt remains.

*266 Ribbed Dome with Mosaics of the Villaviciosa Chapel in the Córdoba Mosque. 10th c.*

*267 Stalactite Decoration in the Hall of the Two Sisters in the Alhambra, Granada. 1353–1391*

Official workshops produced *tiraz* tissues (as the textiles made in state-factories were called), copper and bronze objects which often had zoomorphic features, inspired by the animal-art of the Sassanians, and pottery which at Samarra, Rakka, Rhagae, Gurgan, revived the old Persian art of enamelled terra-cotta, now enriched by the Arabs with the process of lead glazing. In Egypt the Tulunids, vassals of the Abbasids, built large monuments at Fostat which were inspired by those of Mesopotamia (mosque of Ibn-Tulun, 879), and developed crafts there in the form of textiles, ceramics, woodwork and bookbinding. The Abbasids extended their influence as far as Ifrikia (Tunisia) where the Aghlabids in the ninth century undertook some great architectural works (mosques at Kairawan, 836, Tunis, Susa; municipal works, fortifications). At the same time, in Spain, a dynasty descended from the Omayyads of Damascus set up its Caliphate in 929 and maintained an art closer to its Hellenistic origins, the masterpiece of which is the Córdoba Mosque (pl. 264) founded in 785 and enlarged in 848, 961 and 987. The ruins at Medina-az-Zahra (936) contain a palace of that dynasty (pl. 270).

### *Medieval Period*

The art of Islam was superimposed on the old civilizations of the Mediterranean and Asia. From the eleventh century onwards, new elements brought from the interior of Asia by the Turkish and Mongol invasions were to effect some profound changes. The Seljuk Turks who took Baghdad in 1055 remained there until 1250, bringing with them a feeling for grandeur which showed itself in new monumental conceptions of which the vital principle was the vault. They created a type of grandiose

268 *Persian Coat with silk Embroidery. Vienna*

mosque with four *liwan* giving onto the central courtyard; then a type of mosque-school called *a medersa,* a kind of theological university designed to combat the Shiite heresy, and finally the domed mausoleum *(turbeh* and *quoubba)* which was a manifestation of warlike pride. Prospering in Mesopotamia (Mosul, Isfahan) the art of the Seljuks extended into Asia Minor (Aleppo, Konya) and the eastern frontiers of Iran (Afghanistan, Khorasan). The Mongol invasion, following on that of the Seljuks (1250–1500) enriched Iranian art with influence from the Far East and quickened the tendency towards splendour. With the Timurids (1370–1500) eastern Khorasan was to produce the first monuments. The capitals were at Herat and Samarcand where stands the Gor-Emir, the tomb of Tamerlane, built in 1405. Architecture was covered in revetments of enamelled faïence: decorative art became somewhat mechanical, but the Persian miniature was now reaching its perfection.

The impact of the Asiatic invasions, accentuating the split in Islamic unity, resulted in a sharper differentiation between the schools. In Egypt and Syria a Caliphate rivalling that of Baghdad, founded in Cairo by the Fatimite dynasty originating from Ifrikia (970–1169), developed an art which hesitated between the various traditions from Iran. The art of the Aiyubids (1169–1250) and of the Mameluke sultans of Cairo (1250–1520) shows Persian, Seljuk and Mongol influence to have predominated in decorative art. The finest monuments of Muslim art were built at that time in Syria and Egypt, showing a sound architectural sense (use of stone in two shades, sobriety of decoration, pl. 272). The type of mosque associated with the dynastic founder's tomb produced very harmonious works at Cairo under the Mamelukes. To the extreme west of Islam, in Spain and in the Maghreb (Algeria) there developed a style whose unity was favoured at the outset by their common dynasties (Almoravides, 1055–1147, Almohades, 1130–1269), and which survived after the empire was dismembered. This has been called 'Hispano-Moorish' art; its principal monuments are at Marrakesh, Fez, Tlemcen, Rabat, Tunis, Seville (the 'Giralda' of the cathedral, a twelfth-century minaret). At first austere and somewhat archaic, this style, which was but slightly affected by Iranian influences, ended up in an orgy of ornamentation (Alhambra, Granada, fourteenth century). In the early period of the conquest Muslim art persisted in Christian Spain either in its pure state (Alcazar, Seville, fourteenth to sixteenth century) or in a hybrid Gothico-Muslim form called 'Mudéjar' (ducal palace of the Infantado at Guadalajara, 1480–1492).

### *Modern Period*

In Persia, art reached a brilliant level under the Iranian dynasty of the Safavids (1514–1720) which succeeded the Mongols. This was a court art, not very inventive, but which cleverly exploited the heritage of Muslim forms. Shah Abbas I (1587–1628), assuming all the responsibilities of a modern ruler, rebuilt Ispahan according to an ambitious scheme of town-planning, enriching it with mosques and palaces. Following the Iranian type with four *liwan*, the Royal Great Mosque (1612–1640) is entirely covered with faïence decoration both inside and out. The royal workshops made textiles, carpets and ceramics which were much sought after in the West. Decoration lost its geometrical stiffness and used naturalistic features such as flowers and trees. The Chinese taste for porcelain began to influence pottery. Tabriz, in Azerbaijan, became the centre for the official school of miniaturists, who cultivated the Timur (Tamerlane) style.

*269 Relief from the Castle at Mchatta (Syria). Omayyad. 8th c. Berlin*

India under its Mongol dynasty (1520–1800) enjoyed a great expansion in architecture (mosques,

270 *Marble Pilaster from the Palace at Medina-az-Zahra (near Córdoba). 936*

271 *Decorated Leaf of a wooden Door from Egypt. Mameluke. 13th–14th c. New York*

palaces, tombs at Delhi, Agra and Lahore). Muslim India proved to have a monumental sense comparable with that of the West (Taj-Mahal, Agra, tomb of the Empress Mumtaz Mahal, 1630–1647, pl. 273). The innate naturalism of the Hindu soul reappeared in the miniature, which was informed with all the poetry of love and pride. The empire of the Ottoman Turks (1300), which was established at the expense of the Byzantine Empire, apparently hoped to prolong the greatness of Constantinople, after its destruction. After the downfall of Constantinople, now renamed Istanbul, the church of S. Sophia greatly influenced the form of mosques, the tendency now being towards the central plan (mosque of Bayezid by Viheir-ed-Din, 1481–1512; Sulaimaniya Mosque (1550) by Sinan, who built a large number of monuments including the Shah Zasi and Sultan Ahmed Mosques). Decorative art (textiles, carpets, ceramics) increasingly took naturalistic themes from flowers, etc. (tulip, marigold, pomegranate, hyacinth, rose, vine). The art of the Osmanlis (Ottomans) spread throughout their empire to Syria, Egypt, Tunisia and Algeria, to decline entirely in the eighteenth century under Western influence when it was ruined by rococo features.

## *Architecture*

Despite its wide radiation in both time and place, Muslim architecture owed its remarkable unity to a religious faith and an unchanging way of life. Concurrently with the West and Byzantium but over a much greater area, Islam spread vault-construction throughout the world after it had been devised by Mesopotamia and Iran. Although construction with stone materials was almost as much favoured as building in rubble and brick, it was brickwork which dominated all Muslim architecture, resulting in an aesthetic of applied decoration for ornamental effect, rather than a monumental plastic code.

From the very beginning Islam created a type of sanctuary – the mosque – adapted to a religion without ritual, but of which the essential activity was communal prayer. In order to shelter the congregation, Islam imitated the long colonnades in the naves of Christian churches, multiplying them to give the impression of infinite numbers, but placing them crosswise and not down the length of the building (pl. 264, 274 a). The classic mosque was composed of four porticoes or *liwan* framing a courtyard or *sahn* in the centre of which stood a fountain for ablutions *(midha)*. The *liwan* standing at the far end of the courtyard and which served as a prayer-chamber *(haram)* consisted of several naves (or aisles), while the far wall or *quibla* was pointed in the direction of Mecca, marked by an archway or niche, the *mihrab;* a *minbar* made of wood served as a pulpit. Sometimes a large, deep nave led to the *mihrab,* which was topped with a dome (pl. 266). One or several 'minarets' or belfries were used by the *muezzin* for the call to prayer. These minarets took many different shapes. At first they were strong square towers, then in Mesopotamia they took on the helix form of the Assyrian ziggurats. Persia, from the ninth century, created the standard type of very slender tower, elongated and candle-like, with a balcony at the top. Seljuk Persia in the twelfth century invented a second type of mosque on a cruciform plan, no doubts suggested by the old Sassanian palaces; this had four perpendicular *liwan* in the central court, opening their high wide vaults upon it. Finally the Ottoman Turks in the sixteenth century gave the mosque a basilican form with a central cupola, inspired by S. Sophia. The mosque-school or *medersa* grouped four sets of buildings round the central courtyard, corresponding with the four orthodox rites taught there (pl. 274 b). The Mongols introduced into Persia a circular mausoleum surmounted by a dome, which the Egyptian Mamelukes combined with the mosque. The design of palaces still followed that of the Assyrian palace divided into two parts, each of them grouped round a courtyard: the *selamlick* for public activities, the *harem* for private life. The audience or throne-room *(diwan)* opened on to one of the sides of the *selamlick.* The dwelling showed nothing but blank walls from the outside, the few openings being sealed by wooden grills called *moucharabieh.* The interior was veneered

*272 Funerary Mosque of Kait-Bey, Cairo. 1472*

*273 The Taj-Mahal, Agra. Tomb of Mumtaz Mahal. 1630–1647*

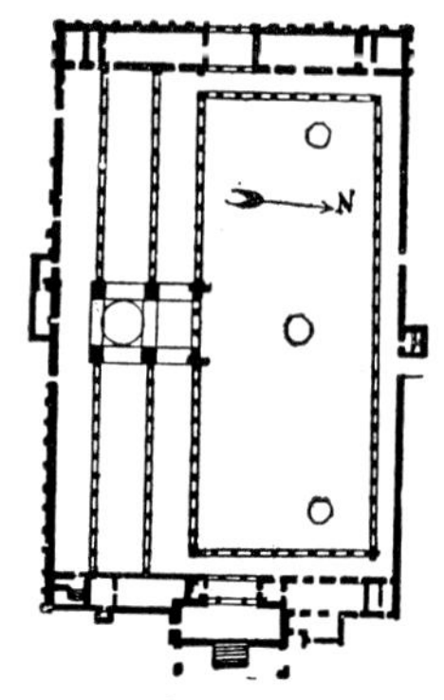

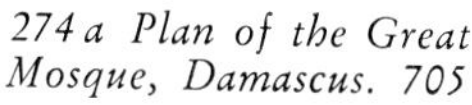

*274 a Plan of the Great Mosque, Damascus. 705*

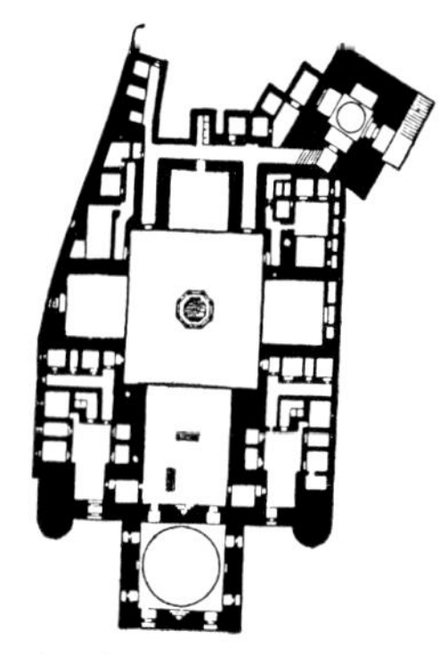

*274 b Plan of the Great Mosque of Sultan Hassan, Cairo. 1356*

with decorations in stucco or porcelain, while often fountains played here and there for coolness. Long before the Christians, the Muslims, who love flowers, knew that refinement in the art of living, the culture of gardens (gardens of the Generalife, Granada). The finest palaces still standing today are to be found in Spain and India.

The Muslims were very skilful in throwing light arches over wide spans, sometimes also using the sectional method of construction tested by the Sassanians. From the tenth century onwards in Mesopotamia and Spain they were using the rib-vault, two hundred years before the builders of the West (pl. 266). They also had astute carpenters who designed complex ceilings with lavish decorations. The Muslim architects, except in a few early Islamic edifices, used the arch in preference to the lintel. Encouraged by their instinct for ornament they gave their archways and vaults all kinds of profiles, both pointed and round: the stilted, the horseshoe, the multifoil, the cusped, the ogee, and the four-centred arches. They sometimes even superimposed arcades (Córdoba Mosque, pl. 264) and intersected the arches.

The structure prepared by the architect had to take a facing of applied decorations which tended to cover all its surface. The constructional elements themselves rapidly became ornamental motifs such as the corner squinch used for the transition from the square plan to the cupola; fragmented and multiplied this feature was transformed into *mukarna* or 'stalactites' which ended by being grafted everywhere: on arches, pendentives, capitals, ceilings, friezes, lintels etc. (pl. 267). The surface decoration, carried out exclusively in arabesque, was done in plaster, stucco, wood, mosaic or, in India, in openwork marble, and in Persia under the influence of the Safavids, in polychrome porcelain which clothed the whole edifice like a robe.

The decorative themes found their source in the foliated scroll-work alive with animals and fruits, common to Hellenistic and Byzantine art (pl. 269, 270). Gradually in both Mesopotamia and Egypt this scroll-work lost all its relief, its design thinned into the purely abstract type of pattern since called 'arabesque'. Arabesque patterns throw up against a dark ground their flat braiding, interlaced in geometrical designs in which the starred polygon plays an essential part (pl. 271). The Muslims also made much of inscriptions of extracts from the Koran in Kufic script.

### *The Minor Arts*

While the peoples of the West were still leading a crude barbarian existence the Muslim princes succeeded in bringing all the refinements of intellectual culture and material luxury to the art of living. They attached great importance to the beauty of everyday things and to the decoration of their houses, and set up workshops in their palaces as well as seeking far and wide for objets d'art and skilled artists. Commercial exchanges became so active between the Muslim countries that the exact origin of old pieces is often hard to trace.

The repugnance shown by the Muslims for representation of living figures hindered sculpture, but in the lay crafts there were none of the limitations that restricted decoration in religious buildings, where the geometrical style alone was allowed. The art of Islam, in a word, maintained into modern times the ancient zoomorphic and phytomorphic (based on plant-forms) decorative style of the East, which it took at first-hand from Iran and Mesopotamia, where it was still flourishing in the Sassanian civilization at the time of the conquest. Thus living forms were suggested only obliquely, through a decorative stylization which stripped them of all reality or representational value. Perhaps the Shiite heresy which at various times took hold of Iran, the crucible of Islamic art, had some indulgence towards this decorative imagery, being at all events less puritanical than was the Sunnite orthodoxy. Calling on both geometrical speculation and the fluid stylization of living forms, the Mohammedans had thus an inexhaustible stock which they exploited to the full. Under Mongol rule from the thirteenth century onwards, Persia showed a bent for human representation which emerged in the highly-developed miniature. In its final phase Muslim art was energized once more by the introduction of naturalistic floral themes which gave a spring-like youthfulness to their ceramics and carpets (pl. 275).

Mohammedan decoration is essentially polychromatic. No doubt weaving was considered as the highest art in Islam. The best tissues in cotton and silk used in the oldest Sassanian decorations are no longer known to us save in fragments, so far as the earliest periods are concerned; these are mostly treasured in Western churches which imported them at great cost for wrapping and preserving holy relics. This art also prospered in the West, especially at Palermo in workshops which the Norman kings of Sicily maintained on a royal scale (pl. 268). The art of rug-making which

*275 Persian Hunt Carpet. Vienna*

flourished in Persia and in Asia Minor gave rise to a brisk trade with the West in the Middle Ages. The oldest specimens remaining only date from the sixteenth century, but earlier Eastern carpets can be studied thanks to the frequency with which they were shown in Western paintings from the fourteenth century onwards. Carpets woven since the end of the sixteenth century in Asia Minor or in the Armenian mountains (Chirvan, Kuba) are designed on a geometric or stylized floral principle; the same is true of Turkestan (Bukhara) carpets. In accordance with their temperament the Persians often enlivened their carpets with hunting-scenes, animal combats, trees and flowers portrayed in a naturalistic manner (pl. 275). They kept alive all the spirit of Hellenistic scroll-work. Their carpets are often very close to contemporary miniatures (Isfahan, Teheran, Shushagan, Khurasan, Shiraz, Tabriz, etc.). Indian carpets imitated the Persian, while those called 'Hispano-Moorish', of which few pre-conquest specimens remain, were on geometrical lines. The eastern Muslim carpets were imitated in China, in the Balkans, and with extraordinary success in Poland.

*276 Large Vase with lustred Decoration. 14th c. Palermo*

277 *Persian Perfume-Brazier. Early 13th c. Teheran*

278 *Detail of a Baptismal Font. Mesopotamian (Mongol Period). Mid 13th c. Paris*

Pieces of pottery have fortunately been recovered in large quantities by digging, or were found concealed in the walls of buildings. The workshops of Mesopotamia (Samarra, Iraq) or Persia (Susa, Rhagae) soon restored to its high place the art of enamelled faïence which had reached such a fine perfection under the Achaemenians. It was they who invented lustred decoration with metallic or mottled sheens, varying from golden yellow to a coppery red, or from brown to green. The best specimens came from the shops at Rhagae, Sultanabad, Gurgan and Rakka in the eleventh, twelfth and thirteenth centuries. Animal and floral decorative imagery they treated with an exquisite fantasy, and they gave little scope to the geometrical style (pl. 276). In the eighteenth century Chinese influence began to filter into Persia, while Asia Minor was to renew its repertory by adding naturalistic floral decoration with a rich range of colour. Lustred decoration spread throughout Islam and in the West resulted in Hispano-Moorish faïence (Malaga, Valencia) which was to survive after the Muslims left Spain (thirteenth to sixteenth century). The working of glass which the Syrians and Egyptians mastered was related to that of faïence and was enriched with enamels, for example in the lamps for mosques.

Mohammedan metalwork began in Mesopotamia, where copper-mines provided the necessary raw material. From the tenth and eleventh centuries the region of Mosul produced bowls, cauldrons and ewers in incised copper or brass. A little later in the twelfth century it began to make brass objects chased with threads of silver, gold or red copper, a technique known as 'damaskeening' (pl. 278). This art subsequently spread to Syria and Egypt. Its patterns are the same as those of pottery. Mixed with pewter, the copper of Mesopotamia gave some fine articles in bronze (fountains, ewers, braziers, mirrors, mosque-lamps, door-panels), the oldest of which are of Mesopotamian origin (animal-shaped ewers) going back to the ninth century and prolonging the zoomorphic art of the Sassanians. The Fatimites of Egypt and the Omayyads of Spain also had bronze-foundries. The objects just mentioned are the only examples of sculpture in the round in Muslim art (pl. 277). The treatment of ivory (caskets) was an offshoot of Byzantine technique, and was a speciality of Córdoba (tenth and eleventh centuries) and of thirteenth-century Sicily. Cairo craftsmen excelled in woodcarving, a technique well developed by the Copts in the Hellenistic period.

*Persian and Hindu Miniatures*

The oldest examples of Iranian painting have been discovered in outer Iran in the sanctuaries of Turkestan which were decorated between 760 and 840 by the Uigur Turks, Manichaeans of Persian origin. Their wall-paintings and manuscripts, showing affinities with the oldest Sassanian paintings of Bamiyan (third to sixth century) and even more so with those of later Mongolian Persia, prove the continuity of an Iranian tradition. However, the first great school of miniaturists in Persia of which we have examples, the Abbasid school of Mesopotamia (twelfth and thirteenth centuries) is of Arab inspiration. It shows strongly accentuated Semitic types, a tendency towards dramatic composition, a dry style, a limited range of colour and a sweeping execution which leads us to suppose that they knew the art of the fresco (*Pharmacopoeia of Dioscorides,* early thirteenth century; *Maqamat of Hariri,* Leningrad and Bibliothèque Nationale, Paris, about 1220, pl. 279; *Fables of Bidpai,* Bibliothèque Nationale, about 1230).

Under the Mongol princes the miniature developed rapidly on a level worthy of the literary, poetic, historical and scientific achievement of Islam. This art was cultivated in the Trans-Oxus region (eastern Iran) then, after the Mongol conquest, in Mesopotamia. The Mongols brought with them a powerful Chinese influence. Their types, costumes and landscapes are Sino-Mongol in character (*Chronicle of Rachid-ed-Din,* Bibliothèque Nationale, about 1310). In the Timurid period (1369–1500) this element blended harmoniously with the old Iranian manner and Arabo-Abbasid art. Springing from such fertile sources the miniature soon showed an admirable versatility of method and a very rich stock of forms. The lyricism of nature (animals, flowers, fields) and social life together with a bent for romance, gave the sixteenth-century Persian miniature some affinity with the cosmopolitan art which prevailed in Europe between 1380 and 1430: French miniatures, the work of Pisanello, the 'soft style' in Germany (colour pl. VI). The centre of that art was then at Herat in Trans-Oxus – now Afghanistan – (*Apocalypse of Mohammed,* Bibliothèque Nationale, 1436). The famous Behzad lived towards the end of the Timurid dynasty, working at Herat from 1469 to 1506 in the service

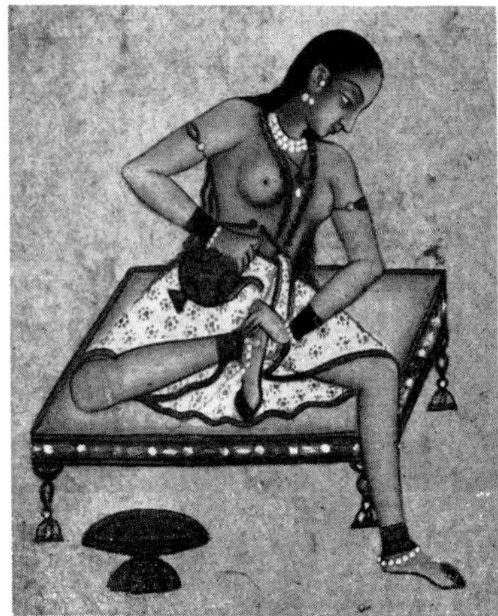

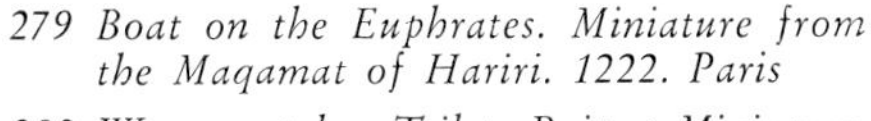

*279 Boat on the Euphrates. Miniature from the Maqamat of Hariri. 1222. Paris*

*280 Woman at her Toilet. Rajput Miniature. 18th–19th c. Paris*

of the last of these kings. Then, after the fall of the dynasty he moved to the court of the first Safavid at Tabriz, where he died in 1529 leaving a whole school of artists (Sultan Mohammed, Ustad Mohammed) known as the Safavid school. This group was remarkable for a certain decadent 'mannerism' (lengthening of forms, twisting of bodies) and an increasing tendency to worldliness and amorous lyricism. The miniature was no longer confined to books and began to be treated as an independent picture. The portrait, introduced by Behzad, became very popular. This school persisted into the seventeenth century, gradually losing its better qualities owing to a slackness of style as well as naturalism (Agha-Riza, Riza-Abbasi, Shafi-Abbasi).

Under the Mongol emperors in India (sixteenth and seventeenth centuries) a very fertile school of miniature developed which turned to Persia for its material, the Mongol princes ordering artists to copy Persian works. But the school was fundamentally different owing to the traditional Indian taste for naturalism which was strengthened by the European influences introduced by the Jesuits. European perspective ousted the Persian panoramic vision; the miniature was usually independent of books, while the portrait became a character-study. Painters sought effects of atmosphere which they suggested in a naturalistic way, varying the light according to the time of day and so on. The sensual eroticism to be found here was as old as the Indian soul itself (pl. 280).

Persian and Hindu miniatures were executed on paper, a technique which the Muslims learnt from the Chinese. Books were dressed in sumptuous bindings (book-binding being probably an Egyptian invention dating from the Hellenistic period). The Egyptians illuminated luxurious Korans with purely geometrical designs.

# VII. EUROPEAN ART IN THE FIFTEENTH CENTURY

After the unity achieved in fourteenth-century Europe through the imposition of Gothic by France, the fifteenth century was one of remarkable confusion. There were two warring principles: the Flamboyant style, which was the final phase of Gothic, and the Renaissance style. France was weakened by the Hundred Years War, and the two creative regions of Europe were now Italy and Flanders, the latter now making its triumphant entry into European civilization.

However, it is not impossible to find some underlying principle in such a rich century, in spite of the many local and national variations and the apparently marked difference of forms. After being a handmaid of a religious faith which tolerated only what could further its own ideals, art broke its bondage to theology and became a means of knowing the external world. The mirror is a common symbol of this new art, which reflected nature, and despite stylistic differences, at least in painting, the same phenomena affected the two parent schools in Italy and Flanders.

The veil of symbolism was torn, but the world as the artist saw it with fresh eyes dazzled him like a marvellous vision. Still deeply imbued with mysticism, the beauty of the universe struck him as the image but no longer the symbol of Paradise; for Fra Angelico, Gentile da Fabriano or Pisanello, as for the van Eycks and the Rhenish painters, virgins, angels and holy hermits walked in the enchanted meadows of spring; at the dawn of an era of positivism the 'dream of love' of the mystic of Assisi yielded its finest flowers.

However, on the intellectual plane the world was soon to be regarded as an object of knowledge and no longer as the subject of sentimental and imaginative outpourings.

The central problem which then worried artists was the conquest of depth and spatial values. A passion for the three-dimensional set sculpture above the other arts; this was the unifying principle of the century all over Europe. Through it Konrad Witz, Paolo Uccello and Rogier van der Weyden were at one. Certainly their methods differed, for the Flemish artists advanced hesitantly into space, letting intuition take the lead, while the Florentines pursued this quest for spatial values rationally and, like surveyors, caught space in a net of geometry. Dieric Bouts in Flanders was perhaps aware of the power of linear perspective, but that was not what the Flemish were after. It was by the sensual expression of atmospheric values that Jan van Eyck was able to suggest immense depths in a few square centimetres.

From now on the artist, with the eye of a reporter, discovered an immense field to be explored, the infinite variety of the forms of the

281 *Hubert and Jan van Eyck. Virgin Martyrs form the Ghent Altarpiece*

world of man and nature. This inquiry was pursued unsystematically by the Northern artists, who built up gradually a vocabulary of gestures and expressions, facial types and natural forms. But for Italy it was an exact science, and Leonardo, the most significant figure in the Quattrocento, dreamed of making painting the crowning glory of human knowledge, since representing the forms of creation implied for him a scientific study of the world.

It was in the early fifteenth century that Italy, held back for almost a century by the Gothic invasion that like the rest of Europe she had no choice but to accept, experienced that great upsurge of creative vigour in the visual arts for which she is famous and which we know as the

282 *Stefano da Zevio. Madonna in the Rose-Garden (detail). Verona*

*VII Jan van Eyck. Madonna in her Chamber. Frankfurt*

'Renaissance'. The Swiss historian Jacob Burckhardt in 1860 defined the Renaissance as an affirmation of the individual, who now emerged from the anonymous crowd of the Middle Ages. From now on the work of art was strongly marked by its author's imprint, and the creative activity of the intellect in the field of the arts was to be considered as one of the finest in the history of man. The artist was promoted from the status of artisan to become an aristocrat of the mind. Yet the time had not come when great isolated workers, commissioned by the society of their time, were to leave their ivory tower to overwhelm mankind with their messages. Setting a distance between itself and the masses, the art of the Renaissance was exalted by the enthusiasm of an aristocratic class of wealthy patrons and intellectuals. It became a princely activity, and now, more than in earlier periods when it had been swept along by the collective urge of society, it came to depend on patronage. Freed from all spiritual or temporal usefulness, the work of art as it became an 'objet d'art' was to be an end in itself. It was made for a pure act of contemplation to which only an enlightened élite could aspire. The fertility and variety of Italian art of the Quattrocento benefited from the political division of the peninsula into rival principalities which resulted in great competition in all cultural matters. The Medicis of Florence, the Aragons of Naples, the Sforzas of Milan, the Estes of Ferrara, the Gonzagas of Mantua, and the Monte-

*283 Paradise Garden. Cologne School. About 1420. Frankfurt*

*284 Konrad Witz. Sabothay and Benaiah from the Mirror of Salvation Altarpiece. About 1435. Basle*

*285 Andrea del Castagno. Portrait of Pippo Spano. Florence*

feltros of Urbino outbid each other for artists of repute. Works of art, valuable evidence of the greatness of man, were now collected by princes as priceless treasures; the idea of the 'museum', a temple reserved for the cult of the beautiful, belongs to the Renaissance.

The art of the Quattrocento was the most heroic attempt that had been made to bring the world down to the human scale. Whatever in the world cannot be grasped by the senses or the human intelligence, all the infinitude of nature and the yearnings of the soul towards the beyond, whatever can be perceived only by mystical intuition and escapes the pure lucidity of consciousness, all this was rejected from a world ruled by architecture and sculpture whose logic is based on the idea of limitation. The Quattrocento went farther along this humanistic road than the antiquity it thought it was reviving; the notion of 'man the measure of all things' must have been powerfully rooted in the make-up of Mediterranean man, to have been capable of asserting itself so strongly after fourteen hundred years of Christianity in which man had lived bowed under the yoke of God. Faith, the need to accept values which the mind considers as supreme, now gave way to that impulse towards knowledge which drives man to accept only such ideas as can be proved true by reasoning. Rationalism was the true principle of the Italian Renaissance; it dictated its every step in the field of thought and art. Dedicated to the understanding of nature, art became a rational pursuit of the appearances of the external world, but this conquest of the visible found itself checked by a speculative inquiry, no less logically pursued, into the abstract 'laws' of beauty. This contradiction caused a tension resulting in a host of creations of genius, such as mankind had never seen before.

*286 Hans Memling. Madonna (detail). 1487. Bruges*

*287 Perugino. Madonna and Saints (detail). Paris*

*288 Master of Moulins. Madonna (detail). About 1498. Moulins*

Even Greek art never had such a wealth of talent – though it is true that Classical humanism expressed itself in philosophical speculations which Italy had nothing to equal. It was in creations in the plastic field that Renaissance humanism found its most powerful expression, its works of pure thought being overshadowed by the revival of ancient philosophy. Quattrocento Italy is perhaps the most remarkable instance of a civilization developed mainly in plastic terms.

Their sharp minds and eagerness for knowledge fitted the Florentines for the task of presiding over the new civilization. The Medici family, and especially Cosimo who first established its power, has a title to the glory of the early Renaissance, which for a century brought such fame to Florence. The first half of the Quattrocento witnessed the final flowering of the Gothic aesthetic in the northern and central provinces of Lombardy and the Marches. Towards the fourteen-sixties in Venetia (Padua and

Venice) a new centre began to develop values which were alien to the intellectualist aesthetic of the Florentines. Sixteenth-century art sprang from the union of Florence and Venice.

The other European countries did not ignore the Italians' brilliant example, but they first had to soothe their nostalgia for a vanishing enchanted world; and that is why Northern Europe of the fifteenth century produced one of the deepest expressions of the Middle Ages. It was not without some anguish that knowledge began to challenge faith in men's minds. The art of the fifteenth century, which gave such prominence to expressing the pangs of death, is evidence of that tragic debate. It is as though the more Italy exalted man's greatness, the more desperately Northern civilization clung to Christianity and sought to diminish man. Italy itself was not entirely untouched by these passionate debates, as can be seen from the tragic and victorious offensive of the Germanic Flamboyant style against the Ferrarese school. The Renaissance spirit slowly advanced against such trials as these. France remained less aloof from it than any other country, and the keen-minded Jean Fouquet is a lay brother of Fra Angelico. However, the situation looked desperate and there seemed little hope of the North emerging from its tangled forest of belated Gothic when, in about 1480 to 1490, the cloud suddenly broke. As though the word had been passed round, artists of every nationality renounced the torments of expressionism, and Italy herself rejected the harshness of a style which was intent on truth alone. At Venice, Bellini, in Umbria, Perugino, in Florence, Ghirlandaio, in Flanders, Memling and Gérard David, in Germany, Holbein the Elder and Tilman Riemenschneider and in France, Michel Colombe and the Master of Moulins devoted themselves to a calm vision of harmonious forms. Resistance was overcome, and through the broken dykes Italy was to overflow into the North; the torrent produced a crisis that was to have enduring aftereffects on the artistic development of all Europe.

## 1. THE RENAISSANCE IN ITALY

### *Architecture*

The great Florentine artists' innovation early in the century was deliberately to cast aside Gothic principles in an attempt to return to the architectural forms which had been developed in Classical antiquity. Since they had never understood the inner form of Gothic architecture they had no qualms in giving up what for them had never been more than a setting for something else. The architect Brunelleschi and the sculptors Donatello and Ghiberti early in the century began studying the remains of ancient Rome, which at that time were still almost intact, and became the leaders in the new reform.

In the field of architectural forms, the Renaissance left behind the complex designs and intricate planes of the Gothic builders, returning to simple compositions with clearly defined volumes and sharp surfaces of which many an example was still to be found in Roman art. The great idea of that time was the central-plan building arranged round a main cupola (or dome), the masterpiece of this type being Bramante's plan for St Peter's, Rome.

*289 Florence Cathedral. Giotto's Campanile; Brunelleschi's Dome (1420–1434)*

Brunelleschi (1377–1446) brought to completion a work begun in the fourteenth century, crowning with a mighty dome (344 1/2 feet to the lantern-light) the crossing of S. Maria del Fiore, Florence, which was inspired by the Pantheon in Rome. At S. Lorenzo (pl. 294) and S. Spirito he left medieval forms behind and gave his churches all the bright harmony of the old basilicas. The contract for the dome of S. Maria del Fiore was competed for in 1417 and the dome was built between 1420 and 1434 (pl. 289). S. Lorenzo, the Medici family's church, was begun in 1419 and swiftly completed. In this building, as in the Pazzi Chapel of S. Croce (after 1430), Brunelleschi returned to the Classical decorative grammar, with Corinthian columns, entablatures, pediments, fluted pilasters, rosettes, scalloping, garlands, cornices, ovolos, denticulation, and pure semi-circular arches.

It remained for Michelozzo (1391–1472), who was a pupil of Brunelleschi and Donatello, to create the typical Florentine palace (Palazzo Medici-Riccardi), a strong stone cube enlivened with Classical decorations and topped with a monumental cornice. Closed off from the outside world in the manner of the Greek or Roman villa, its interior contains a charming pillared courtyard or *cortile* (pl. 295).

Leone Battista Alberti (1404–1472) had the most speculative mind of his time. His researches resulted in the art of Bramante, and he wrote the first treatise on architecture *(De re aedificatoria)*, but he contented himself with intellectual pursuits and most of his designs were carried out by others.

In the Palazzo Ruccellai (1446–1451) Alberti was the first to reintroduce the idea of superimposed orders – Doric, Ionic and Corinthian – followed by the Romans, which he did in the applied decorations of his façade (pl. 292). The basilican church of S. Andrea, Mantua (pl. 296),

*290 Palazzo Strozzi, Florence. Begun 1489*

which was built after his design at the end of century, is an aisleless building which later inspired Vignola's Gesù in Rome. In the Tempio Malatestiano (S. Francesco) at Rimini (about 1446) his façade is based on the ancient triumphal arch.

One of the finest achievements of the Quattrocento is the great ducal palace constructed at Urbino in the Marches for Federigo da Montefeltro. It was begun in about 1455 and finished about 1480, the work being carried out by the Dalmatian Luciano Laurana and later the Sienese Francesco di Giorgio. Decorative sculpture has rarely reached greater delicacy than here. The ducal apartments have several chambers fraught with humanistic meaning: a twin chapel with a Temple of the Muses, a *studiolo* or study decorated with portraits of great men and inlaid-work with symbolic patterns.

The architectural creations of the second half of the century in Florence had not the same splendid inventiveness. Bernardo Rossellino (1409–1464), Benedetto da Maiano (1442–1497) who in 1489 began the finest of Florentine palaces (Palazzo Strozzi, pl. 290), Giuliano da Maiano

*291 Palazzo Vendramin-Calergi, Venice. Finished about 1509*

(1432–1490) and above all Giuliano da Sangallo (1445–1516) all prepared the way for the masterpieces of the great architects of the sixteenth century by their patient researches in matters of detail. At the end of the century the new style developed in Florence spread all over Italy. Lombardy, which had felt the Gothic influence more strongly than any other Italian province, applied it in a diluted form, largely picturesque, in the Certosa, Pavia (pl. 293). Founded in 1396 and built in 1428 by Giovanni Solari, then continued by Giovanni Antonio Amadeo (1447–1552) the Certosa (Charterhouse) is the most famous example of this new style, and it is a pity that the Italian Renaissance was to be known to Europe by this, rather than by Florentine examples. Pure Gothic lingered on in Naples, which was under the patronage of the Aragon family. Venice passed rather late from the Gothic – which like Milan it had known in its Flamboyant form – to the Renaissance manner, which Antonio Rizzo (died 1498) transformed into a flowery, cheerful style in the tradition of Venetian art. Florentine influence came to the fore with Pietro Lombardo (died 1515), a sculptor and architect who, with a sense of perfection tending to Byzantinism, both built and decorated the marble gem, S. Maria dei Miracoli. In lively contrast with the cold straight masses of the Florentine palace – which derives from the fortress – the spirit of fenestrated architecture which had held sway in Venetia in the Middle Ages appeared once more in the Venetian Renaissance palace, whose first completely developed expression is the Palazzo Vendramin-

*292 Alberti (design 1446). Palazzo Ruccellai, Florence*

*293 Window of the Certosa, Pavia. Begun 1473*

Calergi (pl. 291) on the Grand Canal, a work designed no doubt by Mauro Coducci (died 1504).

In the first half of the fifteenth century the ferment of the Renaissance is thus seen to have wrought its work in Florence alone, in an Italy which was otherwise overrun by Flamboyant Gothic.

## *Sculpture*

In the portrayal of figures sculpture was now the major art, for sculptors were twenty-five years ahead of painters in the discovery of the new style, the painters always keeping their eye on the sculptors' experiments. The statue was the ideal of the period. No doubt sculpture owed its prominence to the fact that it was an essentially physical art in a period whose main aim was to give their due to the beauty and strength of the human body. It is also privileged by being situated in real space, and all the arts of the Quattrocento were dominated by an urge to master the three dimensions of space either in reality (through sculpture) or in appearance (through painting). Side by side with the shaping of marble the Italians developed bronze statuary, which incidentally they had never allowed to fall into neglect.

Of all the great masters who made their contribution to the new plastic language, only one was not a Florentine. This was Jacopo della Quercia (1374–1438) who came from Siena. With a minimum of modelling he attained from the very start that vigorous sense of the human body which was to haunt the whole century until it was caught again by Michel-

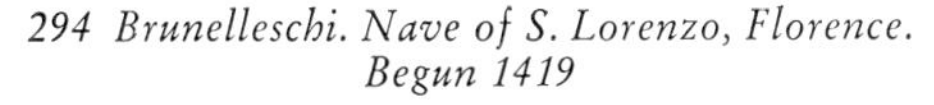

*294 Brunelleschi. Nave of S. Lorenzo, Florence. Begun 1419*

*295 Michelozzo. Courtyard of the Palazzo Medici. Begun 1444*

angelo. The Florentines Lorenzo Ghiberti (1378–1455) and Donatello (1382?–1466) were slower in breaking with the Gothic spirit. Ghiberti kept something of the Gothic sense of the picturesque, its naturalistic spatial lyricism and its canon of elongated proportions, but he was able to give spatial depth to his low-reliefs by the *schiacciato* process of flattened modelling, which he introduced and which consists of giving an impression of great depth even with a very thin base of material, whether marble or bronze, by means of heavy foreshortening in the modelling.

Ghiberti was the laureate of the famous competition for the second bronze door of the Florence Baptistery (1401) with which the great sculptural ventures of the century began; he took the prize against Querica and Brunelleschi who were also competing. From 1403 to 1423 he made this door in a style close to the Gothic, inspired by the first door which had been sculpted by Andrea Pisano in the fourteenth century.

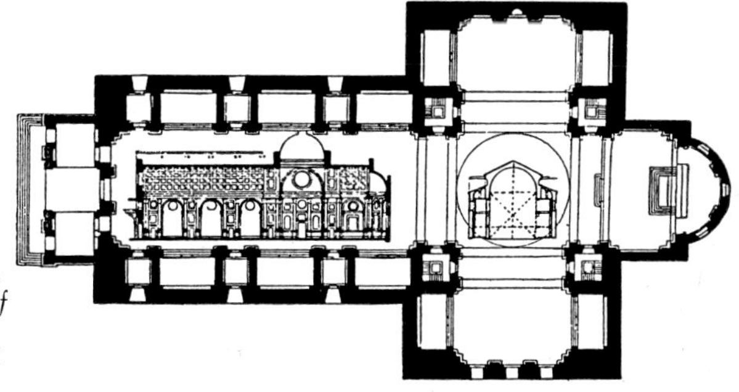

*296 Alberti (design). Plan and Section of S. Andrea, Mantua. 1476*

*297 Ghiberti. Joshua crossing the Jordan and the Fall of Jericho. Panel of the Porta del Paradiso of the Baptistery, Florence*

The third door (1425–1452), called the *Porta del Paradiso* by Michelangelo because of its subject and its beauty, shows his personal art at its very height; exploiting the metal's thickness with tremendous virtuosity, he managed to suggest depth-effects such as are found in painting (pl. 297).

The genius of Ghiberti, like Fra Angelico's, drew him towards the expression of harmony; Donatello, on the contrary, was carried along by a dramatic tenseness and a longing for grandeur. Italian art has always hesitated between these two paths, the first of which led to Raphael, and the second to Michelangelo. Nanni di Banco (1384?–1421) sought his inspiration in antique statuary even more deliberately than Ghiberti had done, but Donatello was the first to use themes taken from the pagan world. Unlike Ghiberti he was blind to the beauties of nature and all his art was dedicated to the praise of the human form, whose inner structure he studied with an analytic keenness which sometimes led him to stress muscles and tendons so that they stood out as if the model was flayed. He freed the statue from architecture, to which it had been subservient since the Middle Ages, and made it into a detached form, valid from every angle, conceived as a volume in the three dimensions of space. He created the carved portrait-bust *(Niccolò da Uzzano).* A soul tormented by his passionate vision of the human drama, he was a direct forerunner of Michelangelo.

*298 Donatello. Annunciation. In S. Croce, Florence, Marble. About 1435*

His early works, for the Florence Duomo (e.g. *St John the Evangelist,* 1413–1415), for Or San Michele (e.g. *St George,* between 1416–1420) or on the campanile of the duomo (*Prophets,* from 1427) were still closely connected with their architectural setting. It was in the course of a visit to Rome in 1432 and 1433, when he was greatly impressed by antique works, that Donatello was freed from his dramatic expressionism. He then began to express the beauty of the human body in the flower of its youth (*Amore-Atys, St John the Baptist, Annunciation* in S. Croce, pl. 298, *Dancing Putti* for the Prato Pulpit and on the Cantoria from the Florence Duomo); yet the bronze bas-reliefs of the Santo at Padua (1444–1448) show a return of his dramatic instinct and a wish to imitate the fluidness of painting. In 1453 he set up in Padua his equestrian statue of the condottiere *Gattamelata* (pl. 299), the image of self-assured power, for which Donatello took his inspiration from Imperial Roman statues. This rider is one of the loftiest expressions of the humanistic pride of the Quattrocento, a symbol of the triumph of intelligence over brute force.

In the second half of the century sculpture in Florence showed the same phenomenon of eased tension as can be seen in painting and architecture. The art of Donatello gave the lead to the whole of the next generation. Luca della Robbia (1400–1483) alone proved unwilling to follow him. In polychrome ceramics he created a religious imagery whose devoutness and fluid style recall Fra Angelico; but he learnt more from the harmony of antique draperies than any of his contemporaries. Mino

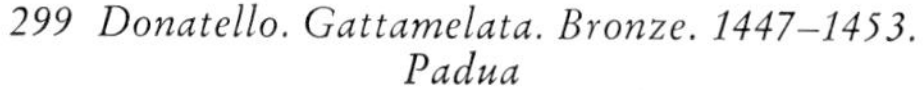

*299 Donatello. Gattamelata. Bronze. 1447–1453. Padua*

*300 Verrocchio. David. Bronze. 1476. Florence*

da Fiesole (1431–1484), Desiderio da Settignano (1428–1464), Antonio Rossellino (1417–about 1478, pl. 301) and Benedetto da Maiano (1442–1497), who all worked in marble, were decorators who did their best to recapture Donatello's gracefulness, but made it somewhat insipid. The Sienese sculptor Agostino di Duccio (1418–about 1481) on the other hand expressed it with a mannerist incisiveness. The bronze-workers found in Donatello a terser sense of analysis of which they sometimes produced a mannerist exaggeration; this was the case with Bertoldo (died 1491) who popularized his master's art in small statuettes, and with the goldsmith Antonio Pollaiuolo (1432–1498). The nearest to genius was Andrea del Verrocchio (1435–1488) who left a young *David* of steel-like intensity (pl. 300) and above all an equestrian statue, the *Colleone* monument (Venice, 1485) which was a reply to Donatello's *Gattamelata* in which the Quattrocento's instinct for power and pride is asserted to the point of bombast.

In the other Italian provinces the Donatellesque manner took root in the second half of the century. There, sculpture turned more readily to decoration and was secondary to the architecture, as in the case of Matteo Civitali (1435–1501) of Lucca, and Lorenzo Vecchietta of Siena (1412–1480). The Triumphal Arch of Aragon which was set up between 1451 and 1453 at the Castel Nuovo was the first sign of the Renaissance in Naples; this great sculptural opus was at one time attributed to Francesco Laurano, an artist of Dalmatian origin (active between 1458–1502) who was helped in his work by a number of other artists. It was Antonio Rizzo (died 1498) who brought the style of Donatello to Venice. Lombardy alone, faithful to its Gothic traditions, remained immune, and the declamatory art of Niccolo dell' Arca (died 1494) and Guido Mazzoni (1450–1518) shows strong traces of Germanic influence.

### *Painting*

It was in the north and, from the end of the Trecento, in Lombardy, that old Italic province of 'long-haired Gaul', that the craze for naturalism first showed itself in the portrayal of animal and floral forms, in the work of such delightful draughtsmen and illuminators as Giovanni de' Grassi. In that northern region of Italy, which continued to be deeply imbued with feudal civilization, the old ideals of chivalry and courtly love which had seduced the medieval imagination flowered once more in the first half of the fifteenth century, when nature became the servant of fantasy. At Verona, Stefano da Zevio (1375–after 1438, pl. 282) and above all Antonio Pisano, called Pisanello (1397–1455), produced the last echoes of the Middle Ages, though Pisanello showed all the feverish curiosity of the Quattrocento in his studies of animals. Pisanello grasped the living arabesque of the animal, the texture of plumage and coat, while paying little attention to anatomical structure, which guided the Florentines in their studies of the human body (pl. 302).

Pisanello's paintings, which are very scarce, consist of little more than a few pictures and the frescoes at Verona of the *Annunciation* in S. Fermo Maggiore, and of *St George rescuing the Princess*, which is treated in legendary fashion, in S. Anastasia (1431). He also modelled and cast medallions (pl. 320), and this experience led him to create the profile portrait (*Princess of the House of Este*, Louvre).

This representational lyricism spread through central Italy of the Marches and Umbria, where it met another important stream, the old Sienese style, to produce that exquisite Gentile da Fabriano (1360–1440) whose masterpiece is the *Adoration of the Kings* (Uffizi, Florence, 1423, pl. 303). This princely procession is imbued with all the charm and fantasy of the medieval mind.

Pisanello and Gentile are the Italian exponents of what we might call

*301 Antonio Rossellino. Madonna. In S. Croce, Florence. Marble. About 1478*

*302 Pisanello. Vision of St Eustace London*

'naturalistic mysticism', a feeling of adoration for the marvels of nature, which in the Middle Ages they called *mirabilia*. It remained for Florence to introduce a more scientific naturalism.

It was only towards 1425 that the Florentine school of painting, which lagged behind sculpture, managed to break its enslavement to a senile Giottesque tradition which had been only slightly rejuvenated by the sincerity of the Camaldolese monk Don Lorenzo Monaco (about 1370–1425?). The founders of the Florentine Renaissance school were Masolino (1383–1447, pl. 304), Fra Angelico and Masaccio. Though Fra Angelico was a Christian painter while Masaccio founded a pagan humanism, both of them belong to the Renaissance in their plastic outlook. Fra Angelico was a meeting-point of styles and ideas emerging from the past

*303 Gentile da Fabriano. Adoration of the Kings (detail). 1423. Florence*

*304 Masolino. Story of Herod. Fresco at Castiglione Olona. About 1420*

but seeking the future, and if he glimpsed a heavenly beatitude he was none the less carried along on the wave of discovery that gripped his generation. With Paolo Uccello he created perspective, and with Masaccio he mastered modelling, expounding the laws of a harmonious composition in his invention of the *Sacra Conversazione* in which he set the saints in a semi-circle round the Virgin, or in attendance at her Coronation (pl. 305). The serene abstractness of his style makes him an early classical master, half-way between Giotto and Raphael.

A late-comer to painting, Guido di Pietro, called Fra Angelico (died 1455), gradually broke away from Gothic illumination. Entering the Dominican friary at Fiesole in 1407 he decorated the friary of S. Marco in Florence with frescoes after it was founded in 1436 by Cosimo de' Medici for the Florentine Dominicans. He was called to Rome in 1445 by Eugenius IV, where from 1449 to 1450 he painted frescoes showing the stories of St Stephan and St Lawrence in the Chapel of Nicholas V in the Vatican. He had a large output and made great use of his apprentices.

In Fra Angelico's work the human being is still that fragile creature who draws all his strength from God alone. Masaccio (1401–1428) was the first in painting to define the plastic and humanistic ideal of the Renaissance without the slightest hesitation. He died at the age of twenty-seven and left little more than the frescoes of the life of St Peter in the Brancacci Chapel in the Carmine at Florence; but this chapel became a sanctuary for the training of a long line of Italian artists up to Raphael and Michelangelo (pl. 306 a). Masaccio was a forerunner of genius who at one stroke found the target which the Italian school as a whole was to reach only fifty years later. Renewing Giotto's ideal of concentrated strength, he heralded the sixteenth century by his monumental sense of composition that points the way to Raphael, and his broad and powerful

305 Fra Angelico. Coronation of the Virgin. Florence

notion of the human body, his heroic and dramatic intensity (pl. 306 b) which only Michelangelo could rival. But his contemporaries went no farther than the experimental stage. They were still trying to find the laws of painting which for them was a problem in itself; they were after a definition of spatial laws, that is to say, how to represent the three dimensions of real space on the flat canvas. They found the as yet unformulated rules of linear perspective and, by their use of foreshortening produced results which recall sculpture, whose effects they tried to reproduce by the device of illusionism *(trompe-l'œil)*, or through the cameo. Paolo Uccello (about 1400–1475) brought a naïve passion to these semi-

*306 a Masaccio. Tribute Money (detail). Fresco in the Carmine, Florence. 1427–1428*

*VIII Filippo Lippi. Adoration in the Forest. Berlin*

*306 b Masaccio. Expulsion. Carmine, Florence. 1427–1428*

*307 Uccello. Rout of San Romano (detail). London*

scientific researches and remained sensitive to the charms of nature. On the contrary the sharp and metallic art of Andrea del Castagno (1390? –1457?) ignored landscape and his world seems to have been one of bronze or marble (pl. 285). He saw everything from the point of view of volume, reducing nature to a pure geometry of his own creation.

The main works of Paolo Uccello are battle-scenes (Paris, London, pl. 307, Florence) and the poorly-preserved frescoes in the Chiostro Verde of S. Maria Novella showing the Deluge.

Andrea del Castagno painted frescoes in a sculptural style for S. Apollonia in Florence (pl. 285).

Meanwhile, the Florentines who followed this generation of pioneers were not on the look-out for new territory to conquer. Painters, sculptors and goldsmiths, Andrea del Verrocchio (1435–1488) or the brothers Piero (1443–1496) and Antonio (1432–1498) Pollaiuolo, still remained obsessed by form in relief. Most of these artists were content with exploiting new discoveries without adding to them. Fra Filippo Lippi (1406–1469, colour pl. VIII) who was a follower of Fra Angelico, expressed a romantic pathos which anticipates Botticelli. Ghirlandaio (1449–1494) fell into a bourgeois optimism, while Benozzo Gozzoli (1449–1497) undertook a facile second version of the 'poetry' of Gentile da Fabriano. Only Alessio Baldovinetti (1425–1499), thanks to his researches into harmonic composition which were all pursued round a main theme, that of the Virgin and Child, shows early signs of that intellectual view of perfection which, 'scientifically' arrived at, could do nothing more than repeat itself – that of Leonardo da Vinci.

With the Pollaiuolo brothers, Piero di Cosimo (1462–1521) and Sandro Botticelli (1444–1510), the end of the century led to the harshness, oddness and morbidities of mannerism, that 'sickness of styles' which always occurs at the end of a creative period. The case of Botticelli is

*308 Botticelli. Birth of Venus. Florence*

typical of the intellectualist frenzy which was then widespread in Florence. This mystic soul, torn between Christianity and paganism, but possessed by the demon of intellect, was condemned to a restless existence. The languishing sadness of his Madonnas, the nostalgia of his portraits, his nervous and troubled style which gives all his compositions a spasmodic rhythm and quickens the edge of his line and the impetuousness of his figures, betrays the deep torment of an art which has reached its

*309 Sassetta. Mystic Marriage of St Francis (detail). 1443. Chantilly*

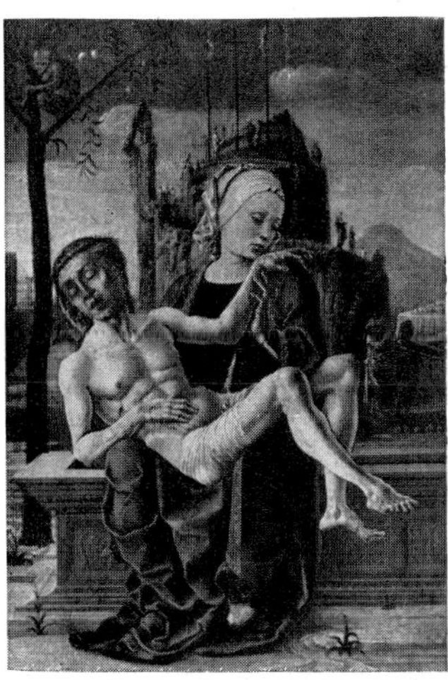

*310 Cosimo Tura. Pietà. Venice*

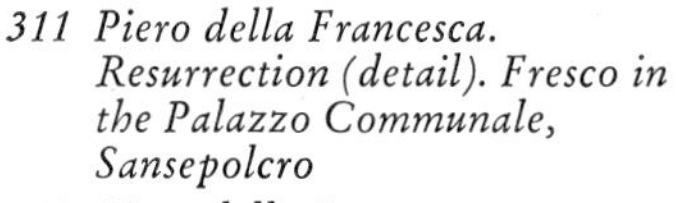

*311 Piero della Francesca. Resurrection (detail). Fresco in the Palazzo Communale, Sansepolcro*

*312 Piero della Francesca. The Queen of Sheba adoring the Holy Wood (detail). Fresco in S. Francesco, Arezzo. About 1455–1460*

limits and can only react against its own impotence in a final spasm of genius.

Botticelli was at first a goldsmith, then a pupil of Antonio Pollaiuolo and Filippo Lippi, and became a religious painter *(Madonna of the Magnificat,* Uffizi, Sistine frescoes). Towards 1485 he began painting themes inspired by antiquity *(Primavera* – an allegory of Spring – *Birth of Venus,* pl. 308, both Uffizi); Savonarola's preaching brought him back to Christianity and he returned eagerly to religious painting.

Siena, in its isolated hill-top position, remained a medieval town into the fifteenth century. Sassetta (1392–1450, pl. 309) and his follower Sano di Pietro (1406–1481) had all the candidness and wonderment of the primitives. Matteo di Giovanni (1435–1495), Neroccio (1447–1500), Giovanni di Paolo (1403–1482) and others finished by adapting the learned art of Florence to the outmoded *cantilena* of Siena.

It is outside Florence and in schools to which she had taught independence, that we must seek further signs of the great movement of discovery which animated the Quattrocento. Piero della Francesca (about 1416/20 –1492) inherited something of the keenness for perspective of Paolo Uccello and Castagno, as well as Masaccio's taste for monumental grandeur. He gave his figures a granite consistency and no artist more haughtily expressed the pride of Quattrocento man (pl. 311). Piero della Francesca's chief work is a series of frescoes in S. Francesco, Arezzo, depicting

*313 Mantegna. Agony in the Garden. 1459–1460. London*

the *Story of the True Cross* (pl. 312). He left also the remarkable portraits of the duke of Urbino, *Federigo da Montefeltro,* and his wife *Battista Sforza* (both Uffizi).

The Florentine view of art was brought to the painters of the north by the Tuscan sculptors, Donatello among them, who came to work in Padua. The intellectualist turn of mind of the Florentines, as it made itself felt in a region where Germanic influences were still active, gave rise to a school of painters in Ferrara who were fired by a quest for the supernatural and whose tense style and fantastic imagination came as a flamboyant intrusion into Italian painting.

The liveliest of these painters was Cosimo Tura (about 1430–1495, pl. 310), who owed something to Piero della Francesca. Francesco Cossa (1435– about 1477) was the author of a series of frescoes in the Palazzo Schifanoia at Ferrara. Ercole de' Roberti (died 1496) and Lorenzo Costa (1460–1535) toned down the pitiless style of Tura and Cossa.

The Florentine school died of anaemia through setting all its faith in the intellect and thus failing to appreciate the gifts of the imagination. The intellectualist leaven of Tuscany, however, working on a powerful imagination, produced the greatest painter of the Quattrocento in the Paduan Andrea Mantegna (1431–1506, pl. 313). He added to the spatial

*314 Mantegna. St James led to Martyrdom. Fresco in the Eremitani, Padua (destroyed). 1449–1454*

*315 Carpaccio. Story of St Ursula (detail). 1491–1495. Venice*

values of the Florentines what Berenson has called 'tactile values'; not content with the visual appearance of things, he tried to give the illusion of material texture. He pushed the mania for antiquities much farther than the Florentines had done, and achieved in paint Alberti's dream of recreating a vision of the Latin world. He renewed the traditional garments and introduced Roman costumes into art, observing them with all the exactness of an archaeologist. Being a northerner he introduced nature into the abstract Florentine world, while submitting natural forms to the decorous laws of architecture and sculpture. His art was a broad synthesis of the many ideals by which Quattrocento man was lured.

*316 Antonello da Messina. Male Portrait. 1475. Paris*

Mantegna's work as it comes down to us is fairly plentiful, but unfortunately the frescoes of the *Life and Martyrdom of St James and St Christopher* in the Church of the Eremitani at Padua (1449–1454, pl. 314), one of the finest achievements of the Renaissance, were almost completely destroyed

*317 Giovanni Bellini. Transfiguration. About 1480. Naples*

by bombardment in 1944. Of his great decorative works the *Gonzaga Family* still survives (in the ducal palace at Mantua) as does the series of the *Triumphs of Caesar* (Hampton Court), paintings in tempera which were intended as settings for the theatre in the palace at Mantua.

Venice, which was long a province of Byzantine art, only threw off that influence in the early fifteenth century. Jacopo Bellini (died 1470), with an inquiring mind typical of his century, was the first to sift in his paintings the mingled influences of Byzantinism, Gothicism and the Florentine 'scientific' outlook, which were struggling for possession of the Venetian school in 1430 or thereabouts. It was then that two streams became apparent in Venice, which were to survive until the dawn of the sixteenth century. Gentile Bellini (1429–1507), son of Jacopo, and Vittore Carpaccio (died 1527), a contemporary of Giorgione, both painted works of a picturesque and other-worldly quality which prolong the credulity of a Pisanello, filled with wonderment both at the real and the imaginary. Gentile Bellini, who made a journey to Constantinople in 1479, came under the influence of Eastern art. Carpaccio gave an ear to Gentile's teaching. He had a taste for narrative cycles and spectacular *mises-en-scène* which he executed for various Venetian societies and confraternities (*Story of St Ursula,* 1490–1498, pl. 315; *Lives of St Jerome and St George,* 1502; *Life of the Virgin,* 1504; *Story of St Stephen,* 1511–1520).

Another group of painters cast their eyes towards Padua where Donatello and Mantegna set the plastic inquiries of the new century in opposition to the picturesque spirit of Gothic art. This tradition was carried on by Carlo Crivelli (died 1493), Antonio (died 1476) and Bartolomeo (died 1499) Vivarini, to end in Giovanni Bellini (died 1516). Giovanni was the younger brother of Gentile, and after beginning with Byzantinism

*318 Signorelli. Fall of the Damned. Fresco in Orvieto Cathedral. 1499–1505*

was drawn away from it by Mantegna who became his brother-in-law in 1453. Taking up the oil technique which had been brought to Venice in about 1575 by Antonello da Messina (pl. 316) he softened the harsh sculptural style of Mantegna, insisting much less on the clear outline of his forms than on the transitions that join them together (pl. 317). By turning away from the analytic outlook of the Quattrocento and towards a pursuit of harmony he helped to prepare for the Cinquecento, and Giorgione and Titian learnt a good deal from him.

Meanwhile in a neighbouring province, while Florence was still sunk in its tense struggle to achieve the impossible, the Umbrian Perugino (1446–1524, pl. 287) was working on the same lines as Giovanni Bellini towards those aspects of the harmonic ideal which were to prevail in the sixteenth century; he was one of the teachers of Raphael. Luca Signorelli (about 1450–1523), also of Umbria, was already haunted by those nightmares of terror that obsessed Michelangelo, and his work contained some of the rudiments of the Baroque style. Everything was now ready for a second powerful drive in Italian art.

Of Perugino's work there remain some frescoes (Sistine Chapel, Rome, and the Cambio, Perugia) and numerous religious paintings. His art

*319 Florentine Cassone*

declined and became somewhat slack towards the end of the century. Luca Signorelli's best-known works are the frescoes of the *Last Judgement* in Orvieto Cathedral (pl. 318). Another artist who came from Perugia, Pinturicchio (1454?–1513), was a follower of the facile and picturesque art of Benozzo Gozzoli. His most outstanding work was the decoration of the Borgia Apartments, carried out from 1492 to 1494 for Alexander VI in the Vatican.

## *The Minor Arts*

The minor arts in Italy during the Quattrocento followed the same principles as the major ones. The Italian decorative sense has always been spoiled by the figurative and monumental emphasis given to everything in imitation of architecture and sculpture. Italian artisans from the fifteenth century onwards specialized, in matters of furnishing and jewellery, in pieces composed of many different materials which they put together like carved or painted objects. Their furniture derives from the styles of antiquity, their tables imitating the Roman *cartibulum* and the coffers or *cassoni* the sarcophagi (pl. 319) while their chairs take the X-shape of the chairs used by Roman magistrates. Decorative pottery which was influenced from the outset by Hispano-Moorish faïence, flourished in centres at Gubbio, Deruta, Urbino and Faenza, but it soon took on

*320 Pisanello. Portrait-Medal of the Byzantine Emperor Johannes VII Paleologus. About 1447. Florence*

an historical or narrative bias. The cult of antiquity also had something to do with the revival of the portrait-medal (pl. 320), of which Pisanello was the greatest exponent. Italy was never outstanding in the art of illumination, except in Lombardy where the French influence was felt. The best Italian achievements in this line were tarots or playing-cards. As for engraving, it came from Germany, by way of Venice. The clear-cut works of the Florentines and above all of Mantegna are masterpieces of copper-engraving.

## 2. LATE GOTHIC AND THE RENAISSANCE IN EUROPE

### *The Flamboyant Style*

While Florence, isolated even from the rest of Italy, was busy throwing off the Middle Ages and developing a monumental art based on Classical models, the rest of Europe was plunged in the excesses of the late Gothic style called 'Flamboyant' because of its sinuous forms (pl. 321).

This style arose in France at the close of the fourteenth century, in the Amiens and Rouen areas. It stemmed from a 'biological' evolution of those Gothic principles which, more rapidly in England than elsewhere, had given rise to the English Decorated or Curvilinear style (c. 1280) which inspired the first continental experiments in the Flamboyant. This evolution was modified by the rationalistic outlook of France. The Flamboyant style spread all over Europe, meeting no resistance except in Italy, where none the less it triumphed in Venetia, Lombardy (Milan Cathedral) and the Kingdom of Naples; but it was checked by the Florentine Renaissance. The most obvious forms of this style were perhaps those to be found in Germany and Spain. England gave up its sinuous style just when the rest of Europe was beginning to adapt it, and towards 1350 invented the Perpendicular style, which is typified by an over-emphasis on stiff, vertical lines and fan-vaults with intricate

*321 Martin Chambiges. Rose-Window in the South Transept of Sens Cathedral. 1490–1497*

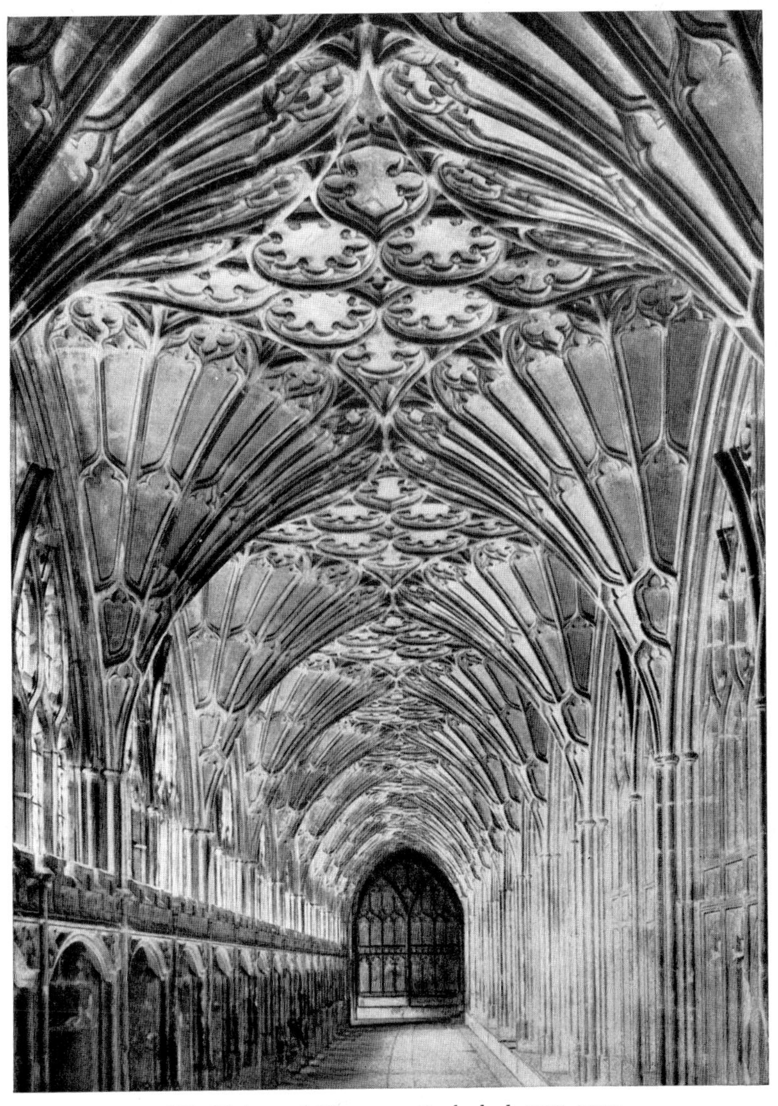

*322 Cloister of Gloucester Cathedral. 1351–1377*

ribbing (much of Gloucester, pl. 322, and Winchester Cathedrals; York Minster, except for transept; Abbey Church, Bath; Divinity School, Oxford; St George's Chapel, Windsor; Henry VII Chapel, Westminster; King's College Chapel, Cambridge).

The fifteenth century did nothing to modify the Gothic structure. Buildings were now more solidly constructed in spite of the light appearance given by the openwork carving of their decorations whose lavishness overlaid the main divisions of the edifice. All the members of these structures assumed an independent life, multiplying at each other's expense, and the moulding with all its complexities became angular. The vaults, whose structure became farther and farther removed from the original design of pointed rib-vaulting, were now covered over with a dense network of non-functional, intermediate ribs which took on either a star pattern as in Spain, or a pattern of interlaced branches as in Germany.

The overseers of these works now did their best to surprise the eye by suggesting instability or some feat of skill by means of dropped keystones, 'cork-screw' pillars, whose twisted effect suggests that they are giving way beneath their load. An overall emphasis on the curve, specially noticeable in the tracery of windows, suggests the writhing of flames (pl. 321) which earned the name 'Flamboyant' for a style which, by comparison with the fine, logical clarity of the thirteenth century, gave expression to a tormented and impassioned state of soul. The same anxiety was to take hold of sculpture. This time it was the Netherlander Claus Sluter who created that style imbued with pathos so typical of the fifteenth century.

### *A New Genius*

Flemish genius appeared as a new artistic force in fifteenth-century Europe. If architecture, whose formulae were invented in France, was still alive enough in that country to give birth to a final change of style, yet the Gothic plastic language was failing by the end of the fourteenth century, when it had already exhausted all its potentialities. It was the grafting of Flemish genius which was to restore energy to France and enable it to prolong the Middle Ages until about 1500.

The first Flemish artists including both painters and sculptors (André Beauneveu, the Limbourg brothers) began by enriching the French school with their talent, as they were attracted by the reputation of Paris. The political fortunes of the dukes of Burgundy, which were now favoured by the disasters of the Hundred Years War, allowed full development of the new style of expression. At the end of the fourteenth century the sculptor Claus Sluter, of Haarlem, was already defining at Dijon the principles of a new art of statuary in which everything was to be governed by emotional expression (Tomb of the dukes of Burgundy, porch and Calvary called the Puits de Moïse (Well of Moses) at the Chartreuse (Charterhouse) of Champmol, between 1395–1404). Sluter freed the statue from architecture. In his hands it is no longer merely a figure applied on a porch or door, but has all the appearance of coming to life

*323 Claus Sluter. Moses from the Well of Moses. Former Chartreuse of Champmol, Dijon. 1395–1404*

*324 Limbourg Brothers. March, from the Très riches Heures du Duc de Berri. Between 1411–1416. Chantilly*

under the stress of some passionate movement that frames its gestures, distorts the face and makes the draperies swirl (pl. 323). The artist rediscovered the antique theatrical approach to drapery which can amplify gestures and expressions; he stressed its billows and folds and reliefs; his intense realistic curiosity turned him into a keen observer of individual types and facial expressions. Claus Sluter's genius invented a whole dramatic repertoire of gestures, expressions and models, which was so fraught with the sense of doom that obsessed the fifteenth century that the whole of Europe adopted it. Strangely enough it was in Flanders that this was to have the least fruitful outcome, and it was from Dijon, where his work was preserved, that Sluter's style spread across Germany and France and into Spain.

Flemish painting emerged from a great international movement which, at the close of the fourteenth century, tended to fuse together the Paris school's linearism and the delicacy of Lombard colouring with the naturalism that arose in the North. The brothers Pol, Hennequin and Hermann de Limbourg accomplished a revolution by introducing the landscape copied direct from nature into their painting. At the same time, as they worked for a French prince, they kept close to a traditional genre and expressed themselves through the medium of the miniature (*Très riches Heures du Duc de Berri,* between 1411–1416, pl. 324). The brothers Hubert (died 1426) and Jan (died 1441) van Eyck freed painting from the tyranny of the book and monumental composition, by creating easel-painting. Together they painted the great altarpiece with the *Adoration of the Lamb* for St Bavon, Ghent, which was finished in 1432 (pl. 281).

After his brother's death, Jan van Eyck devoted himself mainly to portraiture. The van Eycks showed themselves against the Middle Ages and fully committed to the Renaissance spirit by bringing the principle of integral realism into their art. Casting aside the entire paraphernalia of medieval conventions, they translated the symbols of the great theological composition of St Bavon through human characters observed from the life and against a background of genuine landscapes. At the other extreme from Byzantine art, this meant a remarkable effort to represent the supernatural world through the most concrete appearances of the external world. In his portraits (pl. 326) Jan van Eyck knew how to transfer the models who posed for him onto the painted panel with a life-like exactness that no other painter has surpassed. The van Eycks achieved spatial depth at the same time as the Italian Quattrocento painters, but suggested it by different means, using a diminishing scale of tones according to distance (colour or aerial perspective). Whereas the Italians made nature fit their geometrical vision, the van Eycks enveloped everything in a flood of light and atmosphere. These two painters gave such vital truth to reality that their pictures fill the spectator with an almost hallucinatory sense of immediate presence. In order to express such intense realism the van Eycks used the technique of painting in oils, which they perfected and established. Since it makes it possible for the painter to exploit the interplay of successive transparent layers or 'glazes' of colour, this process enables him to render the texture and other qualities of any kind of element or object, whether it be cloth, gold, flesh, sky, water or light itself (colour pl. VII).

Jan van Eyck's was entirely a painter's eye; he saw everything in terms of its fluid and colour values. He was completely free from the tyranny

*325 Rogier van der Weyden. Deposition. Between 1434–1443. Madrid*

*326 Jan van Eyck. Giovanni Arnolfini and his Wife. 1434. London*

*327 Dieric Bouts. Last Supper from the Altarpiece in St Peter's, Louvain. 1465–1468*

of sculpture which gives the brush the edge of a chisel and which dominated the whole century both in the North and in Italy. But after his death the incisive style was to invade Flemish painting immediately. Rogier van der Weyden (died 1467 at Brussels) did not turn to Sluter's example for the principles of his sculptural manner, but found it in the traditions of the more angular French Gothic which he learned at Tournai, his birthplace, a city which had a prosperous school of monumental (funerary) stonemasons dating from the fourteenth century. Rogier's masterpiece, the *Descent from the Cross* in the Escorial (pl. 325), was conceived as a painted low-relief, the figures projecting their shadows on a background of gold. By comparison with Jan van Eyck, van der Weyden looks back to the medieval outlook, with his sharp-edged linear style, his taste for the ascetic, and his lack of interest in landscape, which are all Gothic features. His outlook on life was entirely Christian in its renouncement and mortification, and it was with intense pathos that he portrayed the sufferings of the Passion.

The art of Jan van Eyck, which was perhaps too far in advance of his time, did not leave a very deep mark on it. Only Petrus Christus (died 1472/73) tried to carry on his style while slightly Italianizing it – there being some evidence that he worked in the peninsula where he knew Antonello da Messina. It was therefore van der Weyden rather than van Eyck who created the traditional Flemish style. Dieric Bouts, who died at Louvain in 1475, derived pretty closely from van der Weyden, although he engaged in plastic experiments which are not unlike those of his contemporaries in Italy (linear perspective of the *Last Supper* at Louvain,

*328 Hugo van der Goes. Adoration from the Portinari Altarpiece. 1473–1475. Florence*

pl. 327). The same applies to Hugo van der Goes (died 1482) who also seems to have known Italy (Portinari Altarpiece, Uffizi, pl. 328). After the work of these men, whose style was tensely set in a sort of exasperation of feeling, fifteenth-century Flemish painting ended by relaxing in the work of Hans Memling (or Memlinc, died 1494), a painter of Rhenish origin who settled in Bruges. The symmetry of Memling's compositions, the suavity he gave to facial expressions, his gentle modelling and elegance of line, were perfectly fitted to express that ideal of piety and that feeling of bourgeois security which he had in common with Perugino (pl. 286).

## *Germany*

Fifteenth-century Germany shows a very active though confused artistic production. In keeping with the political division of Germany into minor states and the tendency towards a municipal, provincial outlook, local schools abounded and flourished. These schools were centred on the Rhine and the Danube, spreading into Bavaria, Franconia and Bohemia and as far as the towns of the Hanseatic League and along the Baltic coast. A land of extremes, Germany tended equally towards mystic unreality and

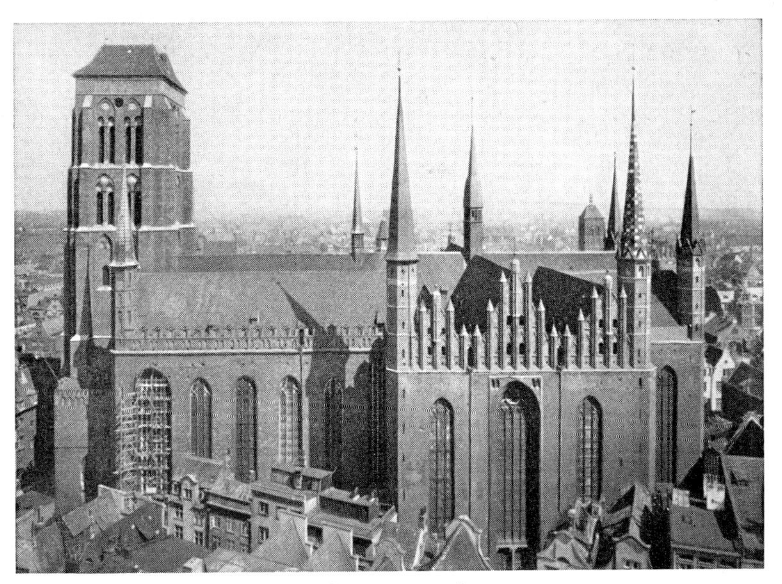

*329 Marienkirche, Danzig. About 1400–1502*

naturalist materialism. The dominant bourgeoisie cared less for the aesthetic quality of a work of art than for its representational values, and expected a work to be didactic, moving and life-like. Mysticism and materialism met in an expressionist crisis which was to remain acute throughout the century.

German architecture lost no time in adopting the Flamboyant style in which it found a vehicle for its own lyrical tendencies. Germany delighted in lavish ornament and openwork decoration, encouraging fantastic vaults with a profusion of decorative ribs, and pierced spires (Ulm, Vienna, Strassburg). The 'hall church' with aisles the same height as the nave which developed in Westphalia in the thirteenth century spread to southern Germany (Liebfrauenkirche, Munich, 1468, choir of St Lawrence, Nuremberg), Austria and Bohemia as well as to the North and along the Baltic as far as Danzig, where there was an outcrop of brick architecture influenced by the English Perpendicular style (town halls of Thorn, Lübeck, Stralsund, Danzig; Marienkirche, Danzig, pl. 329).

Sculpture now made great progress all over Germany, especially in the form of wood-carving which produced huge altarpieces seething with figures and ornamentation. The German plastic principles derived from Sluter, but with more emphasis on expressionism. The enormous output of works was spread over many centres: Nicolas Gerhaert van Leyden (recorded from 1462–1473) at Strassburg and Trier, Hans Multscher

*330 Veit Stoss. Altarpiece of the Virgin in St Mary's, Cracow. 1477–1486*

(about 1400–1476) at Ulm in Swabia, Michael Pacher (about 1435–1498) in the Tyrol, Bernd Notke (about 1440–1509; *St George*, Stockholm 1488) at Lübeck, Veit Stoss at Nuremberg (about 1440–1533). All these workshops, whether in the north or south, showed the same trend towards expressionism (twisting of bodies, convulsive movement of draperies with numerous broken folds), towards a naturalism which led artists to go in search of popular folk-types (Hans Multscher) and even physical deformities (Altarpiece of the Virgin by Veit Stoss, Cracow, 1477–1486, pl. 330), but sometimes also towards a graceful and slightly effeminate mannerism (statues of the Madonna). At the end of the century Italian influence made itself felt through the South and sweetened the harshness of the German style. Adam Krafft (died 1509) of Nuremberg and Tilman Riemenschneider (about 1460–1531, pl. 331) of Würzburg mark the transition from the Gothic to the Renaissance manner.

There was considerable activity in the schools of painting, but it was very mixed in its aims because of the many foreign influences which poured into Germany from every side – the French via the Rhine, the Italian through the Tyrol, the influence of the Burgundian (Dijon) school from the West and South, and the Flemish from the North. In the course of the fourteenth century the clash of Sienese and French contributions gave

*331 Riemenschneider. Tomb of the Prince-Bishops of Scherenberg (detail). 1496–1499. Würzburg*

*332 Master of Wittingau. Agony in the Garden (detail). About 1380–1390. Prague*

*333 Konrad von Soest. Nativity. About 1420. Dortmund*

*334 Konrad Witz. Christ walking on the Waves from the Geneva Altarpiece (detail). 1444*

rise – though with different proportions of each – to the Gothic schools of painting at Cologne (Clarissan Altarpiece) and in Bohemia (pl. 332). The influence of the Franco-Flemish miniaturists subsequently gave Germany a touch of the worldly art of the Limbourg brothers. Early in the fifteenth century Cologne and Westphalia (Konrad von Soest, pl. 333) gave themselves over to a mystic ideal which was markedly ethereal yet naively inclined towards a poetic, pastoral charm (pl. 283). This form of art reached its height about 1430. Its last exponent, Stefan Lochner (between 1405/15–1451) in Cologne, gave it a hint of bourgeois piety.

However, towards 1450 the sculptural style broke into Germany from the North and South at the same time. In the south, the Burgundian style resulted in the popular dramatic manner of Hans Multscher (about 1400 –1467) in Cologne, and at Basle, after 1434, the lofty art of Konrad Witz (about 1400–1446, pl. 284, 334), whose powerful, statuesque density and

*335 Martin Schongauer. Foliage Decoration. Engraving*

*336 Michael Pacher. Resurrection of Lazarus from the St Wolfgang Altarpiece (detail). 1471–1481*

geometrical vision recall Paolo Uccello and Andrea del Castagno and who achieved a strikingly direct representation of landscape. Meanwhile the Flemish sculptural style represented by Rogier van der Weyden and Dieric Bouts came down the Rhine where it met the Burgundian style and penetrated right into Germany with Hans Pleydenwurf at Nuremberg and Friedrich Herlin at Nordlingen. Cologne imitated this with such success that one might well imagine it as coming into the orbit of Flanders rather than of Germany (Masters of the Life of the Virgin, of the Lyversberg Passion, and of St Severin); the bonds uniting the Rhineland school and Rogier van der Weyden are attested by Memling, who brought back to Bruges a breath of mysticism from Cologne. However, in the last decade of the fifteenth century a national German style was developed in the middle-Rhine and in south Germany (Jan Pollack, Michael Wohlgemuth), springing from the mixture of the Burgundian and Flemish styles, which gave to painting something analogous to what the Flemish style gave to architecture; this was mainly achieved by Martin Schongauer (died 1491). Very much influenced by Rogier van der Weyden, Schongauer's medium was mainly the engraving, a new technique for reproducing drawings which gratified the craft-instinct in German artists, their liking for careful workmanship, their passion for infinitely complex detail (pl. 335). It was only at the very end of the century that Italian influence filtered into the Tyrol, where Michael Pacher (about 1435–1498, pl. 336) was inspired by Mantegna, and reached Augsburg, where the elder Holbein (about 1465–1524) was attracted by the harmonious style of Giovanni Bellini.

### *France*

Of all the countries of Northern Europe, France came closest to the Italian Renaissance. Weakened by the misfortunes of the Hundred Years

War, through which she lost the guiding rôle she had hitherto played in European civilization, France gave herself without reserve for a whole century to the excesses of the Flamboyant style in architecture (pl. 337). But the evolution of sculpture shows a progressive detachment from the hard dramatic style of Sluter which, first affecting Burgundy, then descending the Rhone valley, finally made its way into the Midi *(Prophets and Sybils,* choir screen of Albi Cathedral). The setting up of the court on the banks of the Loire gave that region a new importance, and brought to the fore that temperate spirit for which it is renowned. Towards 1460 drapery forms became less rigid, expressionism became milder and the individual character of faces was modified, while artists were now attracted by youth, grace and femininity (pl. 338). Following the demands of the national temperament, pathos was now portrayed more restrainedly, rather by suggesting its inward spiritual meaning, than through its outward, physical and dramatic effects. At the end of the century, after the war with Italy, the native French leaning towards harmony found itself in agreement with the Italian stream, as is shown in the *Entombment* at Solesmes (1496), a masterpiece of French sculpture formerly attributed to Michel Colombe (about 1430–1512).

Taking Europe as a whole, French painting is seen to be, with Italian, the farthest removed from the Gothic outlook. The school of Paris

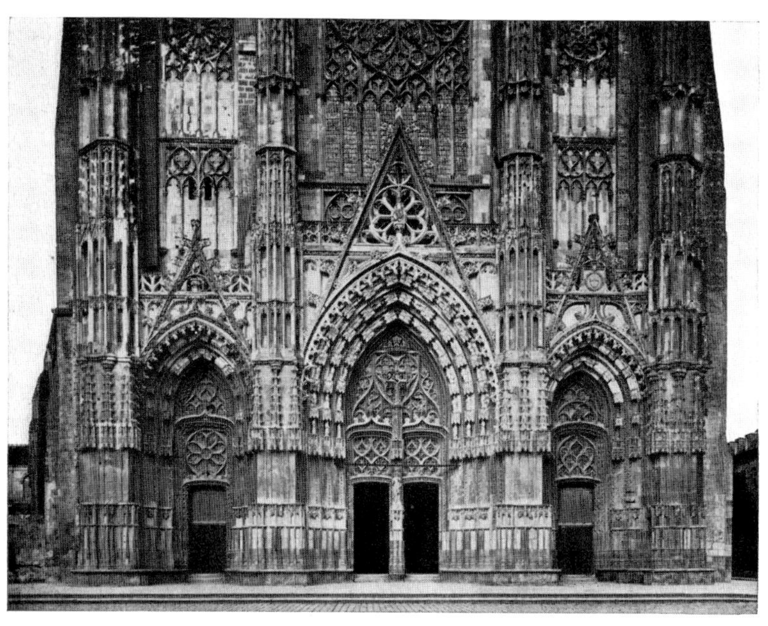

*337 West Front of Tours Cathedral. 15th c.*

*338 The Magdalene.
About 1470. Montluçon*

having been dispersed by the Hundred Years War, the new art centres were in the north, on the Loire, and in Provence. The Valenciennes and Amiens painters followed the Flemish style while slightly toning down its harshness. Avignon, which thanks to its position had already become a great cosmopolitan (Franco-Italian) art-centre in the fourteenth century, produced two of the finest works of the period towards 1450, in the *Coronation of the Virgin* and the *Pietà of Avignon* (pl. 339) by Enguerrand Quarton (or Charonton). The latter painting, one of the highest expression of mysticism, brings together in an admirable synthesis all the intensity of spiritual passion, a monumental rhythm of composition, and an abstract beauty of sculptural modelling, worthy of a Florentine painter of the Quattrocento. The Italian spirit also moved the unknown master who in about 1460 illuminated the *Livre du cœur d'amour épris,* an allegorical 'novel' by King René (Vienna Library). On the Loire, Jean Fouquet of Tours (died between 1477–1481) – who, incidentally, travelled to Italy in 1445 – eschewed the Gothic spirit in favour of the plastic

*339 Enguerrand Quarton. Pietà of Avignon. About 1460. Paris*

outlook of the Italian Quattrocento, of which he contrived to give a French version. He adopted architecture of the classical type, gave up the complicated curves of Gothic modelling in favour of the fluted draperies of the Florentines, and like the Italians became interested in problems of spatial foreshortening while managing to combine a geometrical sense of perspective with aerial colour-perspective in his landscapes. The *Madonna* in Antwerp Museum, one of the most perfect masterpieces of the fifteenth century, is a paragon of harmony to be set beside the Madonnas of Baldovinetti. His portraits have all the grandeur of Italian works, but with a more emphatic truth in them (pl. 341). If he remains a miniaturist (*Heures d'Etienne Chevalier,* pl. 340, *Les Antiquités judaïques,* by Josephus), no doubt of necessity rather than by taste, Jean Fouquet showed France the way to the Renaissance. The tradition of which he was the founder was to be enriched by a fresh Italian strain in the Master

*340 Jean Fouquet. Martyrdom of St James from the Heures d'Etienne Chevalier. About 1450. Chantilly*

341 *Jean Fouquet. Etienne Chevalier and St Stephen. Berlin*

of Moulins who, thanks to his harmonious aesthetic and his pious quietism, is a genius related to Giovanni Bellini, Ghirlandaio, Perugino and Memling (pl. 286).

In the minor arts, France brought the art of tapestry to perfection. Retreating before the English occupation, the Parisian workshops moved to Tours and the North. It would appear that the craftsmen at Tours produced poetic works with a courtly and pastoral tone (pl. 342), while at Arras and Tournai they wove mainly crowded historical scenes in the Flemish style.

342 *Tapestry from the Lady and the Unicorn Series. About 1500. Paris*

It might be thought that fifteenth-century Spain came into the orbit of Italy; but on the contrary she refused to do so and her romantic temperament led her to adopt the Flamboyant style. In both sculpture and painting she was dependent on Flemish and German art, which she was to export even into Italy, through the Neapolitan and Sicilian provinces of the house of Aragon.

The Flamboyant style was introduced by the architects of the North. The fifteenth century saw the creation, probably by Flemings, of Seville Cathedral, a splendid structure with nave and double aisles, which was inspired by a regional type of which Barcelona Cathedral set the first example in the fourteenth century; in the sixteenth century the cathedrals of Segovia and Salamanca were to derive from Seville. The architect Hans de Colonia (Hans of Cologne), who was brought to Burgos by a bishop who had been attending the Council of Basle, built at Burgos Cathedral two pierced spires (1442 and 1458) imitated from those which were designed for Cologne Cathedral. The Burgos workshop produced the first Flamboyant monuments to be found in Spain (Constable's Chapel (1482) in Burgos Cathedral, by Simon de Colonia, son of the Hans already mentioned). Finding a willing soil thanks to the Moorish traditions which were still deeply-rooted in Spain after its liberation, the Flamboyant style now mingled with the Moorish, to create at the time of the Catholic kings the Mudéjar art in which the excess of decoration, taken over from both styles, swarmed over the whole monument. The style of the Catholic kings, sometimes called the 'Isabelline' style, is the first really native expression to be found in Spanish architecture. Enriched with heraldic emblems and Mudéjar features, it is a haughty expression of the triumphant monarchy. The son of an emigrant from Lyons, Juan Güas, built in this style S. Juan de los Reyes at Toledo (1478) and the Infantado Palace at Guadalajara (1480), while Enrique de Egas, the son of an expatriate from Brussels who was overseer at Toledo Cathedral, built the Royal Chapel which

*343 Entrance to the College of S. Gregorio, Valladolid. 1488–1496*

*344 Pedro Berruguete. Ordeal by Fire. Madrid*

*345 Gil de Siloé. Annunciation from the Altarpiece at Miraflores. 1499*

houses the tombs of the Catholic kings in Granada Cathedral. One of the finest monuments in this style is the College of S. Gregorio at Valladolid (1486, pl. 343), whose author remains unknown; the decoration was made up of floral and vegetable shapes as in Manueline art. During the period of the Catholic kings the lay-out of the different parts of the church took on an original character which was to last until the eighteenth century: the choir *(coro)* was placed in the end bays of the nave,

*346 Francisco de Arruda. Tower of Belem (Portugal). 1516*

*347 Diogo de Arruda. Window in the Chapter-house of the Convent-Palace at Tomar*

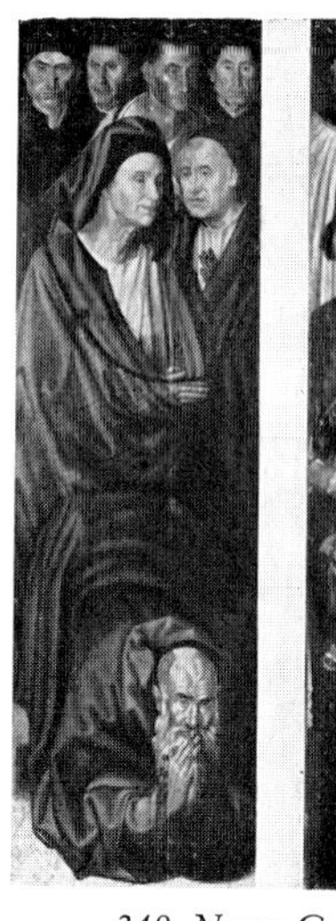

*348 Nuno Gonçalves. Benefactors from the St Vincent Altarpiece. About 1460. Lisbon*

west of the crossing, and closed in with high walls full of carvings; east of the crossing the *capilla mayor* ends in a blank wall, with a large decorated altar in front of it *(altar mayor)*. Exquisite grills or screens in ironwork serve to close off the choir, the *capilla mayor* and the chapels.

Spanish sculpture developed in much the same way as architecture, producing enormous decorative backgrounds, liturgical furnishings, gigantic altarpieces alive with figures, stalls *(sillerias)* and choir-screens *(trascoras)*. A great many artists came from Burgundy, France and Germany to work on these; the greatest was at Burgos, Gil de Siloé, no doubt a converted Jew from Flanders or Germany who, working as easily in wood (altarpiece for the Charterhouse at Miraflores, 1496) as in marble (Tombs of John II and Isabella, in the same church, 1489), introduced a strongly Germanic style, graceful in its mannerism and with a marked intensity of feeling, which gave a start to the Castilian school of sculpture (pl. 345).

Painting was based on Flemish models. In Catalonia Luis Dalmau who went to Flanders in 1431, carried out what amounts to a pastiche of van Eyck in 1445, in the Counsellors' Altarpiece in Barcelona. Jacomart Baço, Jaume Huguet, Bartolomé Bermejo, Pablo Vergos, Fernando Gallegos, were all in the same way disciples of the Flemish tradition. Under the Catholic kings, the Castilian artist Pedro Berruguete (died 1503) who worked for a time in Italy, was to free painting from its Flemish bondage by turning decisively towards the Quattrocento outlook (pl. 344). The

Andalusian Alejo Fernandez (died 1543) tempered Flemish harshness with Italian grace.

Following its great discoveries across the seas, Portugal had a sudden burst of prosperity which in the reign of Don Manuel (1495–1521) showed itself in the rapid strides that were made in art through this ruler's initiative. Portugal then created a style of lyrical exuberance which is unusual in the West, and which reflected the excitement of its great explorers. This is known as the Manueline style. As with the art of the Catholic kings, this style had two phases: the Gothic and the Renaissance. The Manueline style was developed by Boytac in his church at Setúbal and at the monastery at Batalha (about 1509); Diogo de Arruda at the Convent-Palace of the Knights of Christ at Tomar (about 1510, pl. 347); Francisco de Arruda with the Tower of Belem (1516, pl. 346). All these men built the most poetical works in this form of architecture, a kind of naturalistic symphony in stone.

The Spaniard Juan de Castilho was to dry up this creative vein by transposing it into a flat (Plateresque) decorative technique (Monastery of S. Jeronymos at Belem, 1517).

Portuguese painting, like Spanish, was a derivative of Flemish painting. It produced several artists with a sharp eye for realism as well as one of the high-lights in fifteenth-century art, namely the St Vincent Altarpiece (Lisbon Museum, pl. 348). This painting is a portrait-composition of an intense realism suggestive of Jan van Eyck (who visited Portugal in 1428); it was commissioned from Nuno Gonçalves about the year 1460.

# INDEX

The numbers in bold are those of the black and white illustrations
Roman numbers refer to colour plates
National schools of art, the different movements, etc. are in capitals,
place-names in italic, and personal names in roman type